DIARY OF A
CAB MAN
TALES OF A PHOENIX NIGHT OWL

Patrick,

Thanks for a lifetime
friendship. You're a
good man. Enjoy my
ode to cab drivers

Jan

DIARY OF A
CAB MAN
TALES OF A PHOENIX NIGHT OWL

JONATHAN ZISSMAN

Outskirts Press, Inc.
Denver, Colorado

Outskirts Press, Inc.
http://www.outskirtspress.com

ISBN: 978-1-4327-5384-9

Outskirts Press and the "OP" logo are trademarks belonging to Outskirts Press, Inc.

PRINTED IN THE UNITED STATES OF AMERICA

Contents

Acknowledgement

I suppose a lot of thanks are in order here. Finishing a project like this has always been a difficult thing for me. I feel that i have always been a good "idea" man, but sometimes the execution of the idea has been a problem. So, first of all, i would like to thank whomever or whatever enabled me to find tthis masterpiece.

The Discount Cab Company deserves my thanks as well. They didn't have to allow me to drive their cabs. I will spend more than just one or two sentences criticizing things that happened and people during the course of this book. But I appreciate the opportunity they afforded me because, more than anything else, this job was a valuable contributor to my growth as a human being. I saw some things that were at first frightening, but in the end, enlightening.

I have also reaffirmed that I love my family. My dad Lorin is 79 years old and lives with my stepmother Carole.

My older sister Nancy and her husband Bob have two daughters. My brother Eric and his wife Dana have four children and my younger sister Amy, who is married to Rob.

I have many others relatives, but I'm only going to mention two others, my mother Beverly Zissman and her mother Harriet Zissman. I wish my mom were still here. I am thankful that my

92-year-old grandmother is still with us.

I want to thank a large group of friends that I have kept in touch with over the years. Two guys in particular from the Total Research Corporation, Matt Campion and Mark Schuster, are great friends to me. My longtime friends, Dan Lankford, Bill Metzger, Patrick Daley, John Guhl, and Jim Billow, and all the guys from Dewey. My college pals Matt Lepe, Nick Treneff, Bob Hegedus and Jim Katzenberger. And, the people I became friendly with here in Phoenix, specifically, Chuck, Charlie, Scott, Allison and Tim from the Deli, along with Craig, golfer Dave, Utah Dave, Kevin, Meow Mike, Car Mike, Ronnie, wife and Nicholas, and the staff from Hooters Ahwatukee.

I also have to thank my ex-wife Carolyn. She introduced me to Phoenix during our four years together, so if we hadn't gotten together, this book wouldn't have happened. Her brothers, Andrew and David, Andrew's wife, Wendy and their three cumulative children have been so gracious to me in the time I've been in the valley, I haven't been without family.

I would also like to thank Laraine Correll and John Storch for taking the time to edit this book. They came to me, not the other way around, so I am extremely grateful.

I must also thank the Dunkin Donuts on Chandler Boulevard in Ahwatukee. For the last month I was writing this bastion of literary greatness, I was in the store four to six hours per day, and the staff was very kind to me. Thanks guys, you were great!

I also want to thank all of the people who made suggestions on what to incorporate in this book. I got many solid ideas from various sources; other books, passengers, friends and I appreciate all of it. Finally, I have to thank the myriad of people I was fortunate enough to cart around Phoenix during these 15 months, some of whom you will read about shortly. It was one of the most interesting times of my life.

CHAPTER 1

Introduction

I would never have thought I would become a cab driver. I always thought I was destined for a life of grandeur. I'm not sure why I thought that, but I did. Maybe it's because I am a pretty intelligent fellow. I skipped first grade and have always had an aptitude for learning. I remember in college, this one guy telling me about the brilliance of one of his engineering buddies. I looked at him and said, "Bob, he's not any more intelligent than me. I haven't met anybody here that's more intelligent than me." He tried to rephrase what he said, but I stopped him. "Bob, look, I'm not saying I'm a genius, the smartest person in the world or even a great student. I'm not. In fact, I've always been a shitty student. But Andy isn't more intelligent than me. Nobody in this or any other school is more intelligent than me."

Why do I bring this up? Because I think there is one thing that is a constant for every cab driver: the need for independence. While brains are helpful in any endeavor, you don't often come across candidates for a Rhodes scholarship among cab drivers. You do, however, meet a lot of people that need their independence. I'll even take it one step further; it's a need to be alone. I have always been a loner. As a kid, I would walk two miles to the bus stop in Kendall Park, NJ so I could catch a bus to go see a Princeton University hockey game. My brother and I would endure three hours of public transportation each way to go to Shea Stadium to see the Mets. When I was 29 I went to Hawaii by myself because I wanted to go to Hawaii.

I'm not patting myself on the back here. I am making a point. Cab drivers spend 50-100 hours a week in their cabs and are alone for 60-80% of that time. I've waited as many as three hours without getting a fare on more than one occasion. It isn't that way often, because if it were, my mailing address would be Cab 732. However, finding ways to kill time waiting for a call is a necessary skill. In other words, you have to be able to be alone. Everyone can't do that. I think that's why cab drivers seem as angry as so many do. Quite often, being alone means you are lonely as well.

Cab drivers are independent contractors, meaning that we are our own business entities. It is a smart move by the cab company. Eighty to ninety percent of the "employees" of Discount Cab are drivers, so this way, they only have to pay benefits to a few people. Plus, they don't pay the drivers. In essence, we work on commission.

The company leases (or more accurately, rents) the cabs to drivers and we pay for our own gas. You subtract the lease plus gas from your total for the day, and you keep whatever is left over. For example, if the lease costs $100 and you put $50 worth of gas in the car, your expenses are $150. If your billing total for the day is $165, you earn $15 for the day. If your billing total for the day is $265, you earn $115 for the day. If your billing total for the day is $4665, you earn $4515 for the day, although I'm sure THAT scenario has never happened for ANY driver.

There were times I debated describing how we get paid. Somehow, I thought that it would undermine the other drivers.

Then I realized something; most people that ride cabs with some regularity know how the system works, so it doesn't really matter. And, even if the passenger isn't aware of the system, the *only* person that ever loses money is the driver.

The purpose of this book is not to trash the cab industry. There were many things I liked about being a cab driver. For example, I didn't feel like I had someone critiquing my every move. It is difficult for a guy in his 40's to have a boss who is 15 years younger telling him what to do. Imagine having seven people telling you what to do, and it being something different all the time.

I had a lot of situations where circumstance, and occasionally, company personnel, really aggravated me. In this book, I will mention some of them. Any mistake that occurred cost ME money, so it was hard to just forget it when I feel I'm not being treated properly. Once again, my goal is not to insult cab drivers, trash the business or anyone associated with it.

My personality is incorporated quite a bit into this book. I love trivia, sports, tongue-in-cheek humor, professional wrestling, the Ohio State University, New Jersey and my friends and family. You will notice all of these are intertwined in the pages that follow.

I am not trying to challenge freedom of speech by being politically incorrect. In every day speech, I curse a lot, so be forewarned. I also love women and I think about them a lot. I don't have any "type" that I'm attracted to in particular. If anything, I like a woman with an atypical look. Anyway, I thought often about sex, so when an attractive woman got into my cab, it piqued my interest, and I will say so. I also tried to be respectful of peoples' feelings. I don't use the c-word or racial epithets when I speak normally, so I won't use them here. By the same token, showing respect to people doesn't mean kowtowing. I wrote this book to tell stories and I will tell you the stories the same way I would if we were in the same room.

If there was one thing for which I had plenty of time, it was thinking. I was by myself 80% of the time, so I couldn't do much else. That helped me when it came to being the amateur psychologist that cabbies have to be sometimes.

I am going to make one clarification right now. I will refer to Indians from India as Indians and those from North America as American Indians. Again, if I offend someone, it isn't my intention, but this is the way I speak.

First and foremost, I am going to tell you stories of my experiences as a cab driver. I tried to incorporate as much humor as I could without changing the facts. The reason to read this book is to be entertained by stories in this "less than normal" career. I really don't need to change anything. All I'm doing is telling you what happened. By including my insights and thoughts I hope to make these situations that much funnier.

One of the last chapters was going to be a diary of my final 19 weeks as a cab driver, during which I drove all but one day (133 days in total). This has changed from my original plan. Instead of an actual diary, it is now a description of my strategies on a day-to-day and week-to-week basis, how I often saw the same people, other strategies I used to make more money and the way my mood changed working that many consecutive days. At the end of that section, I added less detailed stories that occurred during this time.

I also wanted to give you an idea of some of the things I did when I *didn't* have a passenger. My activities included compiling a list of famous people whose look-alikes rode with me, my personal milestones as a driver and a comprehensive list of photo enforcement camera locations.

Sometimes, certain passengers or adventures were interesting, but there wasn't really a story to tell, so I have included a series of Top Ten lists. Many of these revolve around my passengers, pet peeves, issues and *faux pas*. I think you will find them as humorous as the full stories.

Finally, one acquaintance of mine told me I couldn't write this book without a conclusion. He told me, as a scientist, he couldn't write a paper without coming to some conclusion. I don't agree as it pertains to this "paper", but I did include an Epilog.

I didn't think I had it in me to a write a book. Now that I have, I hope you enjoy reading as much as I enjoyed experiencing the experiences necessary to write it.

CHAPTER 2

How I Became a Cab Driver

The idea of being a cab driver never entered my thoughts until a few months before I became one. I had just turned 46 years old 8 weeks before my first orientation class. I had seen plenty of movies with cab scenes in them, and of course, I watched *Taxi*, the TV sitcom from the 70's that launched the careers of all of the stars of the show, including Judd Hirsch, Andy Kaufmann, Marilu Henner, Tony Danza and, in particular, Danny DeVito. But, I never had an interest in this as a career. So, JUST HOW DID I CHOOSE TO BE A CAB DRIVER?

I was born in Princeton Hospital in Princeton, NJ on April 25th, 1962 at (approximately) 4:40 AM (my mother reminded me of this often, pretty much until the day she died). My parents were playing bridge with friends when her water broke, and I joined the human race about eight or nine hours later. We lived in the same house in Griggstown, NJ my entire childhood. At the time of my birth, I had a sister Nancy, who is 16 months older than me. In the subsequent years, we would add my younger brother (by 2½ years) Eric and my younger sister (by 5 years) Amy.

I remember a pretty funny story that happened shortly after Amy was born. Early one morning, I went down to her crib to look at her. She was rolled over the wrong way, so I turned her head to see her, but she really didn't move. So, I twisted her head some more until I could see her face. Unfortunately, what I next saw was her eyes roll up in her head. I got really scared and turned her head back to where I found it. I ran back upstairs and never said a word about it. Nothing ever came of it, and Amy is fine. About 20 years later at my grandparents' house, I finally told the family what had happened. They thought it was pretty funny.

I would say the root of my being a loner could be traced to something that should have been positive. Halfway through first grade, I was skipped into second grade. I was seeing a psychiatrist because my reading level was so much higher than normal for a six-year-old child. My mother told me this guy wanted to adopt me. This promotion should have been good, but I didn't react to it very well.

Once I got to third grade, a series of things conspired against me. First, my eyesight started to go bad. Since I wouldn't wear my glasses, I stopped paying attention in class (Miss Foley must have turned my desk over five times that year) and my grades were very mediocre. Nancy was a "straight A" student pretty much throughout her entire scholastic career, so I had a tough act to follow. Then, *the coup de grace*, I went from 53 pounds to 83 pounds in six months. Eight-year old kids can be pretty cruel, so I became the butt of many jokes. I would continue to be the butt of jokes, because weight has always been a problem for me. This ridicule really made me feel alone.

My life wasn't entirely bad. Growing up in Griggstown was one of the advantages I had. It was a positive situation that today's kids don't often experience. Griggstown was originally a Norwegian settlement of between 500-1000. It had three sections, the Norseville section, where I lived, Sunset Hill and the Canal. My parents were one of the first non-Norwegian families to live there. We lived on

Park Lane, along with the Olsens, the Vojes, the Langlands and the Johanessens, among others. Near the Canal, Edward Tornquist had a small store that specialized in Norwegian products, mainly fish and dairy products. Plus, he sold candy, so all the kids would go there. We called the store "Eddie's".

The biggest advantage, from my perspective, was the way all the kids around my age (three or four years either way) would play sports and other games together. Baseball and football were played at the field on Leif Ericksson Avenue. We had a basketball hoop attached to the roof of our garage. We played basketball and street hockey in our driveway almost everyday during fall and winter (Some of the kids even referred to our house as "Zissman Arena".) During the summer, at night, we would play "Capture the Flag" or "Kick the Can" in front of the Rubin's house on Lincoln Avenue. We would also go to the Griggstown Church for "Recreation" during the summer, which was a township-sponsored summer activity for kids. What a tremendous neighborhood in which to grow up.

I also had a paper route from the time I was 13 to 16. In fact, for about a year, I had a morning route and an afternoon route. It was the first job I ever had and I was on my own. I guess it makes sense.

I continued to be only a fair student, constantly waiting until to the last minute to do projects, or not do them, and carrying a mediocre GPA throughout high school.

Being last was something I got used to as well. I was the last person announced at my high school graduation.

In February of my senior year, my guidance counselor, Mrs. Ivey, noticed that I hadn't done *anything* college related and she called me in. My dad arranged to meet with her at her house on a Saturday afternoon to discuss my future. My mother made no bones about the fact that she didn't think I was ready for college (and she might have been correct). But, I ended up going to college and I chose The Ohio State University. Like I said, I probably wasn't ready for college, but I'm glad I went. I feel going when I did really worked out for me.

I was no better in college, at least school-wise, than I was in high school, but I felt a lot more liked there. Plus, I was working towards a goal to become a sportscaster. I had the opportunity to broadcast baseball and hockey my senior year. I also became friends with a lot of people and I consider four of them among my best friends. Bob Hegedus and Jim Katzenberger were two former roommates. Bob's father lived in New Jersey, so I saw Bob pretty frequently during breaks, and Jim is from Lansdale, PA, so we have seen each other a fair amount since school. Nick Treneff and Matt Lepe were in my broadcast sequence, and I have seen them around the country a fair amount over the years. I speak with each of them at least a couple of times a year. Matt is the play-by-play announcer for the University of Wisconsin football and basketball teams. Since there are a ton of Wisconsinites here in Phoenix, it opens up a lot of conversations.

Anyway, in February 1984, my senior year, my dad called to tell me he and my mother were splitting up. My sister gave me the head's up that she thought things were bad two months earlier, but I chose to ignore it. This was very traumatic, but there were signs more than 10 years earlier, so deep down, I guess I wasn't really surprised. The real problem, looking back, was that my dad was with someone within days of the separation. Even though I eventually got along with Carole just fine, having her shoved down my throat wasn't easy.

After graduation, I did a number of non-career jobs, including my first bartending job at Pheasant's Landing in Hillsborough, NJ. I was hired there because the manager, Bil Bowman saw my journalism degree and thought I would be a good communicator. I really liked that job, because I learned how to make drinks without having to deal too much with customers. Once I was a good enough drink maker, I got to work in the nightclub downstairs, where the "real" money was. I have had a dozen bartending jobs since.

While I was working at Pheasant's Landing, I also worked during the day at my father's market research company, The Total Research Corporation (TRC). In early 1986, the company was starting major expansion, including moving to a much larger building. I was part of that expansion, becoming part the data processing crew. I worked hard and grew a lot, personally and professionally. Just to give you an idea of my work ethic, I worked through the night when the Mets and Astros played game 6 of the 1986 National League Championship Series that went 16 innings. I listened on the radio while working past midnight. When Jesse Orosco struck out Kevin Bass to end the game, I collapsed from shear mental exhaustion. And, I finished doing what needed to be done.

I also started playing street hockey with a group of guys in Levittown, PA. Among the guys that played were my brother, John Guhl, Jim Billow, Dan Lankford and Bill Metzger. All of these guys would play a significant role in my adult life, mainly because of the friendships I have forged with them.

Around 1988, I moved in with Matt Campion, a co-worker at TRC. He split up with his wife, and he had just bought a townhouse, so he asked me to rent a room from him. I had lived with my mom for the first four years after college, so it was the first time I had lived on my own. Matt and I got along just fine. He is so anal it forced me to think about the *other guy*. I am a better person for it. Plus, he is a close friend to this day.

Right around this time, another co-worker did something that steered me towards broadcasting. John Lesniewski, or "John Le-Driver", as he was called, showed me a flier saying the student station at Princeton University was looking for broadcasters. I was involved with the station, doing on-air and production work until the powers that be saw that I wasn't a student and wouldn't allow me to continue. Fortunately, one of the station managers dropped my name to the local cable company, C-Tec. They asked me to do play-by-play for their football, basketball and hockey broadcasts at Princeton. I did that for three seasons.

The down side was it was my first view of what a cutthroat business sports broadcasting can be. My color commentator was a friend to the son of a former All-American from Princeton, so when the guy lobbied to take my spot, he got it, and I was out. This kind of thing happened to me quite a bit in a 12-13 year period. Since this was the first time, it really hurt.

I also left TRC in 1991. I wanted to do something else within the company, but nothing happened, so I left. I got the chance to bartend full time. I worked at the Rocky Hill Inn for about a year and a half. It is the only job I've ever been fired from where I was at fault. I only just recently stopped feeling guilty about it, but I still can't discuss it. The person to whom I felt guilty just recently passed away, unfortunately.

So, it's early 1993, and I have no job. I went back to TRC on an hourly basis for about three months. Then I got another broadcasting opportunity with WTTM 920 in Trenton. This station was a very popular station in the 50's, 60's, and 70's, but had fallen on hard times since. Dan Lankford was the program director and he brought me in to do some on-air stuff, including sports talk and play-by-play. A local guy, whose name escapes me, brought in a bunch of ex-Philadelphia athletes to do sports talk as well, so I had the opportunity to do radio with Wilbert Montgomery, Vince Papale (the movie "Invincible" with Mark Wahlberg is about him) and half of the Philadelphia Flyers from their Stanley Cup years. All of those guys were gone within six months, because the dude who was bankrolling the whole thing stopped paying them. It was positive for me, because it jumpstarted my broadcast career.

It was during this time I was introduced to Dewey Beach, Delaware. The week after Labor Day every year, 15-25 guys share a condo for five days in Dewey, playing sports, drinking, etc. They are a bunch of great guys, and I am grateful to be a part of it.

By July 1994, I was made the program director of the station. The GM left the company, so Dan took his spot and I moved up as well. I had done quite a bit of sales, created a fair amount of programming and I earned the opportunity. This period, until November 1997, was the best part of my adult life. I broadcasted a ton of games, made a decent amount of money, traveled and made even more friends.

Of course, that came to an end when another broadcasting company bought WTTM. They didn't buy it because they wanted WTTM. They wanted the 50K watt FM that came with it. So, I was out of a job again.

I decided to try my own broadcast company, leasing airtime for specific game broadcasts, and then moving into Internet broadcasting. The same company bought out the station I was leasing airtime from as well, so, I was out of luck again. As I'm sure you can imagine, I don't have a particularly warm feeling towards them.

Shortly after this, I went to the five-year reunion of the 1994 Princeton Women's Lacrosse Team's National Championship at the Tap Room at the Nassau Inn. I knew a number of the players and coaches, and I wanted to say hello. This incident shows how life works in mysterious ways.

While I was there I ran into a woman that worked with my brother's first wife. After a while, she told me that I would be perfect for her friend Carolyn. I hadn't been in a relationship in quite a while, so I agreed to meet her. After 10 days of inaction, I decided if I relied on anyone else setting this up, I might not meet this woman for six years. So I got Carolyn's number and called her myself.

Memorial Day weekend was a significant date during our time together. In 1999, it was when we met. We went to the shore to see this band I liked. We hit it off well. When she told me a sports fact I never thought she would know, and I said, "I want to marry you." She later told me that she told a friend that, "she just met the man she was going to marry". After 15 months, we got married. The wedding was great. So was the honeymoon. After that, not so much. (By the way, if you get married and have a big wedding, do it during the day, and have the cocktail hour BEFORE the ceremony.)

I don't know exactly when things started going bad, but I really started to notice after her mother died in May 2002. I really liked her mom, so I was sad. Then my mom died nine months later and the cause was lost. I'm sure Carolyn decided she wanted out before this, although I can't tell you her reasons. Our lack of communication was, I'm sure, a major contributing factor. On Memorial Day weekend 2003, she spent it with a friend and pretty much ignored me. I guess a blind man could see now.

I will never regret the marriage or say it was her fault. Some of it was, but quite a bit can be put on me. It was truly a shame, because we had so many coincidences in our lives, I thought we were meant to be together.

During the time we were together, I tried to get the Internet broadcasts going, doing a ton of high school stuff in Mercer County, as well as Major League Lacrosse. I broadcasted the first-ever meeting of Lebron James and Carmelo Anthony, at the Prime Time Shootout in Trenton, NJ. But I just couldn't sell it.

I also worked for my last radio station, WBUD, doing high school football and the morning sports. I met a lot of great people there as well. I also met my final experience where a buyout cost me my job. This time, the program director fired me over the phone, because he didn't get to the station in time.

Right before our marriage ended, I started working in management training for the convenience store WAWA. One of the reasons I was hired was I told the regional director I would stamp down garbage in a dumpster to create more space. He really liked me. After six months, though, because of the breakup and other sadness, I left WAWA. I felt like I was having a nervous breakdown.

For some reason, Carolyn and I were going to a marriage counselor. She didn't want to reconcile the marriage. During this time, I did something incredibly stupid. I invested in a candy machine business. Not the huge vending machines, but the plastic ones that give you a handful of M&M's for a quarter. I got 300 of them. The placement guy ripped me off and I charged all the equipment. By the time 2006 rolled around, I had so much debt I had to file for bankruptcy. Fortunately, I waited until after my divorce was final. If she had lost her house because of that, I would have killed myself.

In April 2004, my brother and his best friend from childhood, Peter Bruvik, started the New England Soup Factory. Eric asked me and Peter asked his brother Kenneth, to get involved, and we did. There were two stores in Boston. Eric and Peter decided to try the concept in South Jersey. I was living four miles from the first store, so it was convenient to me.

Over the next 30 months, four additional stores were opened. What didn't work out was the fact that we didn't have enough brand recognition to support that many stores. In January 2007, the company closed. It was a shame, because the product was so good, it should have become a household name.

So, I'm almost 45 years old, collecting unemployment, and miserable. I thought about what to do, and remembered discussing moving to Phoenix with Carolyn when we were together. A large portion of her family was (and still is) living here when we met. I told her I would move here, although, I don't think she believed me. I thought, "I need to start over, why not try Phoenix." I got a mixed reaction from my family, but I made the decision to go. My ex-brother in law, David, offered me a place to stay in Mesa until I found a job and got settled, so, off I went.

After about a month, I started working as a delivery driver for Jason's Deli in Chandler. I moved into an apartment about three miles away in Ahwatukee. I worked there for about 14 months, enjoyed it, and made some friends. I wanted to be considered for management, but that wasn't happening fast enough for my liking. I wanted to drive for both Discount and the deli, but the deli didn't seem to like the idea.

I saw the lime green Discount Cabs all over Phoenix, and I almost went to an orientation about a year before I started driving for them. I had joined a Harry Potter Meet-up Group and the organizer was a cab driver for one of the other companies. I asked him some questions and I decided I was going to try it.

How does one become a cab driver? I'm not sure, but that was how I became a cab driver.

CHAPTER **3**

Glossary

When I decided to write this book, I didn't do a rigid outline, because I realized I would come up with new ideas and thoughts for things to include. Many people gave me good suggestions for things to add or modify. I thought it would be a good idea to add a glossary of terms, so I wouldn't have to explain a lot during the story telling portions of this book. The following are terms, companies and reference points that I will refer to often in these pages. It should be helpful.

Book-in: This means to log on to the system, enabling a driver to accept a call.

C-Book: This is choosing to chase a call that hasn't been assigned to anyone. It is on the screen listed in zone numeric order and is available on a first come-first serve basis. I think I tended to C-Book more often than most drivers. The last six months, C-Booking was harder, because there were fewer opportunities, and everyone's equipment is not at the same level of efficiency.

The Cage: This is the office where all the receipts are

reconciled. This is the place that I have had the least trouble with, especially when I would reconcile with Apollo. It is probably because I gave them the paper work in the fashion they want it, without an attitude. But, here at least, they didn't give me problems.

Call-Box Fare: A number of places, usually bars, have a box attached where an attendant can merely push a button, calling for one of our cabs. If it was a bar, it seemed as if the person for whom the cab was called would leave seven out of ten times before we got there. Another caveat was if the person pressed the button twice, two calls were made. The second driver there was SOL.

Cookie Diet: This was a diet I used to lose 74 pounds during the summer of 2008 (actually March through August). I learned about it from listening to the JohnJay and Rich radio show in Phoenix. The main product is little biscuits that are called cookies (the main flavors were cookie flavors) and you really didn't eat much else. It was a misnomer, in that it really was a deprivation diet. I showed a lot of discipline, although a lack of sleep and the sedentary nature of driving a cab retarded my progress from June on. To me, it was easy, but you have to be in the right frame of mind.

Discount: This is the name of the taxi company I worked for, Discount Cab. It is the largest company in Phoenix. There are many reasons for this, including the easy-to-remember telephone number and the color of the cabs, lime green, which stands out like a sore thumb.

Dispatch: This is the department that sends drivers their assignments. The company refers to this department as the Customer Solution Center. It includes the order takers and troubleshooters.

Electronic Voucher: This is the way drivers are paid when insurance pays for the fare. No money exchanges hands. The amount on the voucher is deducted from the price of the lease. There are two rates for vouchers, $1.80 per mile and $1.45 per mile. We don't get the $2.95 flag drop either. Most of the time, the mileage is correct.

Flag Drop: This is the initial charge, before the cab goes any-where. The flag drop for Discount Cab was $2.95.

Flags: The common term for passengers that are not sent from dispatch. It comes from the fact that in old style cabs, a flag was dropped to start the meter. It sometimes refers to passengers who "flag" drivers down off the street as opposed to receiving a call from dispatch.

FRB: Free Ride Back program. Discount would allow passen-gers that used Discount a free ride back to their car the day after, provided the passenger got the fare number from the driver the previous night. It wasn't advantageous for the drivers, because the company paid us as if it were a $1.45 voucher.

GPS: Global Positioning System. I have used the Garmin Nuvi 200 and 255. This is how I find people 99.7% of the time. It cost me $229. In five months, it paid for itself 15 times over. It has a huge database as well. It is also used to describe the track-ing system the company uses for finding us and sending calls to drivers.

HHV: Hand Held Voucher. These are slips of paper that have a discounted value, generally for senior citizens. The passenger will pay 20-25% of the full fare. They come in either increments of $1 each, or one sheet, on which the driver writes the final amount and charges the passenger 20% or 25%. In Scottsdale, dialysis patients get their entire fare covered. It is one of the best things the city of Phoenix does for the elderly.

IOI line: This stands for Incorrect Order Information line. This is the department that gets called when a driver feels a mistake is made by dispatch. They review it, and you may or may not get a credit on your lease of $5.

JFCS: Jewish Family Counseling Services. This is among the many agencies for people that need counseling for addictions, mental disturbances, physical disabilities, etc.

Lease: Cab drivers are independent contractors and LEASE a car from Discount, and the difference between the lease and total receipts is how much a driver gets paid. There are 12 hour, 24 hour and weekly leases. There are about 6 different types of cars and there are different lease prices. The company is responsible for all cab related costs, except gas.

Magellan: One of the programs within the city. They deal with people who have psychological problems related to health issues. They also deal with other situations, such as battered women. I averaged five fares to and from all offices per week.

MDT: Mobile Display Terminal. This electronic system was responsible for all communications, including receiving fares, credit card payments and messaging dispatch.

MVD: Motor Vehicle Division. This is the agency that handles licenses, registration, etc, for all vehicles in the state.

NESF: New England Soup Factory. This is the restaurant I worked for in New Jersey right before I moved here.

Personals: This was the word used to describe pre-arranged pick-ups. Some guys would claim to have almost nothing but personals. I would question whether that was true or not. I had some, but they generally lasted for two days to six weeks, at the most.

PM: Preventative Maintenance. Every cab has one every 28 days. The Prius ones are less extensive, mainly because no one has been taught anything but oil changes.

QT: Quik Trip is a chain of gas station/convenience stores in Phoenix. It is my best friend. There is 50-75 of them and they are all configured the exact same way. Every item is in the same spot in every store, and each one has a bathroom, the employees are very nice and the stores are all extremely clean, which cannot be said for other convenience stores. I put the Discount zone number right after the letters QT. The following are the locations of the QT's I refer to in this book:

QT84:The corner of Baseline and 48th in Phoenix.

QT85:The corner of Priest and University in Tempe.

QT91:The corner of Highland and 16th street in Phoenix.

QT174:The corner of Camelback and 99th Avenue in Phoenix.

QT179:The corner of Indian School and Third Avenue in Phoenix.

QT271:The corner of Indian School and 30th street in Phoenix.

QT294:The corner of Hancock and Scottsdale in Tempe.

QT308:The corner of Broadway and Rural in Tempe.

QT310:The corner of University and Extension in Mesa.

QT317:The corner of Main and Valencia in Mesa.

QT321:The corner of Baseline and Greenfield in Mesa.

QT328:The corner of Baseline and Rural in Tempe.

QT330:The corner of Mesa and Juanita in Mesa.

QT338:The corner of Warner and Hardy in Tempe.

QT341:The corner of Warner and Arizona in Chandler.

SRPMIC: Salt River Pima Maricopa Indian Community. The Indian Reservation located to the east of Scottsdale. It is directly east of Loop 101.

Terros: One of the rehab programs within the city. They deal with people who have psychological problems related to substance abuse. Many times, the people are required to be in Terros if they are given a DUI (driving under the influence).

Yard Dog: These are the guys that work on the lot where drivers get their cabs. They would check you in and out. During my time as a driver, there were six men that filled this spot. All of them were OK. They weren't the best resource, however.

CHAPTER **4**

Orientation

When I decided to do this job, I was told I had to go to a two-day orientation, which, of course, was unpaid. I went to the Mesa leasing office, where I was told to bring a social security card, driver's license and driving record. I was also told to go to a clinic to give a urine sample for a drug test. I decided I was going to sue someone if they found anything, because I have NEVER taken a controlled substance and I hadn't had a drink in three months.

When I walked in for day one of orientation, there were about 13 people in the classroom. There were two women and 10 other guys. One woman was tall, blonde and attractive. The other was older, shorter and, while not hideous, certainly less attractive. The guys were the assortment you might expect, any combination of the following: short, fat, ugly, missing half their teeth, dressed like slobs, foreigners, etc. I felt like Brad Pitt in there. As you also might guess, most of the guys were huddled around the attractive woman. Dennis, to whom I had spoken the day before about what was needed for orientation, was the guy directing the class.

When the meeting got started, he posted an outline about what we were going to talk about, such as map reading, rules, expectations, what an independent contractor is, reading the computers, business plans, etc.

We were paired up pretty quickly and I was with this dude named Don. He was in the military, and now he was in school on the GI Bill and wanted to make some extra money. He had taken the bus to the cage and I offered to drive him back to his apartment at the end of the day.

Dennis did a really good job of making the orientation a lot less boring then it could have been. There was a ton of drivel that he had to go over, and he did it with enough humor to get us through the morning.

We all went our separate ways for lunch. I was still on the cookie diet, so I stayed to myself (which I probably would have done anyway. I admit, in that type of situation I tend to be pretty cautious). I was still drinking one-two gallons of water a day, so I had to go to the bathroom all the time. This created, what I thought, was a very humorous situation. The bathroom was a 50-yard walk outside from the orientation room. Whenever I went, the water in the sink came out so hard, that I would get drenched, and it looked like I had an accident. But I didn't worry about it, because it was so hot outside by the time I had walked back my clothes were completely dry.

Right before we started the first afternoon session, the attractive woman said she had two kids, which really didn't surprise me. But, she also told us that she was from Long Island and that she was here because she was FORCED to leave there by the law. She had gotten involved with drugs somehow and if she stayed, she probably would have done jail time. When she followed that by saying she had used someone else's urine for the test at Discount, I guess it all made sense. I think that might have made her even more attractive.

For the afternoon session, one of the men who were there in the morning left. I didn't notice it until an hour had gone by. I asked Don what happened and he told me the guy left when Dennis told him he was not permitted to carry a weapon in the car with him. Between him and this chick, I was thinking, "What the HELL am I doing here?"

We saw a whole bunch of videos, showing accidents that drivers had been involved in. There are cameras in most of the cars, so quite a few crashes over the last ten years have been captured on tape. Some of the accidents were pretty horrific, although, when the video ends with someone hanging upside down, it's kind of funny. They told us that the area between the white lines on exit ramps of highways is called the Gore area. It is named after the police officer that was killed when he was hit by a car while parked there, although they didn't *show us* this accident. If you are caught driving through that area, it is a $350 fine.

Some of the company's "executives" came into the room during the afternoon session, in part to introduce themselves, but also, I believe, to size up the new recruits. Two of these people are named Roger. One of them is the driver liaison and was the person I went to with most of my issues.

To end the first day, we all took a couple of quizzes to see how much we learned. This was more of a formality then anything else, because it was open notes, and everyone passed with no more than two wrong. Most of these people got there by public transportation, including Don. I gave him a ride back home and told him I would pick him up for the second class tomorrow.

I was a little late getting out the next morning, so Don panicked and left before I got to his place, trying to catch a bus. Fortunately, I saw him walking to the bus stop (he had left a note on his door), and I yelled across the street to him. So, we got there on time with no trouble.

Everyone was back for Day Two, plus another woman joined the class. She had to reschedule her Day Two for some reason. She certainly had an interesting look. Most of her body that was not covered by clothing was covered by tattoos. Also, she probably should have been covering a larger portion of her body than she was. But, she was nice enough.

Most of the guys were huddled around the cute blonde. We all had become friendly with each other, but the less attractive woman was continuing to get on my nerves. Her husband was a Discount driver, so she had a running knowledge of the job. Most of the time she would blurt out the answers to questions in such a way that it was really aggravating.

Again, Dennis did a good job of making the dull shit interesting to the point that we weren't falling asleep. It was stuff about traffic laws, learning the computer dispatch box, manners with passengers, and then being quizzed on everything we were told. There were two things they talked about constantly. One was that safety was our "number one" issue. And secondly, was there was a learning curve with this job, and that we shouldn't worry if the first couple of days don't net us a lot of money. It will come eventually.

This session went fairly quickly, especially after striking up conversations with the people around me. Most of the seats were taken when Don and I got there, so we were separated. I was talking with the new girl and a dude named Ahmed (yes, Ahmed). By the time we started practicing on the simulators for the dispatch boxes, we only had about two hours left. It is amazing how stressful it was trying those boxes for the first time. They become second nature after only three or four shifts. We took one final written test, and then we all went out in cabs with supervisors to practice a pickup. That went easily enough, although it too was nerve-wracking. I exchanged numbers with four people, mainly because they told us that forming little groups might help. We signed our independent contractor agreements and that was the end.

I spoke with one of the Roger's about the possibility of leasing the cab on a weekly basis, as opposed to 12 or 24-hour leases. He told me that, as a rule of thumb, I would need to do 25 shifts first. He also told me that since one has to plunk down the weekly lease fee ahead of time, he wasn't going to turn down money. That's what I figured. The way I saw it, there were three positive reasons to lease a cab that way. One, I can use the car as if it was mine, meaning I can take it home at night and save myself about 170 miles a week. Two, I only have to go to the cage and reconcile my receipts with Arthur once per week. That easily saves me 5 hours of time. And three, the seventh day is free. Those reasons were enough for me. And I did end up being a weekly leaser, with my tenth shift.

As far as my fellow classmates are concerned, I have only seen three of them, ever. I saw Ahmed once. He was wearing a shirt for the local bus company when I saw him, so I presumed he doesn't work for Discount anymore. I also saw the annoying woman three times, twice at the cage and once on the road, and I might have said hello once. I have also seen the tattooed woman at the cage reconciling two or three times. She is a pretty nice girl. I haven't seen anyone else.

I was told an amusing story about the attractive blond, however. I asked one of the facilitators about her, and he told me that she never drove a shift. What she did do was hook up with one of the other drivers. She apparently gave him a sexually transmitted disease, and stole his wallet and a watch. I guess I'm not really surprised.

I see drivers all the time, and I speak to them occasionally when we are at the same place, waiting for a call. I don't have any feeling either way for any of these people, but we have common issues, so I get into discussions all the time about dispatch, order takers, how insane the rates are on the leases, etc. We are all in the same boat.

CHAPTER 5

My First Day

One of the more terrifying days of my life was my first as a Discount cab driver. I went to the cage at about 5:30 AM. It is generally crowded at that time and I felt pretty awkward standing among a group of guys scoffing at me. I was sure none of them would be any help, so I didn't bother asking. The ladies in the cage were helpful enough, as was Jerry, the yard dog.

It took me about 30 minutes to do all of the checks necessary before I could get signed out. I was told as time went along that would go faster. That was proven true, especially after I started driving the Prius.

After that arduous process, I went out and booked into zone 317. I was in position number 7, so I knew I wouldn't get a call for a while. I waited about 45 minutes and I finally got my first call ever. It was also my first no-show ever, and clearly, it would not be the last. It was to Banner Hospital on Dobson Road, just north of the 60.

My first successful fare was a short HHV in Mesa, taking an older gentleman to a Fry's. It was worth $6. Away we go. Funnily enough, my next fare was his return trip.

The next fare I got after that was my second no-show. It was my first electronic voucher call, and this person told me when I got there, "they didn't want to go." I didn't know enough to be mad. What did make me mad was the fact that when I got back to the car, I realized I had locked the keys in the cab with the engine running. In my first bit of good luck, I was close enough to the cage to where Jerry came out and opened the door. He told me I wouldn't be charged because I was close enough to the cage AND it was my first day. He also gave me a real good piece of advice. He told me: if you're going to leave the engine running, roll down the window.

My next fare was worth $13, bringing this woman and her child to the doctor. It was the lowest value per mile electronic voucher.

I got my first cash fare after that, bringing a guy to the store way out east in Mesa. I got my first tip as well, $2 on a $9 fare.

I kept moving further east, going to the Marc Center on East Florian to pick up this woman and bring her home to Queen Creek. She wasn't very talkative, and she seemed to be unhappy, so I left well enough alone. I kept telling passengers it was my first day, so I guess it's a good thing I didn't get a lot of cash orders.

The hospital I went to next was always a weird place. Some venues have it listed as 1900 South Gilbert in Mesa; others have it as 1900 North Gilbert in Gilbert. I still don't know which it really is, but this was my first credit card fare. The trip wasn't very long but the lady was very nice to me and gave me a $3 tip on a $9 fare. Looking back, credit cards were good because people tended to over-tip when they weren't putting out cash.

The next voucher caused me so many problems. I lost about 90 minutes between looking for the actual location, then looking for the passenger. This hospital is in Apache Junction, but it was sent to me as being in Mesa (I later got this same hospital two other times, but I remembered this case, so I didn't lose anything on those occasions.) By the time I figured it out and got to the hospital, the fare was gone. I lost a whole bunch of time trying to find out what to do. It took 25 minutes before my voice request was answered.

I decided to go back towards to Phoenix. I probably used 15-20 dollars in gas between the no show and going 20 miles back to Phoenix. The Crown Victoria gets only 11-14 miles per gallon.

I got my second and final cash fare of the day. I brought this dude to a store and back. Obviously, he didn't appreciate the weirdness of my first day, because I got no tip. On the up side, it was my biggest fare of the day up to that point.

My next voucher fare was my lucky break of the day. I went to Terros. My fare was this young woman who asked me to drop her off at an auto body shop in South Scottsdale instead of the given destination. It saved me two gallons of gas and 45 minutes of time; because I was that much closer to the cage, and I got paid for 14 miles when I went about five. I had this woman as a fare one other time, about two months later.

My final fare was another voucher, bringing this dude 1 mile from Magellan on 44th street to his apartment. He said about 20 words, and that was enough for me to know he was nuts.

I went to the cage to do my first reconciliation. But first, I had to refill the gas tank and wash the car. I barely drove 100 miles on this first day as a cab driver, but gas was so expensive at this time, I put nearly $45 worth of fuel into the car.

I went in and gave Augie my electronic voucher sheet, my $20 coupon, credit card receipt and HHVs. Humorously, I broke exactly even for the day. I had prepared myself for the possibility I would lose money, so this was a triumph. It's not very exciting, but looking back, not exciting was good sometimes.

CHAPTER **6**

Interesting Stories

Tranny ━━━━━━━━━━━━━━━━━━━━━━━━━

I'm not sure how this story should be categorized. I took a call to a dialysis center that I had been to at least three other times. I was thinking it would be an old man, since the name on the voucher was "Lyle". I got to the center and told the nurse I was looking for "Lyle" and the nurse said he she would be out in a minute. I thought, "She?" and guessed the nurse had just misspoke. But then I heard one of the other dialysis patient's say that "she was on her way out".

When "Lyle" stepped out from the back room, she was a young, beautiful Hispanic woman in tight clothes and looking very sexy. I was stunned that, one, someone named "Lyle" was a woman and, two, someone so young was doing dialysis. We walked out to the car, and I asked if her name was "Lyle", because that was not a common name for a woman. She just laughed, and that's when I started to notice some odd things.

First, I noticed that she was pretty tall, although, that alone is not strange. Then, since she had a sleeveless shirt on, I noticed how muscular her arms were. Considering how skinny she was, that was odd. Then I looked at her face and realized how much makeup she was wearing, especially around the eyes. Then I looked and thought she had breast implants. Then, after we started driving, she was on the phone, speaking Spanish, and I thought her voice was pretty deep for a woman. It was then I realized I had a transsexual in the car with me. I don't care, but it was strange all the same. If you watch the Jerry Springer show, you'd think there are 7.1 million of them living in Los Angeles alone. But, how many can there really be? There can't be that many. Anyway, since she was on dialysis, it was a voucher trip, and she was one of the few people on a voucher to ever tip me.

I Need Razz-ors

There have been times when I just knew that something strange was going to happen. I'm not a genius, I'm not clairvoyant, and I'm not a scientist. It's just a feeling that has occurred at times. Some of those times, I've have been correct. One that stands out was with a guy called Razz.

I had dropped off these fellows at the Chandler Fashion Square, knowing I was going to come back and pick them up in about 90 minutes. I got another call to a supermarket and turned that around quickly. Then, another call took me right back to the Fashion Square brought me right in front of the Cheesecake Factory.

I parked in front of the main entrance and my man was sitting on a bench. I figured he would see me so I just sat there. After 10 seconds, he still hadn't looked up, so I decided to count and see how long it would take for him to notice me. I swear to the highest being, 94 seconds ticked off before he looked up. THAT was when I knew something odd was going to happen.

Well, he was certainly pleasant enough. We talked for a moment. He told me he needed to stop at a CVS and get some razor cartridges. I was OK with that, and I reminded him that the meter would still be running during the time he was inside. He did not have a problem with that.

It took him 10 minutes to get in and out of the store. The issue came up after he got back. After he got in, he started talking about how expensive the disposable cartridges were. I said, "Yeah, I know. Shaving products are one of those things that I have to spend money on, that I hate spending money on." After a couple of minutes, he said, "Boy, I really thought I had enough money to buy razors and get home." Jeez, this guy spent all of his money on razors. He then said he only has $2 left. The meter already says $12. DAMN IT.

Then he starts on a diatribe about how he is an honorable man that went on way too long. He said, "This has never happened to me before. I always pay my debts. I've been the president of the Rotary club in the past. I'm going to go up to my apartment and write you a check. Oh, wait a minute. My ex-wife has my checkbook, so I won't be able to do that, but I will send you a check in the mail. You will have to give me your mailing address."

Now, he was speaking to me so rapidly, I really couldn't digest anything he was saying. The only thing I was sure about was that I wasn't going to be paid. So I just nodded my head and said yes every time he opened his mouth. I have never had anyone follow through and mail me money when they insisted their intentions were good.

Even as we got to the front of his building, he continued to tell me what an honorable soul he is. He insisted that I come up to his apartment so he can show me he was sincere. Now, I know most drivers would have told him to fuck off or they would have called the police. I just couldn't and not because I'm anything special. I am not capable of sticking up for myself without getting frighteningly angry. I really don't like the idea of getting that mad at an 80-year man over $20.

We went upstairs to his apartment and the first thing he does is show me a picture of him with Anwar Sadat, the late president of

Egypt. Apparently, this picture was taken two weeks before Sadat was assassinated. (A quick history lesson, the cleric that approved Sadat's killing, Omar Abdel-Rahman, was also convicted in the 1993 World Trade Center Bombing.) Then, he showed me all of his Rotary club awards and that he was the president for eight years and yadda, yadda, yadda. He told me again how his ex-wife has his checkbook or he would write one for me right now. And, he told me again how honest he is and that this had never happened before.

I asked him when I could expect to hear from him. He told me he would mail me a check tomorrow. I wrote down my address on a post-it, knowing there was a good chance he would lose it. He followed that with the final indignity. He was rummaging through his bag, looking for god knows what. He decided to tell me. He couldn't find his glasses. He assumed he left them in the car and asked me to go downstairs and bring them back up to him. I said, "SURE PAL, YOU GOT IT." I was thinking something completely different.

I went out to the car and looked in the back seat, but I didn't find his glasses. I walked up to the check-in desk, and I asked the guy sitting there if he would call Razz to inform him that the glasses were not in my car. I must have sounded down, because he asked me what was wrong. I told him the story and he was nice enough. He said, "Yeah, Razz is getting a little forgetful. How much does he owe you?" I told him $20. So, this guy told me he would give the money and charge it to Razz's account. Then, the GM of the place came up and he told her what happened. She then gave me a $5 tip. So, I called upstairs to tell Razz I couldn't find his glasses and the front desk was charging his account for my fare. It turns out he knew they could do that all along. Plus, he said he found his glasses *in his pocket*. Thank god I've only got a few weeks left of this shit.

Sister Christian ━━━━━━━━━━━━━━━━━━━━━━━━━━━━━

Sometimes, as men, we think with our penises.   I have no regrets in my life about any relationships I've ever had, other than I wished I had understood myself a little earlier in my adulthood. I have been open-minded to trying friendships with woman, but I get frustrated when I misread what "her objectives" might be.

I was way out in Avondale during the last few weeks I was a driver. I took a call to a house in an area with which I was not familiar. Just to give you an idea of how stupid this area was, the street this woman lived on changed names twice, even though I never made an actual turn. It was so confusing, I almost No-Showed the call. Fate said I could not do that.

When I found Mimi, she told me we had to run a couple of errands and then take her to Wal-Mart. She was about 55 years old and reminded me of Esther Rolle, who I took to block (@). We went to the UPS store for the first stop. She asked me what I thought of Phoenix and I told her I liked it, but I'm not sure I liked it more than New Jersey.

When I said that, she told me she was also from the east coast, just outside of Baltimore. She also said she was on her way back there at the end of the summer. She wanted to be closer to her daughters and she was looking to start an academy where she would be tutoring underprivileged black children. Well, now that's a noble thing to do.

We were going to the second place, a convenience store, when I started telling her why I moved to Phoenix, how I was look-ing for some "sign" as to what to do with the rest of my life. As she was listening, she kept putting her hand on top of mine. I was thinking, "Boy, it seems as if she really likes me." You know what, sex is sex. If the opportunity comes up, I'm going to bang this woman.

As if on cue, she says, "I was wondering, would you like to have a cup of coffee with me," and I said sure. There happened to be a Starbucks in the parking lot where the Wal-Mart was located. She said she would buy, which is good, because as a rule, I hate Starbucks. The problem was she stepped outside for a moment, just as our order came up. I ended up paying for it, because she never offered the money back. It cost me eight dollars for two coffees. I still hate Starbucks.

When we sat down, she was describing her ideas for her academy in Baltimore, telling me she has already encountered a lot of problems with her status. She needs to go back to school to reach a certain level of certification. I asked how long it would take and she said at least one year. I told her how I consider going back to school all the time because each of my siblings has an advanced degree and I don't. That thought usually leaves my head just as fast as it enters, because I don't want to go to school anymore.

I started telling her about this book and how many crazy situations I found myself in, concluding with the story recounted in the chapter, "Danger is my middle name." Then she told me that she used to be a cab driver in Baltimore. She told me a story of how she picked up two couples one night and how they seemed to be a little out of it. She drove them around for a while, and then she realized the two guys had guns and they went in to a store with the intention of robbing it. The two girls were wondering out loud whether they should be with these fellows, and Mimi asked them, "Are you nuts, you should get away from them ASAP." Taking her word for it, the girls told Mimi to bolt and leave the guys there.

Then she said, "You know, I want to tell you the reason I asked you to join me. You said something that got me thinking. When you were telling me how you were looking for a sign as to what you should do with the rest of your life, I wondered why you haven't taken Jesus Christ into your heart. Oh jeez! Have you ever thought about that?" I told her I hadn't, to which she asked why. I said I didn't have an answer to that question.

She had a response to that, as you may have guessed. She said, "I would like you to do me a favor. When you go to bed, just ask Jesus Christ to show himself to you. Will you do that? You don't have anything to lose." I told her I would, knowing full well I wouldn't.

We said our goodbyes and she walked across the parking lot. I got into my car and said out loud, "And I thought I was going to have sex with her." I stopped laughing about 10 minutes later.

(@) I realize the phrase, "who I took to block", made no sense. I will explain it here. My friends from street hockey, Dan, Bill, Jim, my brother and I used to play this game, which I will call, "Do you or don't you". We would take older TV shows that had at least three women as stars. You had to determine whether you would have sex with all three. For example, *Gilligan's Island* was one of the big conundrums. Would you bang Mrs. Howell to get to Ginger and Mary Ann? Well, the show *Maude* came up. Any dude would want to have sex with Adrienne Barbeau. We were considering the pros and cons of Bea Arthur and Rue McClanahan, when Bill said, "Excuse me, I'll take Esther Rolle to block." Our group has used *that* one-liner dozens of times since then, hence my use of it now.

Hallelujah

One particular morning, I was sent to an apartment complex in South Phoenix to pick up a woman who was going to the airport. When I got to the apartment, it took about five minutes for anyone to come to the front door. When she finally did, it was actually her friend. My pick-up was still getting dressed. This was not a good sign.

Janice had a lot of things, and I wasn't sure whether it would fit in the trunk. She had two suitcases and a lot of other clothes that were on hangers and covered in plastic. I carried it all down the stairs and was able to squeeze it in to the trunk and the back seat. The friend was very pleasant, and when Janice finally came down, they said a tearful goodbye. When she saw I was able to fit everything into the car, she was so happy that you would've thought she won the lottery.

We got going and Janice said we needed to make two stops before we went to the airport. The first place was a store at which she was going to cash a check. She started towards that check cashing place and the fun started.

Out of the blue, she started chanting. "Hallelujah, praise the Lord, he is our savior; god blessed is he that follows our holiest leader." At first, I was thinking she was talking to me, until I realized that she was almost in a trance. "Oh, please my lord save me from evil and bless my family." I sneaked a quick look and she had her arms in the air and her eyes were shut. In a way, it was inspiring. In a different way, it was freighting.

What was actually bothering me was that she kept referring to doing things for her "fellow man", and I got the impression she was going to tell me she really didn't have any money once we got to the airport. At this time, I had been a driver for only a few weeks, but I had been scammed a couple of times already, and I was a little more cautious with people now.

We got to the check-cashing place and she went in, telling me a friend worked there and she should be able to get in and out quickly. Almost 15 minutes later, she came back and told me she wasn't able to cash her check for some reason. Fuck.

She told me we needed to go to her storage facility to drop off a bunch of the stuff we had in the trunk. We started towards that place, and the singing started again.

This time, she decided to serenade me with "Amazing Grace". Fortunately for me, she was a pretty decent singer. I'm not a person that cares a whole lot about religion, but I also don't care that others express their religious freedom (I would care if it affected me, but it did not in this case). After a while, I thought about joining in, but I had two problems; first, I really didn't want to encourage her any more and second, I don't know the words to "Amazing Grace".

We got to the storage area and I was able to unload the things she wanted unloaded in less than five minutes. After that, she told me she wanted to go to another store to try to get some money. On the way to our final stop, she went back to chanting.

It was starting to get to me a little, because as far as I knew, she didn't have any money to pay, the meter now said $22, and I've lost about 35 minutes of the day. She almost sounded as if she was holding a sermon. "John 5:17 says blah-blah-blah" and "Mark 21:18 says blah-blah-blah" took us to the place were she was hoping to get some money. She came back out almost immediately, but she didn't say a word, other than, "OK, let's go to the airport".

We were only a couple of miles from Terminal Four at that point, and she actually started talking to me. She was really excited, because she was flying to Albuquerque for a family reunion. She was telling me that her brother had arranged for a really fancy hotel for the 50 people that were going to be there. She also said she was going to see people she hadn't seen in 30 years. I told her how nice that sounded and I appreciate my family more, now that I'm not around them as much.

We pulled up to the skycap for Southwest Airlines and I unloaded the suitcases from the trunk and put them on a trolley. I glanced at the meter and it said $33. I wheeled the trolley over to a bellman and Janice looked at me, waved and said "Thank you so much for your help. She still hadn't paid me. I said, "Sorry ma'am, you still need to pay me." She said, "Oops, yeah, I guess I probably do." I said, "You owe me $35". Then she handed me three 20s and said "Thank you so much, and god bless you." I thought it was going to be a disaster, and it turned out to be the biggest tip I got in my first three months. YOU JUST NEVER KNOW.

Accidents And How They Occur ━━━━━━━━━━

I have seen a few accidents since I have been in the Valley. I heard on a talk radio station that, of the four cities in the US with the most mishaps per capita, three of them are Phoenix, Mesa and Tucson. I don't know if that is true, but it wouldn't surprise me. I think there are many reasons why it could be true.

First, there are a lot of bad drivers. There are many people I would consider bad drivers. The snowbirds (people who are here primarily during the winter) drive 31 miles per hour in the left hand lane. I know they cause a lot of accidents. Generally, they are older people who really shouldn't be on the road anymore.

Also, there are plenty of people who don't pay attention to their surroundings. They change lanes without looking or signaling, for example. As far as bad drivers are concerned, the number one thing (I feel) is that people don't care. I know there are people who CAN talk on a cell phone and drive. I'm one of them. But, when people talking on the cell don't care or choose not to pay attention, they are going to cause an accident.

Some people have told me they think the reason is because there are so many people from so many different parts of the country and each area has its own "rules". I suppose that could be a small part of the reason, but I think that is a pat answer some people say because a lot of people say it.

As I mentioned, I have certainly seen my share of accidents here in Phoenix. This one time I was going to pick up someone near the airport, and I was at the light at Buckeye and 24th. A lot of busses go by there, but this time, a woman in a BMW was turning towards the airport, just as I was looking down at my GPS. The next thing I knew, I heard a loud pop. When I looked up, the BMW must have changed her mind, because her car was smashed against another car that was turning in the opposite direction. I think she decided she wanted to go straight. Unfortunately, she didn't have a green to do that, so she smashed into the other car.

What really stands out for me about this accident is that I came back through that intersection about 5-10 minutes later, and it was already cleared away. That was, by far, the quickest reaction I had seen to an accident since moving here.

This should give you an idea of how often accidents happen because people aren't paying attention. Valley Metro is the bus company that services Phoenix. I don't ride busses, but many people have told me they are inefficient, mainly because of the lack of total routes. Sometimes a 15-mile trip takes 90 minutes, because of transfers.

One of the biggest problems I see is that bus stops are right after traffic signals. It's a problem because, more often than not, there isn't an island for the bus to pull into for pick-ups. They end up stopping traffic in the middle of an intersection, sometimes creating gridlock.

I learned to try to stay away from the furthest right-hand lane if I saw a bus. One time I saw a Volvo following a bus very closely and I remember thinking he was going to hit him if he wasn't careful. Sure enough, 10 seconds later, right after passing through an intersection, the Volvo bounced off the back of the bus. I thought, "How did this guy not see that coming?"

One other time, I was driving in Central Phoenix. I was going to a pickup and moving slower than I would have liked. It was two lanes each way and I was to the right. There were two cars in front of me and two cars in front of the guy in the left hand lane.

All of a sudden, the lead car in my lane decided to make a LEFT HAND turn, crossing in front of all of us. She hit a van and then finished her turn. She went half way up the block before pulling to the side. I thought she was going to leave at first. The van she hit was designated to transport children. Fortunately in this case, the driver was the only person inside. Two things I found unusual happened. First, there was a cop right there at the next intersection to the west and secondly, every car pulled over to be a witness, including me.

A woman was giving a statement and I interrupted, hoping to go first so I could get to my pickup. She said it was fine, so I told the policeman what I saw and left. I didn't think about again until three months later, when I received a subpoena in the mail. Jeez. I called and said I would be there, knowing I might lose up to four hours during an already slow week. I was lucky, because two hours before I had to be in court, the clerk called me and said the woman dropped the court case. Thank god.

One of the main reasons for accidents that isn't discussed is *stuff in the road*. Drivers swerve to avoid whatever it is, then bump into someone to his or her left or right or just lose control of the vehicle. One of the scarier accidents I've seen occurred while I was driving to a pick up on the southern part of the 202 just past the 101. I saw a large object in the road about half a mile ahead of me, so I moved to the right, as far as I could. As I got closer, I could see it was a plastic garbage can. I thought, "What the fuck is that doing there?" Well, to my left, an SUV and an Audi were flying in that left-hand lane. The SUV probably could have pushed the can into the median, but it swerved at the last minute to avoid it. Well, the Audi tried to swerve as well, but the driver lost control of the car. The car spun a couple of times, right in front of me, and smashed in a flat bed semi that was in the furthest right-hand lane. The car bounced off of that, and skidded right in front of me again. I had slowed down quite a bit, so it never came close to my cab. It slid across the highway and into the median. Fortunately, the Audi did not flip, and eventually, came to rest against the fence in the median after sliding a couple of hundred feet. I called 911 to report seeing the accident. I'm not sure whether I was obligated to stay as a witness, but I didn't. I gave them my information, but judging from the fact that I didn't get a call later, I have to guess I wasn't needed. All of this happened because of a GARBAGE CAN in the road. I feel that the DOT is extremely slow to react to things in the road, but that is my opinion. The following is a list of things I have seen lying on the road while driving for Discount:

A box of smashed china
Chairs
A basketball
Full-sized garbage can
Whole tires
Large strips of tires
Full garbage bags
A six pack of beer bottles
A tricycle
Sandbags
A rifle case (I don't know if the gun was in it)
A mounted fish
A trophy
A small suitcase
A log
Wheel covers (Hub caps)
Blankets
Pillows
Baseball caps
Cleats
Part of an engine
Steak knives
Mangoes
Shoes
Road kill
Scissors
Books
Glasses
Gas caps
Part of an AM/PM sign
A yield sign
A case of water bottles

Bales of straw
Weight lifting plates
A mannequin
A couch
Ice skates
Shoes
Mattresses
Box springs
Computer keyboard
A vacuum cleaner
A shovel
Cardboard boxes
Bags from fast food places

The Post Game Show ━━━━━━━━━━━━━━━━━

It's pretty frustrating for me in Phoenix when it comes to sports. The fact that there aren't a lot of true Phoenix sports fans aggravates me, although it is understandable.

Growing up half way between New York and Philadelphia made it easy to be a sports fan. We could get TV channels from both cities, which wasn't common. My mother grew up in Brooklyn and my father grew up in Philadelphia, so factor that in. Between the four major team sports, there were 12 major league professional franchises, so there were plenty of choices. Plus, my home was less than 10 miles from Princeton University, so I rooted for them as well. Finally, I went to the Ohio State University. Sports became my salvation.

Here in the valley, there were no major league teams until 1968 when the Suns became an NBA franchise. The Cardinals, who failed to win in Chicago and St Louis before losing here, came in 1988, the Coyotes in 1996 and finally, the Diamondbacks in 1998. Even though the Snakes won the World Series in 2001, there is not a lot of history and pretty much no tradition. Even the success of Arizona State is sporadic. Just to give you an idea of the varied fan base here, one all sports radio station carries University of Nebraska football.

Last season, the University of Georgia football came to Tempe to play ASU in Sun Devils Stadium. It really set up to be a great game. Georgia was ranked in the Top 10, lead by QB Matthew Stafford, who would become the number one pick in the NFL the next April, and RB Knowshon Moreno, who was also taken in the first round by the Denver Broncos (one other side note, Moreno went to Camden Catholic high school, which was less than two miles from my apartment in Maple Shade, NJ). Arizona State was coming off of a 10-win season, with a lot of that team returning, including QB Rudy Carpenter and DE Dexter Davis, who should be a first round pick in the 2010 draft. Unfortunately, the match up was sabotaged early in the season. The Devils lost at home to UNLV, blowing a fairly large lead to an apparently inferior team, mainly because they just did not play very well. Georgia came into the game playing extremely well. Despite the ominous (and accurate) signs, the ASU fans were hoping for a repeat of the huge 19-0 upset of Nebraska in 1996 (that game is replayed on FOX Sports ALL THE TIME).

The day before the game, I got a call to a hotel near the airport. The fare was a big guy that needed me to bring him two miles to a Starbucks, because he needed a Chai Tea. Not a Thai Chi, but a Chai Tea. He told me he has reached the point that he cannot function without it in the morning.

When we got there, he said he wanted to go into the store, because "The margin for error was greater" in the drive through. That was fine with me. He was in the store for at least 15 minutes, and I had to move the cab three times. I didn't know it that day, but I was getting a hybrid within a couple of weeks, and looking back, I wished I had it that day. By the time he came out, meter read $9.

On the way back, he told me he was here for the Georgia-

ASU game. He played at Georgia in the late 80's and he told me he always goes to intersectional games against good opponents. He shared the name of another former Georgia football player, William Andrews, who had a solid career with the Atlanta Falcons. That William Andrews, sadly, had some trouble after his playing career was done. This William Andrews was doing very well, evidenced by the 100% tip he gave me.

The game was a late afternoon kickoff, so I knew it was going to be a long day. Around 2 PM, I got a call around Cactus and 20th, and it was two guys that were ASU grads that were going to the game. It was a long haul from there, so the fare was outstanding. When you add in the stop at the liquor store, I made a lot of money. They didn't think ASU had a chance in hell of winning, but they were drinking their mini bottles of mudslides, so they were pretty happy by the time we got there. They were also considerate enough to not spill, or leave bottles in the car. This wasn't my only fare of drunks.

Georgia won the game without a lot of problem. Having gone to a major football school, I know the feeling of losing important games. There were plenty of angry Sun Devils fans milling around the stadium. I got a call to pick up three people at a house party three miles from the major intersection by the stadium, University and Rural.

When I got to the house, there were plenty of people outside, but it was dark. I got out and there was a lot of stuff going on. There was a fight that was being broken up, three girls throwing up into the same garbage can and a lot of cursing of Bulldogs. I said I was looking for John. A guy woke from his stupor, got out of a chair and said he was John; he just needed to get his two friends. He started hollering for them to come, and miraculously, they showed up within seconds. John sat in the front and the two girls sat in the back.

I turned around and noticed how hot the girls were. There were pretty angry because of the game and they asked me if I went to the game. I told them I was watching it somewhere else, and the blonde (Donna) started yelling "Fuck Georgia, Fuck Georgia" and she tried to do it in a Southern accent. I started laughing.

They told me they wanted to go to Scottsdale, just east of Scottsdale Road, behind a Food City. Normally, from where we were it would take 10 minutes, even with normal traffic. The streets were jammed.

I was moving at around five MPH when we got out to Rural Road (keep in mind, Rural Road becomes Scottsdale Road at Loop 202, about three miles from where we were). There were thousands of people walking around, wearing either ASU colors (crimson and gold) or Georgia colors (red, silver and black). The Georgia people didn't seem to be gloating very much, but this didn't stop my girls from abusing them. "We're from JOE-ER-JA, we're hicks from JOE-ER-JA, let's fuck some sheep." It was pretty obnoxious.

They were relentless, too. They asked me to keep changing lanes every time they saw someone they wanted to yell epithets towards. In a way, it made me uncomfortable at first, but I thought, "Shit, I did the same thing in college". The girls were making all the noise and I told them, "Just do me this favor. DON'T THROW ANYTHING OUT THE WINDOW", just as the redhead (Cindy) was throwing a can. She stopped in mid-throw, and incredibly, nobody even seemed to think it after that. I appreciated that very much.

About the time we got to Lemon Street, John thought he saw someone they knew. I maneuvered the car to the far right and sure enough, they saw a couple that were their friends. He rolled down the window and yelled, "Hey Doug." The couple (her name was Brittany) turned around and said, "Hey, whazzuuuuup" and John responded with "Whazzuuuuup". I laughed again.

John moved to the back with the other girls and Doug and Brittany got into the front, she sat on his lap. They were pretty drunk. Donna said hello, kissed John and started yelling at

Georgia fans again. "Hey, let's go to JOE-ER-JA, let's go to JOE-ER-JA, Fuck you Georgia. You suck." Not one person yelled anything back at her.

Brittany was trying to ask me a question, but she kept stumbling over her words, and then laughing hysterically. After a while, she slumped into Doug's lap and started giggling again. In the back, Cindy and John were wrapped up, making out and Donna was still yelling at people. Donna then noticed another couple of friends and told me to let them get in. Now, five was the maximum number of passengers I "was supposed" to have in the car. I started to realize I didn't care, because I was having fun. So, Donna hung way out of the window and called to Dave and Joanna, telling them to get in. They squeezed in the back, ending the romance for John and Cindy.

We were still crawling along at 10 MPH when John had a brainstorm; he called his roommate to see where he was. He said we should pick him up too. I said, "I don't think that's a great idea. There is no place to put him." He said, "Don't worry about, they will fit." I probably should have been more forceful, but I went along with it.

John got in touch with his roommate, and he was only a couple of hundred yards from where we were. But this guy said he didn't want to ride with us. John asked him why, but he didn't seem to get a good enough answer. John started yelling at him, and everything got quiet. "Why the fuck not, what's wrong with you." That went on for about three minutes before John hung up. Sure enough, we drove right along side of John's roommate, so John rolled down the window and started screaming at his roommate, whose name was also John. As we passed, his roommate gave him the finger, so EVERYONE started yelling out the window, except for Brittany, who seemed to be asleep. It was totally bizarre.

Not as bizarre as Brittany though. She would close her eyes, then open them, say something incoherent and fall back asleep. Every now and again, Doug would squeeze one of her boobs, and she would smile. Doug was talking to John, and Brittany reached up and rubbed my cheek with her hand. I looked down and she mouthed the words, "I love you". I smiled at her and she fell asleep yet again. I guess I have that effect on women.

After about 35 minutes, we crossed into Scottsdale and Dave and Joanna insisted on being dropped off at the QT 294. They got out and stumbled into the store. John told me they needed to stop at the Food City on Roosevelt. After we went there, we would go to his house around the corner. I was a little worried they would try to stiff me.

They came back out with beer and I drove them home. John asked if I was available later and I told them I was going home, but I appreciate them asking. John asked me for my number for another time, but he never did call me again. That was fine, because I still had a good time with them.

Big Sky Country

I have had a number of fares where the person was from the state of Montana and they all seemed to lead to something eventful, at least in my mind.

The first one was quite a coincidence. I got to this hospital in Mesa that is a problem, because on my GPS, it is considered to be Mesa, when in reality, it is in Gilbert. The address says South Gilbert Road in Mesa, when it is actually North Gilbert Road in Gilbert. I almost always go past it, even though it stands alone in the middle of nowhere.

Anyway, I went into the reception area, and of course, the guy isn't there. I told the women at the desk who I'm looking for, and they checked around for about five minutes, but they couldn't find him. Finally, one of the ladies said thinks she knows who the guy is and that he is walking around with black jeans, a black cowboy shirt, one of those string ties with the medallion holding it in place and a black ten gallon hat. They called him a cowboy. I said "A black hat? Well that explains it. He must be a bad guy." Now, among the three ladies sitting at the desk, one of them was black, and they all gave me puzzled looks. Sensing their lack of understanding, I quickly said, "Sure, the bad guy always wears a black hat", and I started laughing. Fortunately, they got the joke.

Anyway, I saw the guy walking towards us from about 75 yards away. I knew this was my guy, mainly because of the hat. When he got to the information desk, the one nurse told him I was the cab driver. Now, when I am kept waiting, it really bothers me. But I never let on that it does. For the most part, it really doesn't matter. Most people don't care. But this guy was very apologetic. He was visiting his mother in the hospital.

He told me where he was going, and off we went. He felt compelled to tell me about cultural differences between Montana and Arizona. When that shit starts, I get a little nervous. Even though I make joking references to ethnic stereotypes, I don't like the angry "they are what's wrong with society" Neo-Nazi type banter. He said that there are almost no Hispanics or blacks in Missoula (or where ever he said he was from). They don't have to lock their doors at night, or they feel safe walking in town after dark, etc. I'm not sure what his point was supposed to be, but I was thinking he might be involved with a supremacist group.

So, this guy named Don is regaling me with the joys of Montana cowboy living when somehow the subject of the Enron scandal came up. I certainly have become aware in my two-plus years here that corruption leaves NO stone unturned, but that Enron thing really pissed me off. Those fucking guys stole the retirements from thousands of loyal employees (who made them their fortunes) and then the Ringleader dies before doing a minute of jail time. I don't believe that 20 years of hard labor would be punishment enough for what he did. As of this writing, I don't know what happened to the others. (By the way, I am convinced that he is not really dead. When he turns up in 2021 in Costa Rica, I won't be surprised. As a matter of fact, I would love to be the person to find him. That would be a great achievement.)

Well, it turns out that Don's wife was among the people that blew the whistle on the whole thing. He told me to Google the name "Robin Hosea" and I would see what he was talking about. (I looked it up when I got home and a series of stories popped up, confirming what he had told me.)

Robin Hosea was a senior benefits specialist at Enron, who discovered $15 million worth of unapproved expenditures from the benefits department. When she questioned it, she was told to leave it. Don got involved and was told it was none of his business. Later, while meeting with the Department of Labor investigators, she was called by her supervisors and told to keep quiet. She claimed there was only one way they could know she was meeting with them, and that reason: she was being followed. (1)

I have to presume that Don is Robin Hosea's husband, although I don't know it for sure. Why would this guy make that up? It is a pretty vague reference. In the end, the fare was good, and he gave me a solid tip, so what difference does it really make? And, it's a good story.

One of the fares early in my career that made me cry was a woman named Patty I got at a Budget Suites in Mesa. She owned a large horse-breeding farm in Montana, one that was thousands of acres in size. She bred show horses, racehorses and others. But that wasn't the reason she was here.

I drove her to a couple of places like Big Lots and Goodwill so she could pick up stuff like cooking utensils, bathroom necessities and the like. She was moving here for a few months. Finally, I asked why she was here. The answer stunned me.

It turns out that her daughter had been in the hospital for quite a while. The man in her life had beaten her up so badly, she was in a coma. She told me the doctors expected her to recover, and she was here to nurse her back to health. Patty was choosing her words carefully, although I don't know why. I'd be pretty angry if my daughter was viciously attacked. I guess she was trying to control her emotions in front of me.

I felt so bad; I waited from place to place without charging the wait time. That was dumb, but at that point, I was still naïve to the industry. She asked if I would be available to her over the next bit of time, and I said I would be.

Patty called me twice more. It was business as usual the first time, but the second time her demeanor had changed quite a bit. Her daughter's roommate was not being as helpful as she would have liked, to the point where there seemed to be an indifference on her part. As a matter of fact, the two of them spoke on the phone while she was in the cab with me, and it sounded like they would have gotten into a fistfight if they had been in the same room. We got to the daughter's apartment to bring some stuff inside. Luckily, the roommate wasn't there, because this woman was ready to hit her in the head with a shovel. The roommate's boyfriend was there, which could've been just as bad, but nothing happened. I never heard anything further.

In the first couple of weeks I had Prius number 750, I got a call to pick up a woman at the Scottsdale Gateway Apartments. When I arrived, I found that it was a couple that was apartment hunting, because they were moving to Phoenix from Missoula, Montana in approximately a month. I was having a hard time talking to him because she was so friggin' hot. But they were asking me all kinds of questions about the area, what to do, etc. I told them where I was living, but they wanted to be in Tempe or Scottsdale. I dropped them off at another complex about three miles from there and went to the next fare.

I went back to the QT 294 about an hour after that to wait for another call. I was reading, either Harry Potter or a book on the history of professional wrestling. I looked to my right, and there they were, walking towards me. They had just looked at the complex next to the QT, and they asked me to bring them to a place on Baseline and Rural. They seemed to be having a good time (I would be miserable, I hate shopping, no matter what I'm shopping for). I dropped them off at a gated community and told them, "I'll see you later, probably." They laughed and went on their way.

I was leaving the complex, and either there was no sign telling me the gate opens in, or I missed it, because the gate swung into the right front corner of the cab. It didn't hit the car that hard, but it did hit it. It was hard to tell whether any damage was done, because this cab had previously been in an accident and there were dents from that. I struggled with the idea of bringing the car in. I finally decided I would. Of course, I was told I would probably be "charged back" for the damage. I think that was said to scare me, because I wasn't ever "charged back" for it. I realized then though, I won't ever tell them anything like this again.

I stopped at QT 328 once I had gotten back to Tempe, and incredibly, there was that same couple again. They told me they were in that complex for a long time and they wanted to go back to Scottsdale to visit one more place before calling it a day. I took them there and, on the way, they confessed they were having second thoughts on moving here. I asked them why, and they said that moving away from family was going to be tough. I told them that at this point, they would be worse off not doing it. They asked me why I said that. I explained to them that after all the excitement and energy they've invested in this move so far, if they don't go through with it, they will always wonder. Now isn't the time in your life to lament things you did or didn't do. I'm not sure that was a comfort to them.

I took them to their final destination, on Miller and McKellips. I gave them my number and told them I would probably be close, so call me when they're finished. Well, almost exactly one hour later, they called and asked me to pick them up. The hotel they were staying at was only a couple of miles from there. I made a good amount of money from them, and they were fun.

The final Montana fare I had was clearly, to me, the most

intriguing. I got a call to the Department of Economic Security (DES). I'm not sure of all of the things under their jurisdiction, but one of the issues they handle is child custody. The call came to pick up this woman and she was leaning up against a tree when I got there. She came over to confirm the fare and she got in. I was pretty happy when she said where she was going, about 10 miles away in Mesa.

We were making with the small talk and she decided to tell me about her daughter, who was being held in protective custody by DES. I always felt that an agency like this would have the tendency to overstep its bounds, because they have authority to make judgments without facts, because "they are looking out for the welfare of the child". (I wonder how many caseworkers are actually parents.) I didn't know this woman, so I didn't know whether she was being wronged or not.

All of a sudden, she goes, "Look, I'm going to tell you flat out, I'm a prostitute." She blurted it out to me, so I was shocked. It wasn't as if I had never had a prostitute in my cab before. It's just that no one ever admitted it. Come to think it, I'm still not sure why she told me. Maybe, since I was sympathetic to her plight, she felt like she could trust me. Being trustworthy is something I am prideful of, so I hope that was the reason.

Anyway, she told me that business was kind of *drying up* for her in Montana, so she decided to try the Valley. She also told me that she was on the Howard Stern show, about three years ago, arguing with some nut-job super model about whether she is a fit mother or not. When I got home that night, I went to the Howard Stern web site. Sure enough, she was on the show, having that fight with the aforementioned super model. Now, I don't her know from a hole in the wall. But, I can imagine you would have a tough time convincing any state agency that a prostitute could provide an environment that is positive for a child. I understand that way of thinking. In my opinion, though, when the government starts getting involved with stuff like that, someone is going to get hurt. I mean, if you don't know a person, how do you know what they are capable of. I'm sure way too many assumptions are made.

She and I were having a nice conversation and she asked me to stop at QT 310 to grab some beer. Next, I drove to her place and she said she needed to go in the apartment to get some cash. I thought just for a second she might try to dick me, but she came out almost immediately and gave me a good tip. She told me to save her phone number and pass it around to people that might want to use "her services". I put it directly into my phone, saying, "I might call myself." She said, "I look forward to it." "So do I", I replied. I never called her.

(1) "Did Enron steal from employees?" 2002-2-4 CBS Evening News www.cbsnews.com/stories

October 8, 2008

October 8, 2008 was memorable, because of the fares and the things that kept happening that made the day interesting from start to finish.

I got in the cab at 5:50 AM, but I didn't get a call for 45 minutes. I started, as I almost always do, in zone 82, which is where I live. I saw a fare in zone 79 with a C (that means the fare will pay with a credit card). I made the presumption they were going to the airport and chased the call. I was approximately five miles from there, which is a long way to go, but I was correct, they went to the airport.

When I got there, I saw a very attractive woman with two kids and suitcases. She had a British accent and we had a nice conversation on the way. I kept asking questions, hoping to find out if she was married, which she was, of course. It turns out I had driven her husband to the airport two other times for business trips. The kids were maybe 10 and 12, well behaved and cute.

The little girl, in particular, was trying to be cute. Mom kept them from getting annoying, so the trip was outstanding on the whole. Plus, the final fare and tip was $44. That's a great start.

I will either go to the Shell on 44th and Van Buren or to QT 294 after an airport run. This time, I was going to the QT and I got a call to pick up Ray at the Circle K on 52nd and Van Buren. I really hate Circle K calls, because half the time the person isn't there. Ray was sitting on the curb, smoking a stogie when I got there, but it took him a while before he looked at the cab and got up. This seemed strange, but I soon knew why that happened. He signaled to me that he couldn't speak or hear. So I thought, "This should be fun!" He wrote down where he was going, the KFC on Thomas and 40th, so away we went. Now, normally, I would try to start a conversation with the guy, but I thought, "What's the point?" When we got near, he started pointing and waving so I would know where to go, we got there without incident and by the time I had finished my log entry, I saw he was already taking out the garbage.

The next call was about two miles from there, an electronic voucher to bring someone to the hospital at 24th and Roosevelt. This is a good voucher, because there is a good chance that you will get a pickup right at the hospital immediately after the drop off. When I got to the location, the woman was on her way out. I opened the door and noticed that her right diamond earring looked like it was going to fall off. I told her that, but her response was "2525 East Roosevelt", so I gathered that she didn't speak any English. Fortunately, it was a short trip.

I was able to get an immediate fare from the hospital, another Hispanic named Ricardo, who I had picked up two other times from that location. He had a cane, so I had to help him into the cab. He spoke English, so we talked about the car, because he got a kick out of the fact the Prius has a camera that works when the car in running in reverse. I tried to show him some of the other gadgets, like the screen that compiles gas consumption. He had a problem with making some gurgling noises that got kind of an-noying, but no big deal.

My next fare was one I chased down to Baseline Road and Central, but it wasn't very lucrative, paying the minimum. But, on the up side, I only drove 1 mile for $6. This was another fare that I had picked up before (that happens a lot with vouchers). It was a woman and her mother going to dialysis. The daughter sounded, at first, like she had some slight retardation and her voice was really high. I think I realized it was more just a problem speaking, because she said a couple of clever things while we were waiting for her mom. I remembered that her mom took a couple of minutes longer the previous time. Anyway, this pickup went off without a hitch.

I took a risk with the next pickup, because it was in the south-ern part of west Phoenix, and it could have ended up with me driving 7 miles for a $6 pickup. I drove to 49th avenue to a business called Terex. It turns out it was a guy who was flying to Albuquerque to drive a truck back to Phoenix. When I got there, the guy told me he was in a hurry to get to the airport, because his flight was at 11 AM. Well, it was 9:30, so I knew there was no problem. We got off to a poor start, because I had use the bathroom, but that only took two minutes. I was happy, because I knew this was going to be a big fare. He was telling me how he is an independent contractor as well. He told me many sto-ries about how the gas price spike had cost him a ton of money. One, in particular, stood out, when he went from Pittsburgh, PA to Seattle, WA over a five-day period, and only cleared about $300. At the time, diesel was costing over $5 per gallon. There were two things that made the trip kind of a problem. Firstly, he spoke in a real whiny tone. Secondly, and worse yet, was that he smelled like he had been working on cars for three straight days without a shower. There was no problem with getting him to airport, and the fare was great.

As usual, I went towards QT 294, but before I got there, I got a call from a place named the 360 Degrees Rehab, about a half a mile north of the QT, to pick up a woman waiting for a ride home. She was outside when I got there. On the way back we started talking, and she inquired about me driving her friends, who were visiting, around Phoenix over the weekend. She said they don't speak English and she would have to go with them. The language she has in common with them is Esperanto. I told her that I would do it, but I expected to be paid for what my time was worth. She asked what that meant and I said if you want me to go from place to place and wait for them the whole time, $30 per hour would be fair. She said this was pretty expensive and I agreed. But, if I was going to make that kind of time commitment, I expected to be compensated. I also told her that if she got a limousine, it would be $75 per hour. She asked if I could give her a better deal, and I told her no. It is one thing to toss someone a bone when it is one trip, but if I make a commitment for a whole day, I can't do it. She asked if I knew anyone else and I said no. I repeated that I didn't want a misunderstanding and that is the reason I'm setting the rules now. She told me she appreciated my honesty, and she would have her friends call if they were going to use the service. Needless to say, I never heard from them.

I took a break and rode the exercise bike at my gym and came back towards Tempe to resume the shift. I got a call for a girl named Diane at St Luke's Hospital. I got her in front of the hospital and she ran to the car. She thanked me for getting there so soon, because she was forced to listen to a group of nurses and doctors in what (to her) appeared to be a staff meeting. She was very cute, but we really didn't talk about much except me writing this book. She told me there are ways to get the book published where the publisher will advance me money while the book is being edited, because it will take a year to publish the book once they have the original copy. I was pretty sure a whole year wasn't necessary, but I nodded in agreement because it all sounded reasonable. I now realized she didn't have a clue about publishing.

To me, this had already been an interesting day, but it really started to get goofy from this point. I chased a call about six miles to North Mesa. I got to the fare's apartment, and that was kind of weird, because this series of apartments were lettered A-Z, instead of being numbered. I knocked and got no response, so I called the number on the dispatch. Just as the phone started to ring, the door opened and Linda said she would be out in a minute. She came out, and it took her at least a minute and a half to lock her door. I thought "OK" and opened the door to the cab.

As she got closer, I noticed her eyes were wide open and huge, like she was on speed or something. After she got in, she told me she was going to Banner Hospital on Gilbert Road (the same confusing one I mentioned before). She spoke with good diction, something I always notice. I also noticed that she was in a kind of trance, and after we started moving, she was rocking back and forth. I didn't try to speak with her unless I thought it was necessary, and she started mumbling what sounded like "Oh, yah", over and over

Well, that continued for a couple of minutes, and I just drove. Then, without warning, the chant changed to "May-oh-ME". She did that for about five minutes, again rocking back and forth the whole time. I really wasn't concerned, because I just figured she was afraid of being in a car, and that's how she dealt with it. It was weird to watch, though. We were about two minutes from the hospital and she reverted to the first chant "Oh Yah" and did that until we got to the hospital. I asked her if she wanted to be taken to the emergency room, but she wanted the main entrance (which she said, again, with perfect diction). She paid with hand held vouchers and got out. I went inside to go to the bathroom, and when I finished, she was talking with a nurse. I guess she didn't know where she was supposed to be, because the nurse ended up sending her to the other end of the hospital on a golf cart.

I chased another call, more towards central Mesa. I picked up a woman named Rachel, who looked like she was in her 20's, on an electronic voucher. I wonder sometimes about people who are so young going to a hospital. It turns out this woman was, until recently, a Discount Cab driver. She looked at the Prius and told me how cute it was and how she liked the reverse camera. We started talking about the features of the car and, after a while, she told me why she doesn't drive for Discount anymore.

It turns out she has two cancerous brain tumors and she is going for treatment. I just looked at her and said "Oh my god" (I didn't know what else to say). She also said she has had three total tumors in five years. She sounded like she had a pretty good outlook, in spite of it all. She kept saying how she was doing things to keep positive; despite not being able to work, and that she felt that she was going to beat the cancer. It was really hard not to feel sad for her, though.

She then talked about her "step-son". His birth mother, apparently, is a rampaging, drug-crazed, nut of a woman, who is trying to steal the son back from the father (Rachel is supposed to marry this guy in the near future). But, Rachel takes great pride in helping to raise this boy, to the point that she considers him her own. We got to the hospital for her treatment and she told me she would be done in about an hour, if I wanted to wait to try to get that call. I said it was possible, but I wasn't going to turn down a call and she agreed with that.

I did something 10 minutes later that could have proved to be a problem. I had heard about this Pumpkin Pie Blizzard at Dairy Queen and, since I was right by one, decided try it. It was so good! I almost felt like I was making love to it. (In fact...nah just kidding!) Since I did the Cookie diet and lost 74 pounds, I have been very conscious of caloric intake, how much fast food type stuff I eat, etc. The damn thing has about 61,000 calories in it. I didn't want to go back to my old habits, although eventually I did. I promised myself, since it's a seasonal promotion, I will only get two more of them.

My next call was to an Albertson's to pick up Dustin. It was close, but grocery store calls generally are $5-8 dollars, so they don't seem worth it. I got there, and it was a young dude and his grandmother. She wasn't very mobile, so he and I put the groceries in the car, and I helped her in. As usual, they marveled at the camera for backing up, and off we went. We were going to a trailer home park (there a ton of them here). In the end, the fare was only $5, but the woman told him to give me $8, and she went ahead to tell me that she gave me the extra money because I was the nicest cabbie she had ever ridden with and she wished more were like me. I have had many compliments like this.

By the way, I now understand why cab drivers are surly people. A lot of people think they have carte blanche to treat cabbies like shit, so they do. It is tough to be nice to people when they kick you in the head. Still, I have never treated people the shabby way a number of cabbies do. It isn't hard to be nice, carry people's things for them and speak to them with respect. I can't change people's opinion of cab drivers, but I was going to continue to try as long as I was a driver.

At this point, I went back to the hospital to see if I could catch Rachel on her way back home. Unfortunately, I got a note from the safety and compliance guy, asking me to come back to the Mesa cage. "Oh Shit, this can't be good," I thought to myself. I kept wondering what I did, and I started to get really depressed, thinking I was going to lose my job. It was a 20 minute ride, so that made it that much more difficult. When I got there, I knocked on the safety guy's door, went in and sat down. It turns out I got myself worked up over nothing, because he just told me about not wearing my seatbelt and looking both ways before pulling out of a private driveway. Not to minimize these things, but I do wear my seatbelt. The problem was I usually have my arm over the shoulder strap, so it looks like I don't use it. I have become more aware to put the strap over my shoulder, so some good came of this. He told me that I am a low maintenance driver who they are glad to have.

I went back to the QT 294 to wait for a call. The fare I got was a woman I refer to as Candice Many Names. She normally goes to one of the Scottsdale Road clubs where she works as a cocktail waitress. This time, she had a friend with her and they made a trip to the Fry's strip mall on McDowell. It was weird because they wanted me to drop them off at the video store two doors over. That, in and of itself, isn't strange, but I watched them both walk in the alleyway along side of the store. I have a feeling it was something the church would frown upon.

The next fare I got came almost immediately, right back to the apartment complex next to QT 294. It was gated so it took a while to get in. Sometimes the passenger will not give the order taker the code, so you have to wait for someone to open the gate for you. When I got to the correct building, Patrick was outside waiting for me.

We needed to go up to North Scottsdale and it was pretty close to rush hour, so the fare was going to be big. He was picking up his car, so I expected him to be in a shitty mood. I found out that was only partially true.

People often say they don't wish to discuss politics or religion, but I love it. A free exchange of ideas is very healthy. It is also the best way to form opinions, learn when people are bullshitting you, and find out things you wouldn't have known otherwise.

This guy was full of opinions, which I think is good. He went out of his way to talk about Joe Arpaio. Now I have oscillated, for the sake of this book, on how much to discuss this guy. For now, let's just say that, "neither of us care for him."

Patrick was really interesting, because he has a lot of theories on government and the laws they create "for the common good." He particularly was critical of photo enforcement cameras and the DUI laws. We agreed that both of these "laws" were created for the *sole* purpose of raising money.

Then he started talking about woman and how they fuck him over all time. He droned on about how they use him because he has a lot of money. I asked what he meant, and he told me that he spends a lot of time at nightclubs and he never does very well. I said, "You probably do better than you think. A 100% success rate is impossible. Shit, 50% is impossible." I don't know if he felt any better, but it was the truth.

Tales of his love life brought us to the dealer. His fare was $36.75, plus he gave me an $8 tip. I'm having a solid, fun day.

Next, I got a fare near Thunderbird and 90th. It was a really nice apartment complex, bringing this well dressed fellow to a law office. It was a long trip, over to Greenway and (almost) the 51. He was telling me how he got a DUI and he was going to lose his license shortly. There isn't a whole lot you can say to make someone feel better in that situation. He didn't want to talk about it anyway, so I just drove him there. It was another solid fare.

Again, I got a quick call, to pick up this hottie named Brandi. She was tall, slim and had phenomenal, long dark hair. She wanted to go a strip club that was near Cave Creek Road. I never knew that strippers were independent contractors until she told me. She was matter-of-fact about her job. She said, "Look, I'm not a genius, I hate school, and I can make a lot of money doing this." I said, "I'm right there with you. A great skill to have is to know your strengths and weaknesses. Plus, if you enjoy it and you don't get abused, I'm sure you can do extremely well." I've said it many times. I respect strippers. It was a good fare and tip.

The next fare was a woman that was on her way to work. One thing that seems to be true is restaurant workers are the most susceptible to DUI's. You are always going out late, and when you have access to alcohol, you drink it. I would say 10% of the fares are DUI's and half of *them* are restaurant workers. This chick was no exception. It was a short fare with a decent tip.

The next call was difficult, because it was starting to get dark, the street was hidden, and their phone was busy for a long time. I finally found the two women I was looking for. They got into the car and told me that they needed to go to a Cricket (cell phone) store. I wasn't that familiar with North Phoenix, but they directed me to the store of which they were aware. Unfortunately, that one was already closed.

I felt a little uneasy, because they were complaining about that, in addition to the cost of ride and my lack of knowledge. They called an 800 number and we discovered another store about four miles from the first one. They both went in, but not before I explained to them the meter would be running. They didn't seem to have a problem with that.

They were in the store for approximately 15 minutes. When they came back, they hadn't accomplished anything. They didn't seem nearly as perturbed as they were at the other store being closed. They had me drive them home. The fare was decent, but they didn't give me a tip. They did ask if I would help them tomorrow, but I couldn't guarantee I would be in the area. As it turns out, they did call me two other times. I wasn't close enough to pick them up either time.

The next call was to a clinic in a strip mall. I picked up two Indian women, and brought them to an apartment complex near the 51 and Northern. I only spoke with Dasha, the woman's name on the dispatch. She was beautiful and I kept thinking I would love to go out with her. She was very friendly, and had a nice smile. Indians pay with credit cards 99 times out of a 100, and she was no different. I had her as a fare another time, and I picked her up at a hospital. It appears she is on dialysis, which is horrible, especially when the person is so young.

My final fare was bringing this guy and his stuff from Phoenix to Mesa. He was weird. After we loaded the stuff in the Prius, he wanted to take it out and rearrange it. When I asked him why, he said it would fit better another way. "I'm turning the meter on now; do you still want to rearrange stuff?" We got going right then.

On the way, he told me that his girlfriend threw him out and he was going to live with some friends for a while. I asked why he was thrown out; he told me "she was an asshole". I was pretty sure it was more complicated than that, so I played Doctor Freud and asked him to elaborate. He said she expected too much from him. "What the hell does that mean?" He didn't seem to want to talk about it anymore. Fine.

. He asked how I liked driving a cab and I told him it was OK. He also wanted to know what the requirements were, so I told him. I mean, there really aren't any, except you can't be a criminal, or a lousy driver. He said a few ambiguous things, and that made me think that, not only was he a lousy driver, but a criminal, too! I kept that to myself. We got to his friends' apartment and they came out to help move his stuff. He paid with a credit card, but didn't give me a tip. This was one of my most successful and interesting days after 3½ months "in the biz."

The Buddhist Monk

Based on what I was told at my orientation as compared to what I have been told by others since, it is difficult for me to know what rules I have to follow. I have read a number of on-line articles that indicate that what I was told are the rules might not really be factual. I chose not to challenge these rules.

We were told that we needed a specific license to pick up people at the airport. That was easy enough to verify. To me, that's not right. Why should the city and (more importantly) politicians benefit from a company that is providing a service, outside of normal taxation of income? They certainly are not assuming any of the risk involved. And then with weights and measures on top of it, they are making a lot of money.

Having said that, based on some of the things I've seen at Sky Harbour, it's a good thing that licensing exists. I'm convinced there would be murder every month if there were a free-for-all there. There are at least 85 cab companies in Phoenix. Discount alone generally has 200 cabs on the street at any given time. I did have one occasion where I did a pick up at the airport, and brother it was memorable.

I had just dropped off this pompous guy at Terminal Three, when one of the porters came to me asking me to pick up the man she had by the arm. I was going to say I wasn't permitted to, but instead I said OK and tried to get him to hurry into the cab. He had a ragged suitcase, was wearing an orange toga sort of thing and had a wool hat on his head.

I asked him where he was going and he started speaking a language other than English. This is almost always bad. He was trying to "speak with his hands". Now, generally, I'm pretty good at understanding what people in this situation are attempting to communicate, as long as I'm patient. So, I decided to pull to the side until we figured out where he needed to go.

He kept saying "The Temple, The Temple." Now, I was pretty sure he wasn't Jewish, and we weren't in Philadelphia, so that didn't help. I asked him if he had a driver's license and he did. The address on the license said Waddell, AZ, which is west of the 101 near the football stadium. So, now I'm thinking, "Alright, this is going to be a good fare."

I put the address in my GPS, and it showed up about 25-30 miles away, and I asked him if that distance sounded correct. I am not sure he understood, but he said, "Ye-e-e-ah, Ye-e-e-ah", in a really high pitched voice. OK. I turned the cab towards the I-10 and away we went.

Now, 30-45 minutes of driving with a dude that may or may not speak English can be difficult, but I managed. He asked me where I was from, and I told him New Jersey. I might as well have said the Moon. He didn't know where that was, so I told him "very close to New York City." He seemed to understand that, although he asked me two more times. The second time I asked him if he knew where New York City was and he said, "Ye-e-e-ah, Ye-e-e-ah." Then he said something I presumed meant east.

I asked him where he was from and he said something that

sounded like Thailand. I asked him if he was from Thailand, so he showed me his passport, and it was from Thailand. Interestingly enough, the address on the passport was the same as his driver's license. I asked him if he was a citizen of the United States and he said, "Na-a-a-h, Na-a-a-h." Who says communication is hard?

Then, he wanted to know if I'd ever been to Thailand and I told him I had not been there. He said, "Why-y-y-y, Why-y-y-y?" I tried to explain I just haven't had the opportunity. He told me he thought I should go there, and when I asked him why, he told me it was fun. I asked him if he liked it and he said, "Ye-e-e-ah, Ye-e-e-ah." He told me three more times that I should go there. I said, "So, do you think I should go to Thailand?" What do you think he said? "Ye-e-e-ah, Ye-e-e-ah."

He kept asking me questions I could only half understand, and then he would put his hand out and ask me if we were friends. How could I not be a friend with this guy? And I shook his hand every time, after which he would smile and say, "Ye-e-e-ah, Ye-e-e-ah." I thought I was going to bite a hole in my lip trying not to laugh.

When we got to 59th Avenue, something very odd happened. I noticed that he had draped his right arm around the passenger front seat. Then he wrapped his other arm around my seat. The next thing I knew, he was leaning forward and he rested his head on my shoulder. I looked at him and didn't say anything. He just looked up at me and said, "We're friends, right?" He had really sad looking eyes until I said, "Sure we are." He fell back into the seat and said, "Ye-e-e-ah, Ye-e-e-ah." That's when I realized: This guy is drunk.

He became a lot less talkative as we got closer, but he did keep saying, "We go to Temple, we go to Temple." I showed him the GPS as we turned north on the 101, so when we got to Camelback he said, "Ye-e-e-ah, Ye-e-e-ah." We had to go about five miles west of 101, and the GPS was right on target. I saw a place that looked like a water treatment plant that I remembered mainly because, for some reason, there was a port-a-john at the front gate. I asked him if we were friends, and he nodded. Then I told him I needed to use that bathroom. He just smiled. I also took the key out when we stopped. I didn't trust him *that* much.

I saw the signs for the Buddhist Temple as we got close, but he told me to go past it. It turns out he wanted to go to this trading post sort-of place a mile up the road. We went in so he could buy a 30 pack of beer. He offered to buy me anything I wanted. I was on the cookie diet, so water was fine. I was able to snag a couple of pens from the place, though. Plus, he wanted to flirt with the woman behind the counter. I was ready to apologize for him, until I realized that she knew him. He wanted to get the attention of another woman, and I asked if he knew her too and he said, "Ye-e-e-ah, Ye-e-e-ah."

We finally went towards the Temple. When we got to the gate, he had to get out and open it so I could drive the car in. Again, this job puts me in paranoid mode a lot. I was very cautious, and that feeling doubled when five pit bulls surrounded the car. But, they weren't maniac pit bulls, they just barked a lot. My buddy got out of the car and I told him it was $83 (yes, the meter read $83). He handed me a $100 bill, which heightened my anxiety some more. I carry a marker that confirms whether it is a real bill. Fortunately, this one was real.

I gave him the change and he stumbled to his "apartment", which was nothing more than four walls holding each other up. I carried his suitcase into the place, which had a curtain instead of a door. When I walked in, I noticed a bed, a table, some empty beer cans, about 15 pairs of flip-flops and 10 more monk's robes, AND NOTHING ELSE. He collapsed on the bed and he was snoring before I turned and walked away.

I saw another monk as I was leaving and asked if he needed me to re-close the gate. He said he would take care of it. I pulled out of the gate and laughed.

I went to QT 174, which was pretty close to the Temple, to wait for another call. I ended up picking up this older guy that needed me to run some errands for him. After a few moments, I started telling him about the monk I just dropped off. He then told me an interesting story about that Temple.

Apparently, about 30 years earlier, the Temple was the only building that was in the area. There really isn't a whole lot out there now, but in the late 70's, the Temple stood alone. According to him, in 1979 there was a massacre at that Temple, and 12 monks were murdered. It was a huge deal. This guy told me it was four kids who came in to steal things and do some damage to property. In the end, they were caught in the act; they panicked and ended up killing the monks.

I picked up another passenger later who told me a different story. After I told him what the first guy said, he told me it was four guys, but they were associated with the Temple, involved in a power struggle, hoping to gain power within the Temple. They had planned the attack. He also told me it backfired on the leader of the coup, because he was killed a few months after the attack. Intrigued, I decided to do a little research on my own.

After looking for articles in the library and on the Internet, I'm not sure the crime has really been solved. The only things that are definitely true are as follows: that it (actually) happened in 1991 at Wat Promkuranan Buddhist Temple in Waddell, six monks and three others were shot, execution style and it is the largest mass murder in the history of Arizona.

After a few days, clues lead the police to arrest five people who were in Tucson and accuse them of the murders. They were subsequently called the Tucson Five, and, after one was exonerated, the Tucson Four. It was later shown they were coerced into confessions. During this process, the police came across other clues that enabled them to arrest two others. (Three of the Tucson Five later sued the state and won a settlement of $1.2 million. Also, the "mishandling" of the case is considered to be a contributing factor to the failed bid of Tom Agnos for Maricopa

County sheriff against Joe Arpaio.)

Alessandro Garcia and Johnathan Doody were convicted of the murders and sentenced to almost 600 collective years in prison. The initial motive appeared to be robbery.

In 2008, with new representation, including Alan Dershowitz, Doody appealed his conviction, and in November 2008, an appeal was granted. There has yet to be a re-trial. Doody was 17 at the time of the murders, so he has now spent more than half of his life in jail.

CHAPTER **7**

Weird Stories

Loud Talker ━━━━━━━━━━━━━━━━━━━━━━━━━

Vouchers sometimes seem to be a guarantee that something will happen. There are all kinds of patients and people the state feels need help. They also bring out the worst in drivers, because they don't get paid anywhere near what the meter says you should be getting, whether it's $1.80 or $1.45 per mile. Plus, these passengers can create problems. They are often sick, frightened or just out of it.

I got a voucher call towards the end of the day when I was in Southwest Phoenix and the dude's name was Alan. I stopped in the office because there was no site map and I wanted to be able to find this guy without a lot of hassle. There were three women there and I asked where the apartment was located. One of the ladies told me how to get there. I do much better with visuals, meaning a map. I have a very hard time with Mapquest directions, for example. But, if I have the location on a map, I'm fine. All three were talking at me, but one was holding a map, so I asked if could have it. Reluctantly, she gave it to me. I wasn't going to say anything, but I couldn't help myself. I asked, "Why is it a big deal to give me a map?" Of course, nobody had an answer, so I just shook my head and left. There isn't a more useless group of people than those who work in the office of apartment complexes. The only questions they can EVER answer is how much rent you owe, when it is due, what the penalty is for non-compliance and the date. If you ask any other question, the only response is a blank stare, a shrug of the shoulders and these three words: "I don't know". Jeff Spicoli has probably had this job.

So, I got to Alan's apartment as he was coming out of the door. He had on a Chicago Black Hawks jacket and a big smile. He got in and I said, "I guess I know where you're from." He started laughing, but I quickly realized he didn't know what I meant. I asked him if he was from Chicago, but he said no. Then he told me a friend had given him the jacket, and that he was actually from New York. I said that I was from near there and he asked if I meant Long Island. I told him I was from New Jersey and he asked "Is that close to New York"? That is when it occurred to me that something wasn't quite right with him.

We started off towards Avondale, which was about 15 miles from where we were. For some reason, he was going that far to get medication at a CVS. I asked him about that and he said, really loudly "MY DOCTOR USED TO BE RIGHT DOWN THE STREET, BUT HE MOVED TO AVONDALE LAST WEEK, SO I HAVE TO GET MY MEDICATION THERE." Why are you yelling at me?

He started telling me about moving out here from New York and he was still speaking way louder than necessary. I wondered whether he had a hearing problem, but I didn't want to ask. You never know what is going to offend someone.

I asked him if he was a Mets fan and he said, "NO, I REALLY ONLY CARE ABOUT FOOTBALL." So, do you root for the Giants or the Jets? He said, "NO, I ROOT FOR THE KNICKS." OK.

My next question was, "How long have you been in Phoenix?" He said, "FOR THE LAST 10 YEARS. MY COUSINS LIVE OUT HERE AND I'VE BEEN STAYING WITH THEM. WHAT ABOUT

YOU?" I told him I've been here for about 16 months now. He said, "YEAH, ME TOO."

Then I asked what he likes to eat. He said, "WELL, I DON'T LIKE MEXICAN FOOD." So I asked, "Well, what DO you like." He said, "I REALLY HATE MEXICAN FOOD, IT GIVES ME HEARTBURN." I decided to try a different tact. "Do you like Italian Food?" He said, "NO, BUT MEXICAN FOOD IS GOOD."

When we got to the CVS, I told him I would wait for the return trip. He said, "I HOPE YOU'RE MY DRIVER TO GO BACK." I told him I hoped so, too. Alas, I got sent another fare before his came.

Wounded Lambs

Here in Phoenix, people are very conscious of the drinking and driving laws. Whether that is because they really are sensitive to possible dangers or because they don't want to pay the exorbitant fines and suffer the humiliation that awaits them at the hands of a particularly ruthless sheriff isn't important. I am very impressed that so many hire cabs so they don't drink and drive.

Our cab company has a service where we will give you a free ride back to your car the next day if you used us instead of driving drunk the night before. One of many who have used this service is a guy whose nickname is "Q", because the last syllable of his last name is "Q". I gave him rides twice through this program and we had very funny conversations both times. He is the person that gave me the title to this section. It refers to women who have had a bit too much to drink, as in, "Hey Dave, two wounded lambs at the edge of the bar". He also told me about other code phrases that he and his friends use. Unfortunately, I don't remember them. But, trust me when I tell you, I have had more than my share of wounded lambs in my cabs.

I had just dropped off these four dudes back at Mill Avenue and this guy and his girlfriend flagged me down. They were looking for a ride back to Scottsdale, so I thought to myself "Cool; that should be about $20." The girl got in, and it looked like she was wearing one of those pink Donovan McNabb Eagles jerseys I would see back at the Maple Shade Hooters, where I watched NFL games for the three years prior to moving to Phoenix. She was blonde and looked great. I probably couldn't have picked the guy out of a one-person lineup two minutes later she was that hot.

She said something about stopping at Wendy's on the way. At first, I couldn't remember where there was a Wendy's, but it really didn't matter in the end. I was talking to the dude about the Arizona State game and the girl asked if she could smoke, which I said was fine.

We went from Mill through Tempe to 68th street and the girl still hadn't lit the cigarette yet. I looked back and she had a strange look on her face. I was going to ask if anything was wrong, but then I decided I ought to pay attention to the road. About two minutes later, I knew why she had that expression on her face. We came to the corner of McDowell and 68th and I looked back again. Her face was even more contorted then it was and she said, "I don't feel very good."

She then pushed the door open and sort of poured herself out on to the concrete sidewalk. The look on the dude's face was worth a million dollars. It was a combination of shock, embarrassment and laughter. He was afraid because she was lying face first on the concrete and not moving. He was trying to hoist her up and put her back in the car, but she wouldn't budge.

Now, I was at a stoplight and there were cars behind me, so I was waving the other cars on. I'm really glad a police car didn't show up, because there really wasn't any problem. She was fine. Anyway, the guy said I should just leave them, and he would pay me.

Two other girls then came up to them and were trying to be helpful. Actually, they seemed to be trying to help themselves to this semi-conscious woman. I thought they were gay and wanted to get in her pants, but what do I know? They wouldn't have gotten anywhere, though, because as I was driving away, I noticed the girl was still lying face down on the sidewalk.

I stopped at the set of condos in Scottsdale at about 8:45 one Saturday night. I called the dude whose name was on dispatch to let them know I was there. Now, I waited for 10 minutes for them to come out. I went to the door and, of course, they came out to the car the opposite way. I finally found them waiting at the cab. It was a girl and a guy and the girl said, "Are you the cab driver". I said, "Yes" and she told me that was awesome. (By the way, awesome has become, in my opinion, the one of the most over and misused word in the English language.)

Her name was Valerie and his was Chris. She looked very attractive and he looked like he was trying to show off his muscles, his tattoos or both. He told me they were going to a club west of Scottsdale.

Once we got going, it became a classic example of the differences between men and women. She started talking about her friend, Candy, with whom she was very angry. I could tell immediately that she was loaded, and so was he. Valerie was talking about how she did everything for Candy while she was visiting in Phoenix, and all Candy did was criticize her. She said she didn't want to go out and that she was going home.

Chris, on the other hand, was working hard to get her to go. He kept saying that he just wanted her to have fun with her friend.

Well, this was apparently the wrong thing to say. Valerie got very dramatic and continued to complain that Candy was ungrateful. She did everything for Candy, and just because she had too much to drink this day, and wanted to go to bed early, Candy had no right to get so indignant with her and it wasn't fair. She also referred to Candy having "Only Child Syndrome" and said she had everything handed to her on a silver platter. Valerie also said Candy had used her; for what remained a mystery. Valerie must have said, "I'm done with her" at least a dozen times. Chris was trying to be diplomatic, but this just made Valerie angrier.

She started complaining because he wasn't defending her and siding with Candy. Chris just kept saying he wanted the two of them to have fun together. He continued to try to convince her to go out, but she kept responding with "You go out, I'm fine with that, BUT I'M GOING HOME." This went on for another five minutes or so. I was actually pretty impressed with the way she stuck to her guns about wanting to go home.

He finally decided to stop at a liquor store to pick up some beer and wine. I really had just sat there and listened to the conversation. When he went into the store, she started to defend herself to me. I told her she was right, she should be mad. I also told her that Chris wasn't being unsupportive. He just didn't want to fight about it and that's the way men are, we don't want drama-filled conflict. That didn't seem to help, but it is the truth.

So, I started telling her about this book and I told her that this story was sure to end up in it. She was very excited about it and when Chris came back, she told him. He, on the other hand, didn't seem thrilled about it. Too bad for him! I took them about two miles further and let them out, where they were still bickering about her friend when I pulled out of the driveway.

During the three weeks I had the seven-person van, I had some interesting fares. I stopped off at a bar in Scottsdale for a call box fare. The first good thing was that the person was actually there. The added bonus was she was pretty attractive.

It turns out she was a bartender at this place, but she had about eight after-shift drinks too many. Her name was Marcia and she wanted to go to her friend's house in Glendale. So I was thinking, "Man, this is going to be a $60 fare." After all was said and done, I deserved it.

As I was walking her out to the van, I noticed she had on a very revealing dress. It revealed she had very large boobs. I got the impression she was hoping to be picked up, especially consider-ing she had been working before I got there.

Right from the opening bell, I was playing Dr. Freud. She started talking about her horrible relationships with men and I was trying to be sympathetic. She looked really sad and I figured she was just loaded. After a while, I realized she really wasn't that drunk, but I guess she wanted to pour her heart out. Trust me; she wasn't the first fare I've ever been forced to console.

For some reason, she wanted to talk about being a mother, and why she WOULDN'T be a good one. When I asked her why, she burst into tears. She cried, "I was such a lousy child to my parents. I was always getting into trouble and making my parents upset. I drank and did drugs and I still do both. I never finished high school and now I'm 32 years old, and I'm still a fucking bar-tender with no education and no chance to make anything out of myself. How could I ever expect myself to take care of a child?"

I was amazed she could say all of that *without taking a breath*. I tried to think quickly of the best thing to say. "I don't know, you seem pretty compassionate and you want to be a mother, that's a good start," I offered, as she continued to cry. "But, I can't keep a man and a child needs a father and mother," she answered. I then asked her if she would like to hear what I think and she said yes. So I said, "I'm having a hard time understanding what about you could be so terrible. You've been nice to me, you work in a business where you have to be nice to people to keep your job, and you work long hard hours, which take dedication. Plus, you want to BE a good mother. It seems as though you have a lot of what is needed."

Luckily, she noticed that we needed to get off of the 17 by then to get to her friend's house. She calmed down a bit and started smiling. We changed the subject to finding her friend's house and I said that I needed to speak to him on the cell to go to the right place. Plus, he was paying the fare, so I wanted to find him badly. I called him on my cell and he was talking me in, when I noticed she had fallen asleep. Maybe she was drunker than I thought. It took 10 minutes to run his card, but I got paid, and he probably got laid.

One of the first times I drove on a Saturday evening, I got a call to a Mexican Restaurant in Paradise Valley. It was on Lincoln Drive, which is a very narrow road in PV. A lot of the resorts are located on this road and the signs are not easy to see at night.

I got to the valet area of this restaurant and I saw a number of couples standing in the cul-de-sac, waiting for their cars. I called out the name of the guy on the dispatch, but no one answered. I tried the phone number I was given, but it was the restaurant number instead of a cell phone. I told the fellow that answered and he said he would page the man. A couple came out within a minute and they both waved to me, so I guessed they were my fare.

They were an odd couple at first glance. She looked like she was somewhere between 35-45 years old, very tall (at least 5'10") and attractive (I'll call her Tammy). He was shorter than her, dumpy and he was at least 65 (His name was Gary). They were both carrying drinks and laughing out loud. I thought, "This should be a fun ride." It was, sort-of.

They got in and he told me to drop her off at home and then we were to go to the resort at which he was staying. They were laughing as he was telling jokes and I asked if they were having a good night. He said they had a great meal and they were going to a movie tomorrow. He continued on for about 30 seconds and she got real quiet. He looked at her and asked if something was wrong. Based on the 20 minutes that followed, I guessed there was.

Tammy started talking about her financial woes and how she was a single mother of two. He had wanted to go on a vacation with her to Hawaii, but she said she couldn't afford it. He told her he would pay for it, but that was the wrong thing to say. She started crying, saying how she was having a hard time making ends meet, that her kids were turning against her and that the only reason Gary was interested in her was for sex. I thought, "What's wrong with wanting to have sex with you?"

She wouldn't let it go and she kept crying about anything that came up in the conversation. She was pretty drunk and after a while she was really slurring her words. To make matters worse, her voice got louder and shriller. "WHY CAN'T YOU UNDERSTAND WHAT I'M GOING THROUGH?" He was trying to calm her down by telling her he would come over in the morning and help her with her children. Again, he said the wrong thing.

"I'LL BE LUCKY IF I CAN GET INTO THE HOUSE. I DON'T HAVE MY KEYS. I LEFT THEM IN THE HOUSE." He told her if she needed to, she could stay with him at his resort. She was inconsolable. "WHY CAN'T MY SONS BE MORE SUPPORTIVE OF ME? I DO THE BEST I CAN. WHY DO THEY HATE ME SO MUCH?" She also got uncontrollable hiccups at this point, so that made her even more upset, if that was possible.

He was trying to help with the hiccups, but since she seemed to be more concerned with her issues, they didn't interfere with her tirade. "MAYBE I SHOULD JUST KILL MYSELF, HOW MUCH OF THIS SHIT DO I HAVE TO TAKE?" Gary just threw his hands in the air. I was amazed at how long he was able to remain calm. I was getting tired of Tammy crying, but I guess Gary had a large investment in her.

We finally got to her house and she started apologizing to Gary and me for all of the tears. He tried to console her again by walking her to the door. Her one son answered the door when she knocked. She kissed Gary on the cheek and went inside. He came back and said, "Let's get the fuck out of here."

I figured the rest of the trip would be easier, but it wasn't. He started complaining about what a pain in the ass she was to him. He told me that she used to be a Playboy Playmate, but she hasn't done well since leaving. He said he was really good to her, but every time she would drink, she became impossible to deal with.

I brought him to one of the Scottsdale resorts, which took 10 minutes. He complained about Tammy the whole way. I finally asked him, "Why don't you dump her?" He said, "Because I love her." Whatever. Incredibly, after putting up with this nonsense for nearly 30 minutes, Gary tipped me $3 on a $35 fare. I guess I should have considered myself lucky.

How Do You Expect Me To Get In?

Right before my birthday in 2009, I had a very funny pick up. I took this woman home from her doctor's office. She didn't seem to be a person I should worry about, but they never do.

She got into the car, and since it was on a voucher, I knew where she was going. I should have realized that when she started telling me the "best way to go" I was in trouble. I started going down Rural, and she told me to go to towards the 101. When I said that wasn't faster, she got mad and told me to do whatever I wanted. Jeez.

When we got into Scottsdale, she told me to turn down Roosevelt. When I said I was going to do that, she said, "No you weren't." I really didn't want to argue, so I said, "OK". She seemed to realize I was patronizing her, because she said, "You know, if you continue to be rude to me, you're not going to get much of a tip." I thought, "Well, since it's a voucher, I'm not going to get a tip anyway." I didn't actually say anything.

We got to the street she lived on, but it was not a major street. I didn't see it, and she told me that I missed the turn. I quickly made a U-Turn and doubled back. At that point, I had turned off the meter and re-booked in, hoping to get another call ASAP. Sure enough, by the time we got to her driveway, another call was coming through to me.

When I saw the next voucher, I was ecstatic. It was worth $45. I said goodbye to the woman in the car, and she got out. Sadly, I sat in the driveway recording her call and the next one for just a bit too long, and as I was getting ready to leave, she ran back out telling me she couldn't find her keys.

I looked in the back seat for a few minutes and couldn't find them. She said she must have left them in the house. I asked her if anyone else had a key and she said her daughter did, but she was nowhere near the house. I asked her what she wanted to do and she said, "I don't know." I responded by saying, "Well, what do you want me to do?" She didn't have an answer for that either.

I tried to open the front door, but there was nothing I could do. I asked her if the door in the back might be open and she said she didn't know. So I walked in the back. There was a gate that I couldn't open, so now I'm starting to get annoyed. I mean, I've got this $45 voucher and this knucklehead is keeping me here.

I finally squeezed into the back through the gate. I looked for an opening and saw that three of the windows were already smashed. I asked if she was OK with breaking into the house and she said yes.

The door had a smashed window, so I started to pull the screen away from the door and she yelled for me not to do that. I said, "WOULD YOU PLEASE TELL ME WHAT YOU WANT ME TO DO. I CAN'T READ YOUR MIND." Finally, she told me she wanted me to go through the kitchen window.

I said, "Look, I'm too big, I will never fit through that window." Then, she really surprised me, telling me she would climb through the window herself. I asked her if she was sure and she said yes. So I smashed the rest of the broken window out, and I made a note to myself to make sure I bought a pair of gardening gloves.

After I cleared as much glass as I could, I cupped my hands to boost her up to the windowsill. She was no lightweight, but she wasn't huge either. I was able to lift her to the window, and then I had to hold her by the legs so she wouldn't fall. The kitchen table was close enough to the window to where she could slither her way to it, once she leaned far enough through the window.

She was being careful not to over-balance, but she was moving about an inch a minute. I was trying not to laugh, but this took forever. It was probably only a couple of minutes, but it seemed like an hour. Finally, she reached the table and saw her keys. Her two dogs managed to stay out of the way, and I said, "Are you OK, I've got to go." She shook her head yes, so I ran to the cab. She ran out of the front door and thanked me over and over again. I said, "That's OK, but I really have to go." She said she wanted to thank me. I said, "Please let me go then." She finally did.

The Biggest Liar I Ever Met

After I had been driving for several months, I was much more sensitive about protecting my interests. I became able to recognize problem passengers pretty quickly. The contradiction here was that I never really came up with a way to deal with it, other than just accepting my fate.

I got a call to an apartment complex in South Chandler. The name given to me was "Andre, Andy." I got suspicious, just based on that. When I got there, there were two guys, one Japanese and the other American. The American did all of the talking, and he copped an attitude with me almost immediately.

I got out and opened the trunk, and he said, in a really nasty tone, "Could you wait until I'm off of this phone call please?" In hindsight, I should have just called dispatch and told them I refused to take this call because of his attitude, but I didn't. They got into the car and the American guy (let's call him Andy and the Japanese guy Seiji) told me they wanted to go to 24th and Jefferson, which was close to 20 miles.

He started talking about the war in Iraq, and how he was there when those Americans were ambushed, and he was part of the fighting that ensued in Fellujah. He threw out a bunch of numbers and phrases, trying to get me to believe he was there. While he was talking, I was looking at him in the rear view mirror. I thought, "This guy has to be at least 40 years old. He looks old, short, has tattoos all over him and he has five teeth. There is no fucking way this guy was in the military."

On top of all that, he continued to be obnoxious. He said, "You know, I really shouldn't have to pay for this ride. I'm a war veteran and we don't get treated very well. Why don't you help me?" Instead of ignoring him I said, "Well, if you can figure out how to get me paid for the meter rate and my time, it's all yours." He responded with, "You don't have to be a jerk about it."

We got to the light at Queen Creek and the 10 and something really weird happened. He says, "Oh, this is where I threw the garage opener out of the window yesterday." I had a very puzzled look on my face as he got out, looked behind a road barrier, and picked up a small box (he appeared to do that anyway). "That bitch is lucky I don't hold a grudge." What the fuck is he talking about?

As we got onto the 10, he told me he wanted to go to a casino now, but needed to get some money. He said he couldn't cash a check unless the address was printed on the check. He told me they had to go to a copy place to put the name and address on a check. I told him that isn't true, as long as they can identify you with the account number, you can write the address on the check. He insisted they needed to do this, so I said, "So you don't want to go to the casino." He said, "What's with you, I just said we have to copy these checks." Instead of leaving them there, I just went along with it.

We stopped at a Kinko's so they could go in to do whatever this bonehead was going to do. I made sure they knew the meter would be running, and when he said that was fine, I knew it was likely these fuck faces were going to screw me.

After about 15 minutes, I went in to use the bathroom, and when Andy saw me, he started yelling at me. "What are you doing, I said it will take me as long as it takes." I said, "I'm allowed to go to the bathroom." I guess the Japanese guy said something to him, because as I came back he said, "I'm sorry, we should only be another 10 minutes." I just ignored him and went out to the car.

They finally finished what they were doing and said we needed to go across the street to the bank so Seiji could move some money around. I was looking out the window and Andy accused me of watching Seiji so I could steal his password. I turned around and said, "Hey, don't insult me, you've used an hour of my time and you haven't paid me a dime yet." He said, "You cab drivers are always trying to take advantage of him." I just shook my head.

After a couple of minutes, Seiji came back and Andy said to go towards Phoenix. He asked if I would cut him a break since the meter said $50 already. I said, "We're going to 24th and Jefferson, right?" He said yes and I replied, "All right, I will charge you $70." I thought I had just heard Seiji say he had $100. I just want to get these two clowns out of my life and (hopefully) get something for it. I'm pretty sure it won't be $70. But, I'm so tired of these assholes; I know I won't have the strength to fight for the money.

Then this douche bag Andy starts talking about fishing on Lake Pleasant (in the Northwest corner of Phoenix) and how he catches huge fish all the time when he is on his boat. Jeez! I just decided to ignore him. We got to the 10/17 split and veered towards the 24th Street exit. He said, "I need to go to 7th Street." "I thought you said you wanted to go to 24th and Jefferson," I replied.

I got off of I-17 at 7th Street and Andy asked me to pull into the parking lot of a rundown motel – no shit. Seiji gives me a credit card and, as I could have predicted, it failed. Then, he gave me a second card that was practically the same number, and it too failed. I just wanted to cry. Andy started yelling at Seiji, telling him he had to pay me, or they might have to go to jail. I just looked at Andy and said, "Hey jackass, I thought you had a boat. Why is this guy paying for the cab?" He said he "never said that."

Finally, Andy said, "Look, I will give you my cell phone. It's worth $300." Without hesitation I said, OK, I'll take it." One of two things happened. Either he realized giving me his cell was a bad idea because it was valuable, or it was a bad idea because he needed it, so he rescinded the offer.

Instead, he handed me $20 and I said, "The fare was $85. I'll take both." Then he said, "I can give you another $20, or I can give you my number and I'll arrange to give you $65 another time." I took the other $20. Then he said, "You're making a big mistake." I wanted to say, "The biggest mistake of your life will be if you don't get the fuck away from me right now," but instead told him to "Just shut up and go away." I wish I had a shovel to clobber this guy.

Fred Garvin, Male Prostitute ━━━━━━━━━━━━━━

Dan Ackroyd is probably the most successful of the original cast members of Saturday Night Live. To me, he isn't really that funny. But, I believe, he has made the most money. One character he did that was pretty funny on SNL was this character called Fred Garvin. He was dressed all cheesy, with high pants, a plaid jacket, thick glasses and a newspaperman's hat. He looked like a Fuller brush salesman. He would say to the woman, "No ifs, ands or buts about it. You're spending the night with Fred Garvin, (then he would look into the camera) Male Prostitute". Then he would start posing for the woman, and he would have a name for every pose. It was funny. So with Fred Garvin in mind, get this:

I got a call to Phoenix on a Sunday into an area that I was told to avoid at night. I knocked on the door and a dude with gray hair who looked really sick answered and said that the guy would be out in a few minutes. I stood there for a few seconds before I realized that there was music playing that sounded like it was straight out of Studio 54. Then, another dude came to the door and told me that Lonnie would be down in the couple of minutes. I thought I was seeing things, but then, I looked again, and sure enough, this guy's pecker was hanging out of his unzipped pants. I don't think I reacted in a way that would give away anything, but it really disturbed me. I waited another minute, and the first guy came back and said Lonnie was almost ready. I told him I was going to wait in the cab.

Not enough people alive saw what I saw when this guy came out of the house. First of all, he had about four different colors in his hair, which was swooped over like the Flock of Seagulls. He was wearing a t-shirt, which was covered by a black sport coat that was buttoned incorrectly. He had on black faded jeans with beads on them and they were hanging down below his waist. And he (sort of) had on a pair of sneakers that were not on his feet correctly. I had to turn my head to keep from laughing out loud. He was swishing out towards the car, and it looked like he was really drunk. Then, when he got in, his one shoe fell off, and he slipped and tapped his forehead on the door edge. Luckily, it didn't faze him, and he got into the car. Both of the other guys were at the door waving to him. Then he said, "Wait, I want to grab something to "munch on." "Are you for real," I thought. Then he changed gears and said, "Forget it, we can stop at a Circle K on the way." I'm not sure what I thought then. But, away we went.

We traveled about two miles before we stopped. He was courteous enough to ask if I wanted anything, but I said no. He came back with so much stuff; I'm guessing he was stoned on pot. He took out a Hostess pie and ate that quickly. Then, he wolfed down two hot dogs in about a minute. Then he started stuffing a bag of potato chips in. I felt like I should applaud him!

The trip was 10-15 miles, so it was going to be a great fare. We were about half way there when, suddenly, he asked me to turn off the freeway at Camelback Road. What did I care?

We were on the back streets when he saw the person he was looking for. This dude didn't look any less unsavory. He had no shirt and (for a guy) really short shorts. When Lonnie reached him, they hugged and I saw the other guy put something in Lonnie's pocket. I WONDER WHAT THAT WAS. Then he kissed him. I really wanted to leave, but he hadn't given me any money yet. Then Lonnie turned towards me and held up a finger, as if to say, "I'll be right back". Luckily, he did come back almost immediately.

The other dude kissed him again and Lonnie came back over to the car. He told me he wanted to go up towards 35th Avenue and Peoria Avenue. The meter was at $25 and we were still five to seven miles from where he wanted to go.

I got moving again and after a couple of minutes, I looked in the rear view mirror and I noticed his eyes rolling into the back of his head. I said, "Are you alright?" He seemed to snap out of it and said, "Of course, I'm fine." I asked him what was going on and he repeated that he was fine and that I should mind my own business. I said, "Hey, you're in my cab! So ANYTHING that happens here *is* my business." He said, "Look, I don't want any trouble, just take me to 35th and Peoria, and I will be out of your hair." I was getting pissed, so I told him, "You'd better not be rubbing one out, because I'll beat the shit out of you if you do." That was the only time I ever said anything like that to a passenger.

We got to the destination and the fare was $38. He didn't give me a tip.

You're Too Young to Have a Jaguar ━━━━━━━━━━

I got a call to the Palms at Scottsdale Complex, right next to QT 294. This dude comes out and tells me we have to go to North Scottsdale so he can pick up his car. He told me about where it was, so I was pretty happy, because the fare was going to be something like $30.

We started talking about politics on the way and we were both fairly agreeable on most points. He looked like he was at least 15 years younger than me, but we seemed to be of the same mindset. In particular, he was annoyed at the photo enforcement cameras, which basically in his opinion used taxpayer money to tax people more.

Then all of the sudden, he started railing on about his girlfriend, or as he put it, his future ex-girlfriend. He called her just about everything you can imagine. He told me how selfish she was and how she used him to get opportunities for herself and spend his money. I asked him why he stays with her. He said, "I love her."

I told him "It really doesn't sound like you love her." Then he said that I don't understand. I said, "Your right, I don't understand, why don't you explain it to me." So he went on and on about how she always seemed to know the right thing to say, how she was always there for him and how she satisfied him sexually. I decided to play Sigmund Freud.

I said, "If she's always there for you, how can you than say that she is selfish. I mean if she really is selfish, she wouldn't care about helping you." He said, "Well, I guess you're making a good point, but I'm still tired of her." I asked him what he was going to do. He said, "I'm going to keep banging her until something better comes along." OK. What a colossal waste of time that conversation was.

Anyway, we got to the dealership and I noticed it was a Jaguar shop. I said, "You're pretty young to have a Jaguar." He just smiled, paid the fare with a good tip, and said thank you.

About three months later, I got another call to his place, although I didn't notice that it was the same guy until he had been sitting in my cab for a few minutes. I was waiting at the QT 294, so I only had to go about 250 yards to his apartment. It was tough to find a spot to park, but since it was Monday morning, I figured an empty spot was someone's that was at work, so I took one of those.

I started walking towards the apartment and I could hear a dude hollering. I kept walking towards the apartment and he was getting louder. Sure enough, it was the person I was supposed to be picking up. I walked up the stairs towards him and I heard him cursing up I blue storm.

I told him I was the cab driver he called for. He started yelling at me. "Fuck, fuck, fuck, I can't believe that bitch, fuck." I guessed at that point he wasn't actually referring to me. I asked him, "Can I help you find what you're looking for?" He told me he had been robbed. I asked him if he wanted to call the police. He said no, and then explained why.

He said, "I picked up this stripper down the road, and I banged her three or four times. Then we kept drinking and Goddamn, motherfucker. After a brief pause he picked up with "That fucking bitch took my $30,000 watch and money out of my wallet. Fuck!" I said, "Maybe it (the watch) just fell under something." He went in and started slamming things around some more. Then he came out and said, "Man I've got to be on a plane to Denver in an hour. What the fuck am I going to do?"

I said, "Alright, do you want to get on the plane?" He said yes. "So", I continued, "Let's find you a piece of ID and get you over to the airport." He went down to his car and opened the trunk of a Jaguar. He took out some papers, put them in a portfolio and got in the cab. Then he said, "Wait, I've got to get my check book. I don't have any money or credit cards. Oh, shit, I don't have any way of paying you." I told him I felt bad for him and I would bring him to the airport anyway. He looked at me like I was crazy.

As we were pulling out of his driveway, I looked at the Jaguar again and realized it was the same dude from a couple of months ago. He had calmed down after a few minutes, but that was when I realized how shit-faced he was. He was still babbling on about the woman that stole his watch. He swore he would never pick up a stripper again.

He also said he had to pay me to take him to the airport. He took out his checkbook and wrote me a check for $20 (the fare ended up being $17). He asked me how to spell my name, and I ended up saying one letter at a time.

At that point, I felt it was my duty to coach him on how to be able to get on his flight. First of all, speak as infrequently as you possibly can. They will not let you on the plane if they realize how wasted you are. Second, if you have to speak, use one-word answers. Third, don't get too close to anybody. You smell like you've been drinking all night. Finally, drink some water.

When we got to the airport, he nearly fell flat on his face getting out of the car. I don't think anyone saw it, but to be sure, I gave him some peppermint gum. He got his suitcase out of the trunk and went inside.

That weekend, I had a pickup about half a mile from where I picked him up. It was a young woman headed out to a nightclub in Scottsdale. We were talking, mainly because she told me we had to stop to pick up a friend. I was telling her about my boy getting his watch stolen. She said, "Is his name (she said his name)?" I gave her a puzzled look and said, "Yeah, how do you know him?" She said, "Because he's an asshole, a womanizer and a drunk. He's a little rich boy and his daddy pays for everything."

When we got to her friend's house, the first thing she did was tell her friend the story I just told her. They both laughed hysterically. When I dropped them off at the bar, they said, "You just made our night." Poor bastard.

Motocross Party

I had just driven all the way to Maricopa, bringing a bunch of drunks from Jersey's in Chandler (which is one of my personal hangouts) to the next phase of their pub-crawl. I was pretty tired and I got back to Ahwatukee by around 10:30 PM. I was driving towards my apartment and I got a call close to it, so I figured I could get another quick one and call it a night. Not this time.

In Ahwatukee, there are a series of houses that are (sort of) hidden from the rest, almost into South Mountain. As I pulled back in there, it was really hard to maneuver the Crown Vic, because a zillion cars were lining the streets. I couldn't really see the house numbers at first, but then I saw this enormous sign with the picture of a motocross guy on it. I figured, correctly as it so happens, this was the place I was looking for.

My first stroke of luck happened when I didn't do something. I was rolling back down a steep road, trying to park, and I saw a guy lying in the road, and I DIDN'T hit him. It took me a couple more minutes to find a spot, but I finally did. I ignored the dude in the road and the people yelling at me, and I walked inside. I really wanted to stay, because this was as close to a Hollywood party as I had ever come.

When I got inside the door, I couldn't believe the size of the house. There were people everywhere, the music was blasting and I didn't know who my fare was or what he looked like, only that his name was Ted. I asked a couple of people if they knew him and they did, but we couldn't find him. I walked around and a chick in a bikini fell into my arms, because she tripped. She said something that was either "Thank you" or "Fuck you", I really couldn't tell. I walked into the kitchen to see a series of people doing lines and one was considerate enough to ask if I was interested. I said, "Maybe later. Right now, I am looking for Ted. Do you know him?" One person told me he saw him out at the pool. So, that's where I headed.

There were 200 people in the area around the pool and there was more debauchery going on. There were at least five couples, two threesomes and one larger group having sex. It was awesome. The most any woman was wearing was a bikini, and there were plenty of nude people not having sex, just drinking, smoking or snorting (I guess cocaine is not really "deader than dead"). I even watched this hot chick doing a line off of some other chick's belly. That was fun to watch.

I still couldn't find Ted though. I was getting annoyed, mainly because I knew he was there. But, I walked to my car with the intention of getting a no-show. As I got to my car, three guys walked up to me saying they needed a cab. I just presumed they were who I was looking for, and off we went. After about half a mile, another cab pulled up, and a sour looking driver claimed they were his fare. It turns out they were. So they got out of my car and into his. I went back and tried to find Ted.

I was going to walk back inside, but a guy came running up to me and told me he was the fellow for whom I was looking. And he was, thank god! I didn't just waste an hour of my life. He said he had five others coming and it would take a while to gather them up. I told him I was going to turn the car around.

After a couple of minutes, two tall, shit-faced women came strolling out, along with two really short women. One of the taller women said she couldn't find her husband. Ted asked, "Where was the last place you saw him." She was in mid-sentence, when she looked across the street and realized the guy who was passed out lying in the street was her husband.

Ted and I walked over, and Ted confirmed it. He stood over him, slapping him lightly in the face, trying to wake him up. He wasn't moving. His wife came over and started yelling at him. Still nothing. Ted and I tried to pick him up, but he was total dead weight. His wife threw a beer on his head, but that didn't work either. I asked, "Is he even alive?" His wife said, "He'd better be." Now, that's love. After another dozen slaps and a couple more beers on the face, he started moving. We were able to haul his carcass off of the street towards the car. He started giggling and seemed to be snapping out of it.

There were six passengers altogether, and, even though I wasn't "supposed" to take more than five, I didn't really care. What did concern me was what I noticed after everyone was in the cab. The two really short women were actually 11 and nine years old. I was thinking, "What the fuck are these little girls doing at that kind of a party?" It turns out that Ted's girlfriend, the mother of the two girls, is also the ex-wife of the guy throwing the party, and he wanted his daughters there, for some reason.

I started driving towards the main road and Ted (the only person sitting in the front aside from me) told me we were going to Gilbert, probably 20 miles from there. This was going to be a tremendous fare. You can't tell me I didn't earn it, because the women started bickering immediately.

Ted's girlfriend (let's call her Alice, and the other couple are Bob and Carol) started bitching because she said they should have left two hours earlier. Ted said, "I told you that my parents were more than willing to take care of the girls, we had it pre-arranged. You were the one who insisted on bringing them." Alice responded by saying how they wanted to see their father and vice-versa (she was too loaded to actually say vice-versa). Ted said, "OK, but don't get mad at me." That comment made her yell even louder.

"Why can't you ever back me up? He wanted to see his daughters; he's a good father. Your parents are always trying to create problems. They just don't like Tom." Ted was doing a tremendous job of keeping me from getting really mad. The girls were just talking to each other. Bob and Carol weren't helping either.

Bob kept trying to take Carol's clothes off. He said how much fun it would be to have sex in the cab. She would suck his face for a little while, but then he would grab her between the legs and she would yell at him. "How come you didn't do that in the house, before you fell asleep in the middle of the street?" yelled Carol. He acted as though she just made this stuff up. "Why the fuck do you think you're drenched in beer, you dumb ass? That's how we woke you up", but he just said, "I don't know what you're talking about." Ted said, "Hey, there's two young girls in here, watch what you say." Carol told him to fuck off. WOW.

This type of bickering went on the entire ride. I couldn't believe how long it seemed to be taking. Ted decided to drop off Alice and the girls first. He was the only reasonably coherent person in the car. He got out, helped the three of them out of the car and into the house, kissed them all and got back in. Bob and Carol had already passed out in each other's arms in the back seat.

We started towards the next stop, Bob and Carol's house.

Luckily, they never moved again and Ted directed me to their place. We got there in about five minutes and Ted helped them in through the garage. He came back and I was thinking that thankfully, this safari was coming to an end.

When he got back in, Ted said, "Let me ask you, I been thinking about this since I dropped the girls off. I want to go back. What do you think? That party was still rockin' when we left." I didn't even hesitate. "Hell, yeah I'd go back. In fact, I would be really disappointed in you if you didn't, especially after what that bitch just put you through." He didn't seem to care that I called his girlfriend a bitch. He said, "Good, let's go."

For me, this was great. I would be bringing him to within two miles of my apartment, so I got paid to go home. Plus, Ted and I had a lot of laughs on the way. So the trip went by quickly. The final fare was $83, plus he threw $20 on as a tip. I had been driving less than a month, but it was the best day of my career to that point.

DAWWWG KILLER

Nutty dog owners; where to begin? You know, people who prefer their dogs to human beings. I saw a woman that looked like Imogene Coca, who was a pretty big star in the beginnings of television with Sid Caesar, but is remembered by the majority of people 40 and under as Aunt Edna in National Lampoon's Vacation. As the Griswold's are driving her to Phoenix, Clark accidentally ties her rabid dog Dinky to the bumper of the car, and of course, the pooch gets mangled. Later, at a drive-in restaurant, she says, "Had to go to a cheap restaurant, huh, DAWWWWG KILLER"! This still makes me laugh out loud and that is the reason for the title of this section.

On my third day on the job, I went to pick up a fare at a vet in North Phoenix, just off the 17. I walked in and called out the woman's name. She told me that it would be about five minutes.

At that point in my "career", I wasn't so concerned about time. She was very pleasant about it, but then five minutes became 20 minutes, and I started getting annoyed. She apologized again, so at least, I thought, she's not a selfish bitch. She was playing with this other dude's dog, calling him by his name and chasing him around the kennel. The guy didn't seem to mind, but then she wanted to feed him something and he said no, because the dog wasn't permitted to eat for another two hours or so. She said, "One little snack won't hurt", and, of course, the guy got furious. She then started acting as though he was being completely un-reasonable, telling him he wasn't really an animal lover. He told her to fuck off, and I turned my head to laugh. At that point, one of the nurses came in and got everything settled with her dog and off we went.

She was one of those chatterboxes who talk way too much, and it was pretty obvious she was a little off the wall. She started saying how much she missed her dog, and I thought "We just left 60 seconds ago". She started talking about all of the dogs she has had in the past, so I chimed in with my stories. I told her how when I was living with my buddy Matt, he had a huge white dog that looked like a polar bear. There was one time, we were sitting on the back porch drinking beers, and Matt poured some beer on the concrete and Beau (his dog) lapped it up. After the third time, Beau looked at us, contorted his head, and let out the biggest doggie belch I had (and have) ever heard. We fell out of our chairs laughing. For some reason, this woman (we'll call her Stacy), didn't see the humor in it. She looked as though I had waved dog shit under her nose. I said, "You don't think that's funny"? She said, "How can you feed beer to a dog"? I thought, "Let's change the subject".

Luckily, she likes to talk about her dogs. The one she had just dropped off is one of her five. Apparently, her Yorkshire terrier named Mel has some psychic abilities. Stacy said this dog told her that the pain she was feeling at one time was cancer. So, she went to the doctor, and sure enough, she was diagnosed with lymphoma. She then told me that the ensuing treatment cured her, and that Mel helped her during the treatment. I asked her how. She said that she would forget about appointments and the dog would bark a specific way to let her know she needed to go to the doctor. Also, when Mel would bark a different way that meant she was spending too much time lying down and she needed to get up and start exercising. Not only that, but Mel would bark another different way that meant she needed to her take medications. I said maybe a calendar would help, and she actually said, "Oh no, my dogs are the only thing I need".

Then, Stacy started to talk about her other dogs, because she didn't want them to feel left out. I rolled my eyes, but unfortunately for me, she happened to see this and, of course, she got really angry with me. "You don't know anything about dogs, who are you to judge me"? I said, "What did I say?" She was screaming now. *"What the fuck kind of cab driver are you, I love my dogs and they are brilliant animals. You wish you had that kind of a relationship!"* I'm just sitting there wondering what is going on. She continued with the assault. *"My dogs are fantastic. They can do tricks and they come when I call them. You know why? Because they love me, and I love them! Just because nobody cares that much about you, you think you have the right to criticize me!"* I said, "Whatever I said, I'm sorry." As if the explosion wasn't weird enough, she then said, "That's OK, I know you don't have anything against dogs. I'm just glad you have seen the error of your ways. Do you want to see some pictures of my other dogs?" I have now truly entered The Twilight Zone.

I was hoping we were close to her house, because this whole thing was starting to bother me. When she showed me the pictures of her other dogs, I made the mistake of saying her bulldog was a little unusual looking. As soon as I said it, I thought, "Oh shit," and I was right. *"What do you mean unusual?"* she said. *"He is not an ugly dog, he's beautiful. He has those beautiful, sad* eyes and that cute face. *Why do you hate dogs so much?"* I told her that I don't hate dogs, but she didn't buy it. She said, *"You know, you are the cruelest person I've ever met. People think I'm crazy to be so attached to my dogs. But, it's people like you that are crazy. How can you not love a dog that is that cute?"* God, please help me!!

When we got to her place, I was thinking I might have to call the police to get my money. The fee was $25, and I was expecting the worst. When I pulled in, I turned around to tell her the fare, and she had a huge smile on her face. I said the amount and she handed me $30, told me to keep the change and that she hoped to see me again in the future. Lying through my teeth I said "I hope so too, goodbye."

The next dog person I picked up was Susan, just after I started driving the hybrid. She had two dogs and she was taking them to a Pet Smart for a bath. It took her a couple of minutes to get out to the cab. When she did, the dogs were tying her up in knots, running around her, barking in that shrill sort of poochy-dog bark. She told me she wanted get to the shop before 5 PM, because her discount ran out at the end of the day, and appointments weren't taken a moment after. She was finally able to get the dogs in the car and the smaller of the two started climbing into the front seat. She seemed to find that amusing and I guess I did too. The dogs didn't seem to pay much attention to what she was saying, but she pulled the little one into the back seat with her as I pulled out.

She started talking about how she was going to enter them both in dog show at some point and I mentioned that I was from New Jersey and that I had seen the Westminster Dog Show on TV for years. She told me that was her goal for the big dog. She also said the dog is starting to realize its potential. I asked her how she could tell. She said the dog told her. Jeez.

I must have rolled my eyes, because she said, "You don't believe me, do you?" I tried to sound as sarcastic as I could when I said, "What makes you say that?" I probably shouldn't have tried to provoke this fruit loop, but after my encounter with that Stacy woman (and listening to some "pet psychic" on a local radio show), I was fed up with this nonsense.

"Nobody believes dogs can communicate directly with people, or the other way around, but I understand 'Lexi' and 'Eli'", she said. "I always know exactly what they are trying to say." We were at a light, so I turned to respond, and looked directly into her fabulous cleavage. I was certainly distracted – great boobs always distract me – and instantly this Susan didn't seem as nutty as Stacy.

While waiting for the signal to change; the small dog climbed into the front seat with me. I didn't care; I like dogs as much as anyone. I was rubbing him on the belly and he seemed to enjoy it. Susan told him to come back into the back seat. When the dog didn't respond, she got a little louder and more assertive with him. "Eli" still just sat there on the front seat, letting me play with him. Susan got even louder, now (pun intended) barking orders at him. I took my hand off of his belly and he climbed into the back.

She said, "See". I said, "See what?" "He does exactly what I tell him, he understands me perfectly", she concluded. I thought quietly for a minute, and then for some reason I said, "He didn't move the first three times you told him to move." "Sure he did, you were holding him down, preventing him from moving", she responded. I shook my head, but continued to argue, "No I didn't! I was scratching his tummy. I couldn't have held a gnat down with what I was doing."

She would have none of it. "I'm telling you, these dogs understand everything I say". Luckily, she was a controlled sort of nut – with above-average cleavage – and she didn't get angry.

We got to the Pet Smart in time, so she was happy and told me to be back in about 90 minutes to pick her up. I said sure. Then I drove back to Ahwatukee.

Narcolepsy ━━━━━━━━━━━━━━━━━━━━━━━━━━━━━━━━━━

Drivers only have so much control over the types of people they can pick up. For example, I will not pick up people in certain zones after dark. There is a portion of South Phoenix between 16th Street and 19th Avenue that is too dangerous after the sun goes down. You have no idea when voucher customers are going to say, "I don't feel like going" after you've chased a call seven miles and it took 20 minutes to get there. A lot of drivers claim they have piles of regular customers, and the really full of shit drivers say they have 10 regulars that are strippers, all of whom just "LOVE" them. But on the whole, it is the luck of the draw. As much as I love to talk, I wouldn't have ever imagined that I would get as many passengers as I do that simply fall asleep.

I got a call on a Sunday morning, and typically, I expect the majority of Sunday calls between 8 AM and 2 PM to be people going to the airport, or going to pickup their car from the previous evening. Phoenicians are very good about avoiding drinking and driving, although, based on the number of DUI's, you wouldn't think so. But, this dude was going back to pick up his truck and he told me so. I thought that was strange, because there were four trucks parked in his driveway! I guess one can never have too many trucks. Plus, he looked like a combination of the Marlboro Man and one of these brooding gothic guys. Mine is not to question why – and off we went.

We started talking about what he had done the night before, and he was telling me how he and his friends were hanging out with this group of girls and they were drinking like crazy, doing shots and beers three or four an hour, and I thought, this could be a cool story. He sure as hell smelled like he had been drinking that morning right before I picked him up, much less 12 hours ago. Just as he started to tell me about what this one friend of his was doing with his tongue to some girl, his cell phone rang. I figured he would be on the phone a while, because he said it was that friend he was just talking about, but as I looked up, I saw him sort of swirl his head around like he was going to start talking to me again. But he answered the call, so I focused on the road. He said hello to his friend, then a couple more pointless things, and then nothing else for about a minute. Then I thought I heard him snoring. Sure enough, the mope's head is resting on the seat, and he's grinding away like a buzz saw! He just passed out in mid-sentence while talking to his buddy on the phone. I could actually hear his buddy calling out his name over the phone. I started to laugh to myself, and five seconds later he's talking again as though nothing had happened.

Obviously, the dude on the other side of the call realized something was weird, because he started asking what was wrong. My boy responded by questioning him, saying "What are you talking about?" and then, he nodded off a second time, snoring even louder. The only time I had ever seen anything even remotely similar was at my old radio station in Trenton, NJ. The weather guy had slipped on a patch of ice outside. He crawled back to the door, telling me that he had fallen and broken his leg. We were all panicking, but he calmly told us what to do, calling the paramedics and getting to a chair. When the ambulance got there he passed out and started snoring really loudly. When we reminisced about this, we both laughed out loud, but at the time, it wasn't so amusing.

Narcolepsy is an ailment that, until this cab ride, I thought was probably a myth. They made a really funny bit on Saturday Night Live about it, during a take off of the Phil Donahue Show. But the narcoleptic in my cab was amazing. He saw the look on my face and said, "I didn't get a lot of sleep last night". When we got to where his car was located, I asked him what had happened with the girls from the previous night, and he said "What girls?" I said "Never mind, hope you enjoyed the nap, that'll be $13."

A valuable lesson I have learned, for the most part, is that the outlying areas are more trouble than they are worth. You have to drive 10-20 miles to get there and, though they are decent fares, quite often they are not worth more than $15-20 dollars, so you get less than $1 per mile (that is my personal Mason-Dixon Line for collections). It's even worse when the person isn't there, or couldn't wait, or some other excuse for not being there when you arrive. Then, you're really screwed, because you are out in the middle of nowhere with almost no prospects for another call.

Zone 396 is south of Hunt Highway in Queen Creek, which is further southeast than Gilbert. They tend to be voucher calls, which make them even less desirable. This particular zone gets maybe four calls per day. This one afternoon, I was fairly close to this zone, so I decided to take a call that popped up. I should have sensed my impending problems, when I found out the fare was to the furthest-most point from where I was, about 15 miles. There are no Interstates or loops near there, so I had to deal with it (some drivers will figure out a way to void the call. I don't do that. When I make a commitment, I stick to it).

It took me 20 minutes to get there. The final destination was a house at the end of a dirt road. The place had toys all over the grounds out front (there was no grass to speak of), and there were two cars in the driveway. No one answered when I knocked. This was really disturbing, because I didn't have a contact phone number (as a rule, electronic vouchers don't have phone numbers – something about privacy issues). I waited five minutes and walked around to the back and knocked on the sliding glass door. Again, there was no answer. As you can imagine, I'm starting to get pissed off. This was a $45 voucher, so not only was I going to not get that money but I'm also at least 25 miles from a decent call area. To top it all off, I have to piss like a racehorse.

I decided to handle this one issue at a time, starting with the nature call. I walked around to the side of the house, looked around as best I could for prying eyes, and let her fly behind an air conditioning duct. I really couldn't hold it.

I then went back to the car to get a No-Show. This really

messed up my plans, because I had a scheduled pick-up in 45 minutes, and if I waited any longer I'd be late for that call. This no-show was going to be a problem, because I was in a bad zone for the computer to work. Sure enough, I had to drive around to get the message to go through. After waiting five minutes, during which I was screaming at the computer, wondering why the no-show took so long, they disapproved it. Now, I'm fuming. They sent another message, though, telling me to call the passenger, and they gave me a phone number.

I called the number they gave me and the woman who answered told me that I needed to pick them up at a supermarket that I had passed on the way to their house. I asked her, "How I was supposed to know that", and she said that she always meets the driver there. My response was, "There was nothing on the dispatch that said that, and if that was the case, why didn't it just have the address of the store as the pick-up point?" Had she been able to read my mind, my answer would have been a bit more graphic. But, she said she was picking up her son and would be at the store in a couple of minutes. I was pretty unhappy, because I should have been traveling for 20 minutes towards the final destination by now. Just for my edification, I asked dispatch for a voice request, just to see what they would say. I knew it was merely a formality, because they said they knew nothing about the change of pick-up spots. I swear I've never seen an operation like this where no one EVER helps anyone.

Anyway, it took me about five minutes to get to the shopping plaza, and I parked by the KFC, as I had arranged with the woman. I expected her to be there when I pulled in, but she wasn't. I figured it would be only another minute or two. After 10 minutes, I started yelling at the computer terminal. I guess in Queen Creek, "a couple of minutes" mean something different then everywhere else. If she had been at the house when I got there, we would be half way to the destination already.

She finally pulls up in the hunk of crap car she drove and

asked if I was her cab. Thinking something sarcastic, I confirmed that I was. I then asked if all four people in the car were going with me, because I would have to move stuff from the front seat to make room. She said it was just the two young girls, so that worked out. Then, incredibly, she asked if we had time for her daughters to grab some food from the KFC. Now, normally, I would just be wishy-washy and tell the person it was OK. But, since I had been pushed as far as I could by this point, I told her "We are already getting started 20 minutes later than we should be. We don't have time." She responded with "They're hungry, though." Again, the only reason I didn't backslide was because I was pissed. I said, "It would take a minimum of 30-45 minutes to get another driver out here. I'm leaving right now. If they want a ride with me, they had better get in." They did.

The problem, or so I thought, was that they were going to be crybabies for the whole trip, which was 25 miles. They had pissed me off so much; I was ready to start yelling at them. We had gone about 500 yards, and I looked into the back, and they were screwing around with I-Pods or video games or something, so it looked like I was in the clear. Five minutes later, I heard them talking and then, just as suddenly, I didn't. It looked like they were trying to sleep, so I didn't think anything of it. Then they started talking again. I looked in the rear view mirror, and the younger of the two had her head resting on the seat back, seemingly out cold. The older one was just looking straight ahead. I was thinking, "Are they fucking with me?"

They never said anything directly to me during the course of the trip, other than replying to my asking them for direction specifics. As we got close to the destination (I was constantly looking at my GPS since they were in their own little world), I turned around, because the older girl was now snoring and I needed to wake her up so she could direct me. For one moment I thought the other girl was gone, because I didn't see her head, but I thought no, that couldn't be true. When we got to New Leaf, I turned around, and the other girl had fallen back asleep and the younger girl was curled up on the floor with her head resting on the seat. I had to practically yell to wake them up. They both got up, grunted a goodbye and left. I also found three candy bar wrappers under my seat about an hour later. I never chased a call to that zone again.

Firewater

I apologize in advance for any upcoming lack of politically correctness, but almost every time I had a fare who was an American Indian, they have been drunk, so what am I going to do?

I got to a hotel in Scottsdale, looking for a woman. I walked in and told the desk clerk her name and she said there was no one with that name in the hotel. At that time, an older man walked up to me and informed me that he was the fare. I told him the name I was given was a woman's, so he said OK and walked away. I kept trying to figure out what could be the problem while I waited and this dude came back and said he supposed to go with me. That's when I realized what the problem was; the stupid new automated system still had glitches. When a number is recognized as a repeat number, it continues to show the name of the original caller. I thought, "This guy must be my fare." So, I told him that and off we went.

I opened the door for him and he sat down, and as soon as I got in I was overwhelmed by this incredible stink. "Why can't you take a shower?" I thought. We started moving and I asked him where he wanted to go. He said, "Discount Liquor", which was half a mile up the street. I assumed that he wanted to go there and then right back to the hotel. When we got to the liquor store, he told me he would be right back. As he was walking inside, I saw a huge stain on his pants in his crotch area and down his leg. I said, "Jeez, this guy pissed all over himself. No wonder he smells so bad." I didn't have any disinfectant, so I sprayed the seat and the rest of the car with air freshener. Now I'm thinking how I need to get this guy out of here as quickly as possible. On the surface, that sounded like a really good idea, but when he returned he told me he wanted to go out to the Salt River Pima Maricopa Indian Community (SRPMIC), all the way out on Indian School and Mesa. Now what do I do? I look at the bright side. The fare will be decent; I'll just have to hold my breath.

He started directing me to the place. Then he opened up a beer. I gave him a sharp look, and he said, "You mean I can't drink this beer." Now, I really didn't care, but since he is stinking up my cab, I wanted him to feel bad. I said, "Well, I guess it's a little late now for you to ask for my permission, ISN'T IT. I don't care, do what you want, and just keep the beer low so no one sees it." Then I turned and smiled at my handy work.

For about two minutes, the car didn't smell so bad. But, eventually, the smell overpowered the air freshener and I felt sick again. I tried to drive as fast as I could to get to his house, but as usual, construction and police presence interfered with that. This guy didn't help very much. He was swinging his bottle around in the air when he thought I wasn't looking, spilling beer all over the back seat. I said, "Are you trying to get me arrested?" He said, "No, I'm sorry." I told him to sit there and not move. Before he stopped moving, he rolled down the window, and threw the bottle out. Obviously, I know how to influence people.

When we got to his house, he told me he had to talk to the guy inside. I decided I would let him do that before he paid me. That might have been a mistake. As I waited, I looked around and saw stuff all over the yard. There were tires, bikes, toys, trash and a car engine. I decided that at the first indication that this guy wasn't going to pay, I was going to load this engine into my cab. That'll fix him.

He came back out and I told him the fare was $22. It took him at least three minutes to count out the money, and I was standing next to him the whole time, smelling his urine-soaked clothes. I really started getting nauseous, and after I left his driveway I had to pull back over and puked. It was the first and only time in my cab-driving career that I vomited.

Another time, I went on a call to a bar in Scottsdale called the Playa. I went inside and discovered that my fare was another drunken American Indian. He told me he was ready to go as soon as he finished this beer. I told him I would wait outside in the cab.

He finally came out 15 minutes later. He tripped coming out of the door. He told me he was going to a house "on the reservation." There is a drive-through liquor store on McDowell right by the 101. Almost every time I drop off someone on the other side of the highway, they want to stop there first. This time was no different.

After we went through there, he told me he wanted to go to Indian School and Alma School. I really don't like the radio on when I have passengers because they almost always want me to play DJ for them, and it's very distracting. He asked if I could put some music on, and said, "Do you like Rush", because I had the CD "Rush Chronicles" in my player. He said, "I love Rush." That's one problem solved.

The song "Bastille Day" came on which, in and of itself, wasn't important, but this joker started singing and playing air drums. I had to turn my head so he wouldn't see me laughing at him. I was pretty sure he wouldn't see it because his head was shaking and his arms were flailing all over the place. Of course, he didn't know any of the words, so I just laughed some more.

I could listen to this CD nonstop, so I skipped to "Freewill," which I enjoy. Once again, he became Neil Pertt and was drumming his ass off. He was going crazy, banging into the window, pulling on the front seat, making a lot of noise. It was all I could do to pay attention to the road. It's difficult to understand the words when Geddy Lee sings sometimes, but I'm sure this guy wouldn't know the words if he had the lyrics in front of him. It was very funny.

When that song ended, he said, "Play another great song." So I skipped ahead to "Closer to the Heart," which is one of my favorites. As soon as he recognized the song, it started all over again. This particular song starts much slower than the other two, but he didn't seem to care. He was acting like it was just as fast.

We got to his house and he said, "That was awesome." Maybe it was, but not quite awesome enough for him to leave me a tip.

The most lucrative pick up I had from the reservation was a group of four American Indians that were going to run a series of errands. Three got in the back and a very large woman got in the front. Two of them already had beers in their hands. At this point, I was fairly new to the job, but I said it was OK, as long as they were careful. Had I been more knowledgeable, I would have said otherwise. My main reason for saying this is because they couldn't have cared less about being careful and that seems to be the feeling most of the time, regardless of who is in the cab.

We went to a bank first, so they could cash their casino check. Most of the "reservation" Indians receives a monthly check from the Casino Arizona, or so I believe. For some reason, the Wells Fargo branch we stopped at wouldn't cash their checks.

Undeterred, we went to the next place, Target. Two of them stayed in the car and the others went in. The two in the car kept talking, but I couldn't understand what they were saying. Whatever it was, it must have been funny, because they just kept laughing. After 10 minutes, the others came back.

Next, we went to a pawnshop. All four of them went in. I didn't know enough to worry about them ditching me, although since they had some stuff in the trunk, there really wasn't much to worry about. They were only in the place for about five minutes.

I guess they weren't loaded enough, because we had to stop next at a bar so they could do some shots. They asked me if I wanted to come in and join them, but I took a pass. I don't do shots as a rule, and certainly not while on the clock with people I don't know, but I thought it was nice of them to ask.

After the shots, we naturally proceeded to a Burger King. We went through the drive through window. They got $85 worth of food. They ordered 30 whoppers!! It was totally unreal! I'd never seen anything like this before. And all the while, they just kept laughing.

The meter said $60 at this point, so I was pretty happy. We made our way back to their house, but we stopped at the infamous drive-through liquor store I mentioned earlier. They got a bunch of beer, and some ready-made cocktails. They opened them before we left the parking lot.

At this point, I had gotten kind of tired of them, because they were giggling the whole time, and I didn't know that they weren't laughing at me. They asked me to put on the radio, and they all were singing whatever song was playing, which really made things worse because none of them could sing worth a shit! I'm sure they knew that.

When this sojourn to heaven finally ended, the meter said $78. They took all of their stuff from the cab and the trunk, and they gave me $85 and told me to keep the change. The whole trip took less than two hours, so it was worth it.

CHAPTER 8

Stories That Affected Me

Just Like Dana

I remember a lot of inane details about people, place and things. As such, I come across quite a few coincidences.

I went home to New Jersey for Thanksgiving and was returning to Phoenix for my first shift on December 2nd. Not five minutes before I left my dad's house to go to the airport, my brother called and told us that my sister-in-law, who was eight months pregnant, went to the hospital because of (what they initially thought was) a kidney stone. They eventually found out that there are some issues with her kidneys and that she was going to be in the hospital for a little while, although there didn't seem to be any tremendous long-term concern. She was probably going to have to deal with some physical pain.

On that first day back, I chased my first fare because I get impatient after sitting for 30 minutes. I had to go seven miles to Baseline Road and Central. I saw her name was Lily and I thought, "She sounds cute". Sorry, I'm a heterosexual man.

We really didn't say much to each other for the first couple of minutes. But I noticed that she was pregnant when she got in the car, so I asked her how far along she was. She said eight months and two days, and I was very surprised to hear that. I would have guessed five months, tops. We stopped at a light and I turned around to ask her another question. Then, I really looked at her and I thought, wow, she's beautiful. Again, I'm a man.

Anyway, I asked where we were going and she told me to a specialist because she was having problems with her kidneys. It was interesting. I already knew that kidney stones are excesses of calcium, but if I remember our conversation correctly, they often occur because of a lack of iron and taking in too much calcium will deplete iron, and then the excesses of calcium form the stones. Since women tend to be more iron deficient than men, that would explain why women tend to get kidney stones more frequently. She also said she thought she was eating in the proper fashion, but that cheese, yogurt and milk were a large portion of what she ate.

I asked if this was her first child. Lily said it was her fourth. Then I asked her how old her other kids were and she said ten, seven and five. She also had mentioned that she was having a C-section on December 25.

"You're not going to believe this", I said, and then told her that my sister-in-law was having a C-section on December 31, she also has three other children age seven, five and three and she just went into the hospital for what she thought was kidney stones, but it might be something worse. What a crazy coincidence.

Can't You Do Anything Right?

One of the more bizarre fares I've ever had came on a Saturday morning, my first call of the day. I had been waiting for a call for more than two hours, so I was anxious for a good fare. I picked up this fellow at an extended stay-type place near my apartment. He seemed normal enough, but was also a little disoriented. He apologized, saying that he was going to "have" me for most of the morning, because he had errands to run. Hey, if you pay me, I'll drive you anywhere you want to go.

He told me that he wanted to go to a Cricket Store because he had lost his cell phone. I have seen these stores all over, but I didn't remember one very close to where we were. He insisted that there was one near 40th and Chandler, so I drove towards that intersection. When I got there, I couldn't find it. He insisted it was somewhere in the area, but after the meter got to $15, he decided we should move on to the next errand.

The next phase of our sojourn was to go to a police station in South Phoenix, near the confluence of I-17 and I-10. It took quite a while to get there, which, from my perspective, was fine. On the way, we were talking about our ex-wives. Needless to say, we were laughing our Asses off. I felt bad for him, not so much because of the busted marriage, but because he started telling me about his health issues.

He had been involved in the limousine industry for a number of years and he was in a solid management spot. He was going to be moving into an even higher position when he started having fainting spells. It got to the point where he had to leave his job to take care of himself. He was clearly depressed, because he had no prospects for a job when he got healthy. Plus, there was no guarantee he would be cleared to work again.

Anyway, we got to the police station, and there were no cars in the parking lot. He didn't really tell me why we were there. He just said that he had a bunch of his belongings inside. I walked up to the intercom that was next to the gate that surrounded the building. Someone answered my page, saying there was no access to the building for non-employees until Monday. I went back to the cab to give my fare the bad news. He said, "They take my stuff and then I have to jump through hoops to get it back."

He shrugged off that disappointment, and said he wanted to go to this particular Mexican restaurant to get some lunch. He was still a little disoriented, so we kept making turns that led to nowhere. We would get to a spot and he would say, "It's right up the street from here", but I couldn't find it. After about 10 minutes, we finally came across the place he was looking for, but it was closed for renovations. I turned my head away to laugh, but when I looked back towards him, I thought he was going to cry. I asked him what he wanted to do, and he said, "How about shooting me". We both laughed, but I found out later that maybe it wasn't a laughing matter.

He said he wanted to go to the Cricket Store on Indian School and the 51. Fortunately, I remembered this store and we got to it pretty quickly. He went in, and I sat there wondering whether I was going to be paid. If there is ever a situation to expect the screw job, it's this one. In fairness, it didn't seem as if he was trying to get over on me. After a couple of minutes, he came back out and told me they couldn't help him, because he didn't have any documentation. OK, we are zero for four. He was so disconsolate, he said, "I just want to go to a hotel. Is there an extended stay near here?" My GPS told me there was one about two miles from where we were.

I took him there and waited for him to check in. He came back and asked if I would help him on the fare, but I said it would come out of my pocket, so I couldn't. He seemed to be OK with that and paid the full amount, which was more than $80. He didn't tip me, but a fare that big is good enough.

I picked up this guy two other times. The first one was a short trip to a Lowe's and back. He didn't remember me at first, but after I explained what happened the previous time, he did. The second time was a much longer trip. He had a voucher, and it explained a lot.

When I got to the extended stay at which I had originally picked him up, he was still in bed. I was kind of pissed, because it was a $50 voucher, and I had been skunked for the first 90 minutes that morning. But he crawled out of bed and said he would go. When he got out of the apartment, I noticed he had stitches on the side of his head, next to his right eye.

He told me that a blood clot had popped there and he had undergone brain surgery. He kept saying he had "this zipper" going up his face and laughing about it. That was funny, but then he talked about wanting to die. Now, I have had many people say stuff like that to me during my time as a driver, but this guy sounded like he meant it.

The doctors had told him that he shouldn't be drinking at all, either. He made a joke about that, and he kept saying how he likes vodka and that's all he really wants to do. We joked about that for a while, and I went back to that "theme" many times, hoping to cheer him up. I then started talking about sportscasters who drive me crazy, and made fun of them, and he laughed some more. Then, it was on to ex-wife jokes, and he laughed some more still. I don't know what kind of an impact I had on his overall mood an hour from then, but I wanted to try to help. I liked this guy, and it's hard not to feel for someone who seemingly had their life snatched away from them, through no obvious fault of there own.

We got to the counseling location, and I told him I would try to be in position to give him the return ride home, and we talked a little while longer, until the office opened up. I didn't get that return trip, and I never saw him after that. I hope he is OK.

Free Parking...Not

I love America. It is the greatest country in the world. It is called the land of opportunity and it certainly is often enough. There are zillions of stories where people made something out of themselves when the odds seemed to be stacked against them. Sometimes, however, I think it should be called "The Land of Our Opportunity, *because we are going to take our share from you, somehow or another.*"

I got a call to the Circle K on Elliot and Priest. It was this very young blonde woman dressed in scrubs. She told me she needed to go to the tow lot across from the Tempe Market Place on Rio Salado and McClintock. Her car had been towed and she needed to get it and then get to work, which was south of Chandler.

We got to talking and she told me how she parked illegally, thinking it was going to be a quick in and out thing. She was very mature about it, telling me it was her own fault and that she had learned a valuable lesson. She asked me how much I thought the fare was going to be and I told her $25. She said, "Look, I don't have enough money, but when we get to the tow place, my ATM card is in my car, I will run in and get it and then I will pay you." I thought for a moment, and then I decided to give her the bad news.

"Look, honey. I'm going to tell you what is going to happen, and I'm not telling you to upset you. You just need to know that you have a serious problem." I then informed her that she would not be able to get her car out. Tow lots ONLY accept cash when cars are impounded and her fee will be at least $100. Plus, they will not allow her to get into her car until she has paid the fee. On top of that, if she doesn't get the car out tonight, they will charge her a storage fee if it sits there for 24 hours (or maybe even 12 hours).

Her reaction truly amazed me. It was clear she had no idea about the racket *that is the towing industry*. But, she just calmly acknowledged what I said and asked what would be a good idea for a plan of action. I thought, "Man, this chick must have had great parents." Not only did I feel bad for her, but also I was pissed at these local thieves. I'm guessing there is a loophole in the law that allows these "Agencies" to drive around the city and tow cars for shits and giggles. I'm also sure that cash only is the rule because there is something not quite right about it. That way, there is no record of the transaction.

I felt that I could trust her. So I said, "Look, this is what I'm going to do. You are going to need more than $100. I happen to have that on me. I'm going to give you the money. You can get your car, and then, we will go to an ATM so you can pay me for the ride and reimburse the money for the tow." She thanked me as we closed in on the destination.

I also told her, "You can bet your house what the dude you talk to is going to look like. He will be about 5'7, weigh about 290. He will have a sleeveless shirt on, showing off huge arms with tattoos all over them. And his hat will be on backwards. Plus, he will be smiling the whole time and sound like he's from Brooklyn."

Sure enough, everything I told her was going happen, did happen. We were there about 15 minutes. She had to be at work in 45 minutes, so she had time to get to the bank and get to work. She told me, "I already told them I might be late. I certainly wasn't going to not pay you." That was nice of her.

We got to the bank and she took out $200. The fare was $30, but I told her I felt so bad for her, I was only going to charge her $25. So with that and the money I had loaned her, she owed me $140. She handed me the whole $200 and said, "I can't believe how nice you were to me. You deserve all of it." I was stunned. She drove off and I just sat there for about five minutes. I don't think about Karma, but if there is such a thing, that was it.

Just to give you an idea of how frequently this happens, I had three other passengers that I brought to tow yards to pick up their cars. Each story was pretty much the same. Each time, the passenger had no idea they needed cash to get their car out. I didn't get another $60 tip, but I felt good that I was able to help them.

Kill 'Em with Kindness

One of my favorite experiences occurred on a Friday night. I had a good day in total. I thought it was going to be a disaster at first, but I did extremely well from 2 PM on. I was driving back to my apartment and was ready to call it a day and I saw a call in zone 81, which is directly south of my apartment. I figured, what the hell, I might as well take it.

It turns out I was seven miles from it. As I was getting close, I also realized I was nearly out of gas. I had a Crown Vic at the time, so I had to fill up. Dispatch had spelled the name of the street incorrectly, so I couldn't find it on the GPS. While I was at the gas station, I called the woman to inform her as to why I was running late. She didn't sound very happy.

The street that she lived on is one of the many in residential areas that break up and start over again somewhere else. It had just gotten dark when I found it. I drove by the house very slowly; slow enough to where people started shouting for me to stop. At this point, I had no idea there was anything wrong. They opened the passenger side door and a guy started screaming at me.

I discovered that this couple had luxury box seats for a Diamondbacks game. The wife told me she made the cab reservation yesterday. She continued that they needed to be there at 6:45 and it was now 7:05. Then, her husband took over. He was screaming again, saying, "I want to know what you are going to do for me. I'm not getting in the car until you make me a deal."

Now, there were many things I could have said, beginning, obviously, with "here's my deal: I leave and you go off and fuck yourself." But that's not really my style. The truth is, he might still be waiting for the cab had I not picked up that call (by the way, making a reservation 24 hours in advance for non-vouchers, I have found, is not a good idea. Things happen, and it's no skin off anyone's teeth). I could have said, "Sir, I really don't care to be spoken to in that fashion, and I really want to help you, so if you calm down, I'll see what I can do." Since there wasn't really much I could do, and considering the way he treated me, I was pissed, but I understood his perspective. I'm the representative of the cab company, and he got screwed. I'm sure I've been in a similar situation, so it wasn't hard to understand his feelings.

What I said was, "Alright, I will give you the fare for half price." He shut up immediately. They got in the cab and we started towards the ballpark. The woman started asking me questions, and I tried to get her to realize that it wasn't my fault that the order got messed up. It worked, because she said, "Oh, so you don't know what fares you're taking until a few minutes before?" Her husband still didn't say anything.

About a mile before the ballpark, I heard them whispering, but I didn't hear what they were saying. I asked where they wanted to be dropped off, and he said right by the ticket office. I got there at about 7:30, looked at the meter, which said $31.90 and said, "OK, here we are, and that will be $16." He looked at me and said, "Look, I'm going to give you the full amount. I really appreciate your kindness and your attitude." I thanked him and drove away. I turned on the radio to listen to the game, and I realized the game started at six as opposed to seven. I hope he was still in a good mood.

I picked that couple up two more times. The first time I took them to the airport. It turns out she works on the Fiesta Bowl committee and they were going to a game at the University of Alabama to scout for the 2009 game. When they came out to the cab with three suitcases, he said, "Can you guess where we are going?" I said, "The Diamondbacks game?" He laughed, but I don't think he remembered me.

The second time, they wanted to ride the newly opened light rail to a party in downtown Phoenix. I picked up one of their friends and they talked about Nebraska football the whole way. Which was fine, I'm in my element talking sports. In this case, though, I just kept my mouth shut, because they got so many facts wrong.

Meth Chick

I have met people, as fares, and I just can't believe the trouble they've gotten themselves into. Meth Chick is one of those people.

I got this call to a house in Scottsdale. It was the August, so it was really hot outside. A young woman had what looked like cuts all over her face, no shoes on her feet and a furry blanket wrapped around her like she was in Winnipeg in February. She told me where to go and exactly how she wanted me to get there. She sounded like she had a cold, so I thought that's why she has the blanket. But, then I thought, why isn't she wearing shoes?

I wasn't sure where I was going, but, since she was directing me, what did I care? We were talking for a few minutes and she told me she was going to the methadone clinic to get her fix. That kind of stunned me. I am pretty naïve when it comes to drug use and the symptoms thereof, but she was pretty cavalier about it.

When I get into a situation like that, I have a tendency to ask a lot of questions. I'm curious about addictions, people's health, etc. Quite often, I end up putting my foot in my mouth, because I don't know what questions will offend people, and since I have no desire to hurt anyone's feelings, I presume the other person will know that as well. Obviously, I can't really know that.

When we got there, I asked her if they had a bathroom and she said they wouldn't let me use it. I told her, "That's OK; there are couple of trees out here." She laughed and walked away. I'm not sure whether she thought I was serious or not. I got out and walked behind a tree that was blocked by a wall and did what I had to do. One thing about this job is that it has allowed me to leave my mark throughout the Valley.

It took her a long time to get back to the cab. I made another joke about going to the bathroom. Then I said, "Please don't think less of me". She laughed again and we started back. She was telling me how she had gotten addicted and that she was starting to get back to normal. She had been clean for 26 days at that point. I can't really relate to those milestones, but I tried to be encouraging. She kept sniffing like she had a cold, and it was really distracting me. She seemed to be irritated by this visit to the clinic, because she was complaining about the person who gave her the medication.

When we got back to her house, she started cursing herself because she didn't have any shoes on and the sidewalk was going to be hot. She paid for the fare, which was $35, with a credit card and got out, dropping her bag. I started cursing myself, because I didn't give her my card.

About a month later, I picked her up again for the same reason. It was after Labor Day, but it was still really hot. She was again shoeless and wrapped in a heavy blanket. I asked her why she didn't have any shoes and she said, "Oh, I always forget them." But she didn't ask me to wait so she could go get some shoes. I was thinking I should call her Joe Jackson.

After we had gotten back out to McDonald Drive, she said to me, "Ooh, you're my favorite driver. You're the one who drives real fast." This is only somewhat true. I just don't drive real slow, trying to run up the fare. I have noticed that many people comment on how cabbies will drive too slowly, or take longer routes, anything to run the meter up as high as possible. I refuse to do this, perhaps to my moneymaking detriment, but I also have a conscience. Anyway, she made it clear that she appreciated it.

When we got to the clinic, she told me it would be about two-three minutes. After about 30 seconds, I realized I needed to piss again. I hesitated for a couple of minutes than noticed the tree I used the last time, and thought "What the hell". I was now hoping for one thing: that I beat her back to the car. I did.

I wasn't going to tell her when she got back in the car that I had again used nature's toilet, but I did. What is the sense in hiding great accomplishments? Once again, she laughed. As we left, she told me that she needed me to stop at McDonald's.

When we got to the drive-up, she ordered a lot of things; three Egg McMuffin's, four hash browns, cinnamon bites and two big breakfasts. I was thinking, "Jeez, I thought the drugs curbed your appetite." When we got rolling, I asked her if these drugs make you really hungry. I guess she figured out why I asked her that, because she told me she was buying food for three people. She also said that you got sweepstakes game pieces with the hash browns. I couldn't help thinking, I wish I had met this girl under better circumstances, because she is a very nice person, easy on the eyes and it's a shame she is going through this stuff.

After downing a large portion of the food she bought, she offered me something, but I said no. Amazingly, she finished almost all of it before we got back to her house. This is one of my favorite people, but thinking about her kind of makes me sad.

Nearly 10 months later, I took my final call of the day at a hospital in North Scottsdale. I called the number on the dispatch and the woman on the other end directed me to where she was waiting. When she got in, I realized it was Meth Chick. She was trying to cover up the fact that she was crying, but maybe she wasn't, because it was obvious. She told me she was visiting her boyfriend, who had relapsed, and that they had a big fight.

She mentioned how long my hair had gotten, and I told her I was going to donate my hair to "Locks of Love" until I found out it has to be 10 inches long, which I had no intention of doing. She also remembered that I was writing a book, and about my "tendency" to urinate "where I'm able, when necessary". We laughed about that, and for the rest of the trip we talked about publishing, editing and promoting the book. She indicated she would buy it when it comes out.

She told me a few things about her situation, so I thought it was strange that she wanted to stop and get some beer. I hadn't had a beer in four months, so maybe I was a bit jealous. But, she had been clean since the last time I saw her and she looked like she had gained some weight. I knew a woman back in New Jersey that I was very fond of and she had a similar problem with a drug addiction. Her weight gain was the first sign of her recovery. I hope Meth Chick makes a full recovery and has a happy life.

I Just Want Five More Minutes With My Dad ━━━━━

I have numerous stories about health issues that people have had when they were my passengers. In a way, this story is one of them, but I chose to separate it, and I think the reason will be obvious.

I went to the American Legion hall in Chandler. I tend to have philosophical differences with members of these "organizations", because they are generally very conservative in their thinking. Not that it matters much, but I have, on occasion, had disagreements with members of these fraternities while doing this job. This time it was different.

I waited outside for a few minutes, and a dude who looked like he was about 35 years old came and asked me to roll down the window. He told me his name was Bill and then he said, "Would it be OK if I had five minutes more inside with my dad?" I had no problem with that. As soon as he walked away, I thought, "Shit, this isn't going to be good."

He got into the cab and told me he needed to go to the airport. I felt better, because it was going to be a $40-$50 fare. Then he started talking about why he was there.

He told me he never met his dad until he was in his early 20's. Apparently, his mother and father had a huge falling out before he was born and she decided Bill would be better off without his father in his life. To his credit, Bill's dad (Jack) respected her wishes. Personally, I don't think any guy is better off without a father in almost any situation.

When Bill finally did meet Jack, they didn't really spend a lot of time together for the first few years. When the first 20 years of a person's life is formed through the perspective of one parent's eyes, it is hard to form an unbiased opinion. It seems as if Bill's mom continued to speak harshly about Jack. Eventually, Bill decided that he would rather get to know his dad than not know him regardless of his mother's feelings.

In the last few years, Bill and his father started to become familiar with one another and, consequently, a lot closer. That's pretty heartwarming, considering the fact that Jack is here and Bill lives in Washington State.

Unfortunately, the reason Bill was here was because Jack is dying of inoperable cancer. When I met Bill, his dad only had a few months to live. He was stoic about the situation, but he was also understandably sad. He really didn't have him in his life for most of his first 30 years, and now, time is running out.

The worst part of this story is Bill's mom. She can't let her son have quality time with his father without making it all about her. This made Bill angry, as he explained, "I told her, if you are going to say negative things about him, then WE are not going to have a relationship. If you can't get over your feelings, that's your problem. I want to spend whatever time I have left with him without you interfering." I'm not sure what happened with that, but if she was so selfish that she couldn't respect that, then she's forgotten what it means to be a mother and she doesn't deserve to have her son in her life on those terms.

I dropped Bill off at the airport, and he thanked me for listening to him. I said, "That is one of the most gut-wrenching stories I've ever heard. I feel bad for you. Thanks for sharing that with me. It takes a lot of courage to deal with all of that."

About a month later, I picked up a guy at an apartment complex less than a mile away from the American Legion Post. I realized it was Jack, so I asked him if he had a son who lives in Washington. He looked at me like I was crazy, so I explained how I knew him. He told me he was impressed that I remembered the story. I told him it's hard to forget that kind of story. When he got out I wished him good luck.

A couple of weeks later, I brought Jack from the Post to his apartment. I reminded him of our previous meeting and he remembered. We talked about his illness. It already seemed as if he had lived longer than he was supposed to live. He told me what a good kid his son was and I told him that Bill feels that same way about him. I saw him hold back a tear. I felt good for both of them.

My Top Ten Best and Favorite Passengers ━━━━━━

There are passengers that I consider "regulars" and they are the ones that have left me with a particularly important memory or that I just really liked.

Quite often, I picked up people who were in their late 70's, 80's, 90's, and even a few past the century mark. One of the centenarians was a woman named Adelaide, who I picked up at a condo in Scottsdale. I would always pick her up at around 8:30 on a weekday morning at the same place. She would be sitting in her garage in a chair, ready to go. Five of the six times I drove her, she went to the same church about two miles away.

She was always smiling and had a very cheerful attitude. She was in remarkable health. She doesn't use a cane, she heard pretty well, she could see where we were going, and her voice was clear. She was always excited about going to church, and she was always very upbeat.

She would laugh at nearly everything I said, and she was very funny herself. The final time I gave her a ride, she had turned 100 just a couple of weeks prior. She said her family was still throwing her parties. She just laughed and laughed. I can say without fear, I would want to be like her. It also dawns on me with passengers like Adelaide; I never know if this will be the last time I will see them.

During my first summer as a driver, I picked up a father and son from Kuwait. They were staying at The Buttes, a top-flight resort built into a mountain in Tempe. The father, Hamid, was helping his son Khalid, matriculate into ASU, to study, if I remember correctly, agricultural finance. I took them to a Target and they took my phone number, asking me to come back to pick them up. That was a pretty decent fare and Hamid asked if they could call me over the next series of days.

They no-showed me the next time I was supposed to take them somewhere, because a friend gave them a ride. I was pissed, but I received another call the next day, and that one worked out. They decided they could rely on me, so I got calls almost everyday for the next week.

Some of the time I felt an inability to communicate, especially with Khalid, because his English wasn't great, but it went pretty smoothly. I tried really hard to give him little tidbits of information to make his acclimation to Phoenix and college easier. One day, I brought Khalid from the ASU campus in Tempe to the one down by Williams Field Airport in South East Mesa and then back. That trip was particularly satisfying monetarily.

I also ended up helping Khalid move into his apartment near The Buttes. These apartments were new, built in the time that I have lived in Phoenix, and they are beautiful. By the time Hamid was ready to go back to Kuwait, they had spent more than $400 in my cab.

I brought Hamid to the airport and he thanked me one last time with an extra $50 tip. That was tremendous. He also thanked me for "being a true gentleman". That comment made me feel even better. Khalid called me one more time, to bring him to the MVD to get his driver's license. I haven't seen him since, but why would I if he has his own car. He was a really nice kid and I hope he does well.

I felt a particular kinship to another fellow that I have mentioned once or twice before named Reggie. He bares a striking resemblance to Forest Whitaker. I picked him up about five times in Chandler, plus I gave his wife a ride to church probably another five times.

Our conversations were always interesting because was obvious that he's a reasonable, educated and open-minded man. Those are the people I relate to the best. We talked politics a lot, especially those issues that affect people in the Valley. He was also interesting because he had particular tastes that didn't seem to match the meat and potatoes impression I had of him.

One thing that stood out to me was he drank Evian water.

When I saw the six cases of Evian he had bought during one fare, I presumed that was for his wife. He told me the difference between Evian and ANYTHING else was enormous. One time, after I dropped him off, he said, "It's too bad it's not 15 minutes from now, my wife needs to go to church. I told him I would wait. So he gave me a 75% tip for that delivery.

I didn't get a lot of calls down to the Foothills, a fairly wealthy area southwest of where I live in Ahwatukee. I loved to chase calls down there, in zone 78 and 79, because they were generally lucrative.

The most frequent call came off of Desert Foothills Parkway, from this 25-ish guy named Evald. I probably had him as a fare 10 times. He is a really interesting guy, because among other things, one of his parents is from Iceland. Or maybe it was both parents.

He works at a restaurant near me, and every ride I ever gave him was to work. He spent a lot time in New York before he moved here, so we could have a relative conversation. The last time I saw him as a passenger, we were discussing other drivers, because he and his roommate take a lot of cab rides. We laughed when I told him the one cabbie that works near Ahwatukee looks like Mookie Wilson, something only a New York Mets fan would know. I have seen him out and about a few times since I left Discount Cab.

I have had a couple of people that were favorites of mine even though I drove them only once. One was a young woman named Missy. She was a voucher passenger from the Magellan in Mesa. The obvious reason to say she was a favorite was because the voucher was worth $139. I ended up taking her all the way out to Kearny, which was a 76-mile trip.

This trip was beneficial to me because I took a lot of pictures on the way back. Kearny is south of Florence, a town southeast of Phoenix with a huge mine. It is out in the middle of nowhere, like most of Arizona. It looked like a place where they could have filmed some of those old westerns, or the Brady Bunch Grand Canyon episode.

Missy was way more together than most of the people I get from Magellan. She smiled and laughed the whole time we were in the cab. She also told me that she was genuinely afraid of a lot of the drivers she had, but that she felt very comfortable with me. She also let me know part of the reason she was going to Magellan.

I think she was kind of ashamed of her past, because she told me she was in prison for a while, which she chose instead of doing community service. That must have been some really shitty community service they offered her! She was living with her grandparents out in Kearny during her probation. She didn't tell me exactly what happened, but I'm pretty sure it was drug related. It seems like lots of young people get mixed up somehow in that stuff. Every now and again, I just feel like I could help one of them, and she was someone I could help. I almost asked for a way to contact her, but I didn't. I never saw her again, either. A lot of guys knew about her voucher, so you were lucky if you got it.

I was up in North Scottsdale on a Sunday afternoon and got a call to a resort. I picked up this older guy, probably in his 80s, and he asked me to bring him to a church up towards Carefree. He name was Karl.

We started talking, and it turns out he went to Rutgers. That came out when I told him I was from NJ. He then said to me, "Did you know Princeton and Rutgers played the first-ever college football game?" I answered with my own question, "Did you know the final score was 6-4?" He laughed.

I'm not sure how it came up, but he told me he was in the military and fought in the Battle of the Bulge in World War II. This particular battle was fought in Belgium. The goal of the Nazis was to capture Antwerp, Belgium, split the Western Allies forces in half and force them into a treaty that favored the Axis Powers. It was actually named the Ardennes Offensive. It began on December 16, 1944 and ended on January 25, 1945, and was the unofficial beginning of the end for the German army. Even though the Allies were caught off guard and suffered nearly 90,000 casualties, the Germans eventually retreated and three months later, Hitler was dead (this paragraph is according to Wikipedia).

There aren't a lot of WW II vets left. I knew one in Maple Shade who just couldn't talk about it, because he lost so many friends there. Karl wouldn't talk about the battle, but he did tell me about General Patton.

Karl had a fairly close relationship with the General. He had a lot of respect for him and took his suggestions quite a bit. This was interesting to me, because the great coach of the Ohio State University football team, Woody Hayes, was another guy who loved Patton.

Karl told me a how he was going to take French in college, but then his mother told him that if he wanted to learn French, he should go to school in Paris. Then, someone else told him it would be advantageous to learn German instead of French, so he changed again and went to school in Heidelberg.

He was going to do training in the field, but his father suggested that he should be trained in chemical warfare. His reason for this was that if he was trained in this discipline, he could get out of situations a lot easier. That made sense, and Karl said he was able to work his way out of three or four scrapes because of what he learned.

Karl might have been the most interesting fare I ever had. I brought him back to the resort and he gave me a great tip. I thanked him for his service to his country. I do that every time I meet someone in the military. I feel I owe that to any and all veterans.

During the last three months I drove for Discount, I drove a fellow named Ron around on a handful of occasions. The first time I had him in the cab, he was with his mother. The other times, he was by himself. He is probably the most even-tempered, pleasant fellow I've ever met. He didn't come across as a guy for whom I should feel bad, but it was hard not to be sympathetic towards him.

On that first occasion, I brought him and his mother to the store, but the times he was by himself, I was bringing him to a psychologist because he suffers from epilepsy. He can't work because of it. He's here in Phoenix trying to work his way around it.

The fact that I like him comes, in part, from the fact that he is from Palmyra, NJ. During the last four years I was in NJ, I lived in Maple Shade, the town adjacent to Palmyra. So, we had a lot to talk about. In fact, he made me feel better about myself. There is a sports broadcaster who is a constant reminder to me of how I didn't go very far in that field, or at least as far as I would have liked. It's nothing personal; he's a good guy. I just know I'm as good a play-by-play announcer as him. Every time I hear him on-air, I want to cry. But that's my problem. Anyway, Ron told me he doesn't like him.

I ended up taking Ron to this psychologist and back a couple of times, plus I brought him to the MVD and back another time. I was impressed at how stoic he is about his affliction. Acceptance is probably the hardest thing, but he has a really upbeat attitude and personality.

During that same time period, I would bring the owner of a restaurant in Ahwatukee from his apartment to his restaurant. I probably took him eight times in total and he always gave me $15 on an $8 fare. That was a great thing.

Chaz was really entertaining to me. He said he had a customer that had an issue with "bodily function control." Coincidently enough, I had picked this other guy up a few times and sure enough, the next time I gave him a ride, he left his mark in the cab. I needed to spray the car endlessly. I told Chaz about it, and we both laughed.

There were a couple of times I brought his girlfriend Tina to the bar after having brought him there earlier. The first time, she was bringing a set of golf clubs to him. She was making jokes about the golf clubs the whole time and we had a good laugh about that. The next time I saw Chaz, I told him I had brought her to the bar, and he said, "Yeah, she brought the wrong clubs."

Another local regular to me is this fellow named Jack. I had his fare many times. He is a big fan of my book project, mainly because he is also trying to get published. Generally, I would give him and the woman he lives with rides from the Bashas' near my apartment to their home about 1.5 miles away. During the last few months I drove, he would call me to see if I was available. We still keep in touch.

For an eight-week period in spring of 2009, I drove around a couple whose first names are Pat and Ross. They are snowbirds from the Detroit area. They were a perfect example that all octo-genarians are not grouchy.

The first time I got them as passengers, they wanted to go to the Scottsdale Fashion Square. I brought them there and I just figured it would be an easy trip. When we got there, he asked me for my phone number for when they wanted to go home. I gave it to him, but I wasn't counting on a return call. When he did call me, I was close to the mall, so it worked out.

We talked about the cab industry, and I was telling them about some of the stupid things that would happen to me. They were a great audience, laughing at practically anything I would say. When we got to their condo, Ross asked me if I would be available to them for a couple of doctor's appointments Pat had coming up in Chandler.

Apparently, they had a driver the over the previous several years, but that guy had recently quit. I guess I reminded them of this guy, because they wanted me to assume his role.

They are an interesting couple. They were both widowed a number of years ago and met through a church group. I thought it a funny coincidence that Pat had three sons and one daughter, while Ross had three daughters and one son. One of Pat's sons lives nearby.

Ross was a big sports fan and he seemed to be amazed at

how much I knew about the history of baseball, football, etc. He would get a big smile when I would dust off some unimportant fact. In fact, one of times I was waiting for Pat's appointment to finish, he walked out with a Sporting News magazine for me to read. How could I not like these people?

They were getting ready to go back to Detroit at the end of March when Ross broke his hip. At first, he said he fell, but Pat later told me that what really happened was that his hip was very brittle and it finally gave out (this is common), causing him to fall.

For the next several weeks, Ross was in a rehabilitation center in the middle of Old Town Scottsdale. I would pick up Pat at their condo at 9 AM and bring her to the center. At 5 PM, I would pick her up and bring her back home. Though there were times when her son would come to Scottsdale to drive her, I was her ride about 90% of the time. She basically was an everyday customer. She was amazingly even tempered about things, but you could see that she was worried about Ross.

Her son called me frequently to make sure I was taking care of her, which I certainly understood. When I told her how much he would call, she said, "I'm going to wring his neck." It was so cute.

On April 15, they got the go ahead to bring Ross back to Michigan, where his rehab would continue. Two days before they left, I had Pat as a fare for the last time. She handed me an extra $50 and gave me a big hug.

I called them a few times to see how they were doing. The last time I spoke with Ross, he really seemed to be in good spirits. I hope they are still doing well and, without a doubt, they will forever stand as my most favorite passengers.

Damn, this job is hard to take sometimes ━━━━━━━━

One of the things that I realized while working this job is how sad real life can be for some people. I bring people to and from the hospital every day and I am constantly amazed at how people deal with the horrors of their lives. There are thousands of people in Phoenix who know nothing but pain, confusion and medication.

I picked up this woman named Deanne from the Magellan office on Cave Creek, which is located in zone 231. I would go there at least three times per month, so I had no trouble finding it. This woman met me downstairs (normally I have to go upstairs to get fares) and, as I opened the door, I noticed how timid she appeared to be. She is probably 50 years old and was very thin and wearing baggy sweat clothes.

We drove for a while before either of us said anything, but I asked her how she was doing and she didn't waste any time telling me her problems. Deanne told me that she wasn't having a good time, because she really had no place to go and was having problems with her medication. She told me her caseworker told her she couldn't work because she wasn't ready, and that she was going to start collecting social security insurance to the tune of $635 per month. I asked her how she was going to be able to survive on that amount. $600 a week is hard enough to stretch, $600 a month is impossible. She said her caseworker told her she should able to do it. Insurance covers a lot of her expenses, but still, she wouldn't have much more than $200 a month for everything else. Then I asked her where she was going next, and she said the street name to which I was bringing her. I already knew that, so I asked her where *exactly*. She got this ashamed look on her face and said, "Oh, I'm going to this shelter." It turns out she was forced to live at a shelter for battered women. It is in a building that has a ton of security and has no markings on it, to make sure no undesirables can find it. I had been there before and recognized it once we got there. She said she thought she would only have to be there for a week, but I couldn't help but think she might be better off staying there longer.

She seemed so scared that I felt this would be a good place

for her. I don't know whether she was battered or not, but I was sure that I really didn't want to know. I dropped her at the back gate and told her that maybe I would see her again. She said she hoped so and said goodbye. I pulled the car to the side and started crying. I felt so bad for her that I pondered chasing her down and giving her some money, but she had already gone inside.

Another time I went to a hospital near Seventh Street and McDowell. I was getting frustrated, because I wasn't provided with a good indication of where this person would be. I asked a couple of people and finally was able to locate the proper door to enter. She was sitting in a wheel chair in a dressing gown when I met her.

She looked really tired and had some raggedy stuff. I helped her in the car, and I noticed a bandage on the right side of her head, and that her hair was really short. I thought she had undergone an operation, but I figured that if she wanted to tell me, she would.

We had a fairly long ride, so I tried to engage her in small talk. She was pretty talkative and cheerful at first, but then, almost as quickly, she got to a point that I thought she was going to cry. I was trying not to ask what was wrong, because I was afraid of what was bothering her. It wasn't some emotional thing.

The bandage was covering a wound from a 380 pistol. A man she claims she didn't know had shot her in the head! She was never in danger of dying or suffering brain damage or anything like that, but her head had been opened up and the recovery was taking a long time. I'm sure the emotional recovery would take years. She was really upset about the fact that she couldn't even look normal, what with the shaved head and the bandage. She did start to cry when she talked about it. I was really uncomfortable, because I just didn't know what I could do to comfort her.

This would have been bad enough, but then she started talking about the place she was living. She was assigned to this house by one of the state agencies. Apparently, she didn't have any family in the area that could (or would) help her. The person with whom she was living was treating her very poorly. She said she wasn't in any physically danger, but was instead being verbally abused on a regular basis. I didn't know how true it was, but you have to be a pretty horrible person to kick around someone with a gunshot wound to the head. I asked her when we got there if I could do anything for her. She said she would be OK and that she was going to stick it out and within three months she would be fine. I wasn't so sure.

I had a passenger in the spring of 2009 that made me as sad as I could ever be made to be. There are two pickup places at the Magellan office in Mesa. The other office is a JFCS location, and that's where I picked up Jane and her 11-year-old daughter Sara.

It was a fare to Scottsdale, an $18 voucher, so that was good. Jane got into the cab and buckled Sara in. I looked back and saw the expression on the kid's face. She was smiling, but I could tell that she had Cerebral Palsy. I smiled back and then confirmed the address with her Jane. Sara responded before her mom did, but all she could really do was make squeaking noises. This was really unnerving at first.

Jane and I were talking about a bunch of mundane things like the weather, and Sara would try to interject, but all that served to do was frustrate her mother. Sara asking questions about getting a hamster, because her father promised her she could get a hamster. She was really excited about it, and her mom just kept telling her they would talk about it later.

My first reaction was to be a little annoyed at Jane for dismissing her kid like that. She seemed to show only a surface concern for Sara, reacting to her obvious needs and "displaying" just the minimal amount of sympathy for her. I'm not sure whether I thought about this while they were still in the cab, just after they got out, or not until a bunch of days later, but my opinion changed.

Why would I judge Jane harshly at all? How do I know what it is like to have a child like Sara, knowing you are going to have to take care of her for rest of her life? I can't even begin to imagine the difficulty in that. How can it not be hard, if not impossible, to not get a little indifferent to every little need? You also have to consider the anger and resentment that would build up after years of NEVER being able to consider yourself first. What a difficult life that must be!

Anyway, Sara started tapping me on the shoulder to talk to me. This made it difficult to drive, because I knew she didn't understand the necessity for me to concentrate on driving more than talking to her. I tried as best as I could to do both, and she just kept smiling. I was actually starting to understand what she was saying. It's amazing what listening can actually do.

Jane stepped in and asked Sara to let me drive because we were going to be home soon. When we got to their house, Sara and Jane both said goodbye. I got out and helped Sara unbuckle her seat belt, and when she saw me opening her door, she smiled again. I helped her out and shook her hand and said goodbye. Jane mouthed the words "Thank you" to me. If I was able to give her a few minutes of rest, I was glad.

The most striking memory of this pick up came right after that. Sara was leaning on the cab to support herself as she walked towards her mother. She turned to me again, and waved with a huge glowing smile on her face. That made me smile and wave too. I started to climb back into the cab, and she said goodbye again, replete with her million-watt smile. As soon as I saw them step into the house, I burst into tears. This kid just broke my heart.

Subsequently, I told dozens of passengers about this kid. One woman with a very biblical way of looking at things told me that the reason this (illness) happens to people is to test the compassion of others. I'm not sure I buy that explanation, but whether it's true or not, the experience made me feel better about myself.

Insurance pays for a large percentage of the fares I took as a cab driver. Whether it was people with physical ailments or mental ailments, approximately 25% were for rides to the doctor.

One afternoon I found myself in Peoria and I got a call to a house. It took 10 minutes before I could get anyone to answer door. I had just called for a no-show when a gentleman who spoke with a European accent finally answered the door.

I told him I was supposed to be picking up a woman named Olga. He told me that she would be ready to go in about five minutes. It was only an $11 voucher, so I really didn't want to wait too long. The guy told me Olga was going to the dentist. As she was coming out of her room, the guy pulled me aside and told me that I really have to pay close attention, because Olga has Alzheimer's disease.

He told me that she would ask me the same question over and over. He was right. She asked me if I would be coming to pick her up. I told her someone would be coming to get her. Then she asked me my name and I told her. Unfortunately, that was the conversation for the entire trip. Olga did four more rounds of those two questions and we finally got to the dentist.

I helped walk her in to the office and asked the nurse to reassure her that someone was coming to take her home, which she did. After I got back to my cab, I started to cry. Then, I saw the nurse run out. She was checking whether Olga left her wallet in the car. Of course, we soon discovered Olga had it the whole time.

This really stuck home with me, because my dad's mother was like this before the affliction was given the name Alzheimer's disease.

I've seen some pretty terrible things. Below is a comprehensive list of physical and mental ailments of my passengers over a 15-month period:

Gunshot wound to the head
Parkinson's disease
Gunshot wound to the stomach

Dialysis (Kidney failure)
Stab wound to the stomach
Down's Syndrome
Physical battery
Pregnancy
Alzheimer's Disease
Brain Tumor
Blindness
Cirrhosis of the liver
Cataracts
Pregnancy
Prosthetic leg
Kidney stones
Multiple Sclerosis
Paralysis from a Stroke
Anterior Lateral Sclerosis
Gangrene
Ovarian Cancer
Tourette's syndrome
Brain damage
Deafness
Blood poisoning
Broken hip
Lung Cancer
Skin Cancer
Cerebral Palsy
Fibromyalgia
Hip replacement
Epilepsy
Gastric bypass
Meth addiction
AIDS
Broken arm
Broken ribs

Missing arm
Diabetes
Seizures
Missing leg
Brain aneurysm

CHAPTER **9**

The Me Section

You Wanted to See Me, Sir? ━━━━━━━━

From Day One, I tried to follow the rules, as I understood them. I'm no angel, but I wasn't interested in screwing myself over. Sometimes, I think the cab company would just call me in to create fear, so they could exert a level of control over me. I had my share of meetings with the bosses.

The first time I got called in, it seemed to come out of nowhere. I tried to figure out what was up, but I just couldn't remember doing anything I shouldn't have. When I got to the cage, I waited for the safety guy, and he had me look at a video that showed me not wearing a seat beat. Now there are many occasions where I don't have my belt on until I start rolling. One time, I had to slam on the brake almost immediately after I got started, so that video was recorded. I do admit, that maybe 1% of the time, I'm moving when my seat belt isn't fastened, so I couldn't argue with that video.

The second time, it was seemingly the same situation, I couldn't figure out what was wrong. I told the passenger in the car what was going on, and he told me to tell them to "fuck off". I wasn't going to do that, even though I would have enjoyed it. Anyway, when I got back to the cage, it was the same thing: I wasn't wearing my seatbelt, according to them.

I didn't understand how that could be, until I looked very carefully at that video. My arm was draped over the strap. I pointed this out to the safety guy, but he argued that this was worse then not having the seatbelt on, so I just said yes, yes, yes and got on with my life. The problem with these "lessons" is that I lose time and money doing the *mea culpa* while these safety guys get boners over finding new and creative was to justify their salaries.

Right before Thanksgiving 2008, The IOI line was instituted to reimburse drivers for mistakes that weren't their fault. We were given the minimum for each mistake, but at least it was something. I was one of the first to use this "service" regularly. I told many other drivers about it. My frequent use of this line eventually came back to bite me in the ass.

One particular day, I got three consecutive fares that had mistakes. I was livid and I felt I was justified. I had called the IOI line after each occurrence. By the third one, I was so pissed off that I concluded my message by screaming "COULD YOU GUYS GET IT TOGETHER OVER THERE?"

I didn't think about it until a few days later. I saw on a message board in the cage, a request for me to report to the safety office. I ended up speaking to Roger the driver liaison. He told me that the IOI office decided that I have "anger management problems", based on the message I left for them. I just started to laugh.

After he was done reading their "findings", I got my say. I told them I had just received three straight fucked-up orders and I had every right to be upset. But then I got to the real point. "Is this guy a clinical psychologist? I want to see his degree right now, and for that matter, what the hell does that even mean, 'I have anger management issues?' Does he even know what he's talking about? Not only that, but why am I not getting a call from *them*?"

Roger just shrugged and said, "Hey, don't shoot the messenger."

When he found out that I was going back to New Jersey in a couple of days for Thanksgiving, he told me that was a good thing, to get away for a while. When I came back, I had ELEVEN credits to my account. When I pointed this out to Roger, he just shrugged again.

About three months later, I actually spoke to the IOI office. I specifically requested a phone call. The reason was the new automated phone service was creating a lot of duplicate orders and big problems. I wanted to speak to them about it. They told me they "knew there were glitches" and that "it was being worked on". What bothered me was they put the responsibility of being proactive against the glitches on the drivers' shoulders.

Shortly after that, I had an issue with the Glendale cage. I got a flat tire about four miles from there and was towed in. I was told they would let me know when the tire was fixed. I saw the safety guy there, so we talked for a bit and I told him why I was there. He told me it shouldn't be too long.

I sat outside his office where he could see me the whole time. I didn't want to ruffle any feathers since this wasn't my cage, so I just sat quietly. After almost two and a half hours, he finally said, "They should be done by now," and he went to check. It turns out they finished my car 90 minutes earlier, only no one bothered to tell me! I said, "Are you kidding me?" He just said, "Have a good rest of your shift and be safe out there." Thanks a lot!

The driver liaison did something that pissed me off only once, which is actually pretty impressive. I had this one passenger who, through circumstance, ran his credit card three times during the same trip. Discount has a rule that says more than one charge on the same card within an hour has to be approved. Well, he didn't get around to checking it for two weeks, so I lost $25 because of his laziness. When I confronted him about it, he basically told me, "Too bad, it's gone." What next?

Unfortunately, the photo enforcement cameras ticketed me

twice. Nobody can tell me those cameras aren't rigged. It is claimed that they are set to ticket you if you are going 11 miles per hour over the posted speed limit. There are many reports that certain cameras fire off at lesser speeds. I know I wasn't going 11 miles per hour over the limit on the first ticket, which I got on Rural Road in Tempe.

I am pretty sure it's illegal for the cab company to give my information away so the city can send me a ticket, although I certainly don't blame them. If drivers knew they wouldn't have to pay for these tickets, they would break the traffic laws all the time.

Anyway, the safety guys didn't make a big deal out of the first one. After the second one, I was told that if I got one more of these tickets, they wouldn't be able to contract me anymore. I was thinking, "That's bullshit." What was even bigger and deeper bullshit was being told that I had to take an online safety course. They told me it would cost $35. When I looked it up, the cost was actually $165. I finally decided, "Fuck that", they can't make me spend nearly $200 on that. I guess I was correct, because I never heard another word about it.

About a month before my last shift, the IOI office specifically requested to meet with me to discuss issues with the IOI line, how you get credits, etc. They had asked the 10 or so people that frequently called the IOI line to come in for a brainstorming session. When I got to the cage, the IOI meister was with two other drivers. I sat down and listened to their conversation. I really didn't want to be there, because I knew I was leaving the job soon, but I felt somehow that I owed it to the other drivers to express my opinions.

After a couple of minutes, I knew it was a waste of time. Every other time an issue was brought up; this IOI guy told us that the issue wasn't the Solution Center's fault, because of, whatever. I thought, "You know, you aren't here to determine fault. You are supposed to be listening to driver's issues, writing them down and trying to come up with solutions down the line." If I had cared about the results, I would have said that. But, I sat there for 15 minutes, fulfilled my "obligation" to show up, and then I left.

Tuesday with Murray ━━━━━━━━━━━━━━━━

There is an award-winning book written by a sportswriter named Mitch Albom called *Tuesdays with Morry*. I met the fellow I'm about to talk about on a Tuesday, so...

Towards the end of my time with Discount, I started talking a lot more with other drivers. By nature, we are entities unto ourselves. Sometimes, I would see guys at gas stations and convenience stores and we'd talk about business of the day. I never really got to know anyone, however. The first real in-depth conversation I had was with a driver that I called Murray. I'm not sure that his name was really Murray, but to me, *he was fucking Murray!*

I met this guy about four months before I left the company. I was at QT 294 waiting for a call. Murray pulled up and we started to talk. Now, based on my impression of cab drivers prior to becoming one, this guy was exactly how I would describe a typical cab driver.

I'm not sure how it happened, but he started "telling me his secrets" from 20 years on the job. He basically implied that the cab company isn't very honest with drivers as far as what we are obligated to do. For example, I was told at orientation that we must run the meter at all times. Murray told me that wasn't true. We, as independent contractors, can negotiate a price ahead of time whenever we want, except on vouchers. As long as the price is agreed upon, anything is fair. In that situation, it's a good idea to get the money up front. Then, turn the meter on and off. The only thing we can't do is charge MORE than it says on meter.

Turning the meter on and off quickly is called rapid metering. If you do that, an automatic message will come back, asking if you picked up the passenger. Murray told me that dispatch has no right to ask that question. Once again, they don't have any say. If you do that on a voucher, and don't pick up a passenger, you could get in trouble. Other than that, it's not an issue.

The most intriguing thing he told me was about the contract itself. According to what we were told by the company, once we accept a fare we are obligated to take it. What Murray explained, however, was that dispatch automatically breaks the contract as soon as they "force" us to take a fare. They do not give us full details as to the pickups, until AFTER we accept it. We only get the zone location and the distance from where we are at the time of the call. And even that isn't completely accurate. Each pick up is considered an individual contract. Since we don't have full information, we aren't contractually required to make that pick-up. I believe drivers use this knowledge to get out of $6 vouchers and supermarket calls. I never turned down calls, even after I learned this. But, I don't blame guys for doing anything they feel they have to do.

Murray opined that most of the office people have never driven a cab, and the ones that have, did so a long time ago. Now, you don't have to be a genius to figure out the problem with that scenario. Drivers will never have a voice in the office looking out for them. That is probably why cab companies DON'T hire from within. When there are bosses that don't understand the business because they have never been in the trenches, it's pretty hard to get any sympathy from them. It's hard enough as it is, even with smart bosses! Shit, even the late Gene Upshaw, who played in the AFL and NFL for 15 years, seemed to side with the owners, when he was in charge of the NFL's players union!

Murray also told me "he was sure" that the other large company here (which owns, among others, AAA and Yellow) was eventually going to purchase Discount.

He also suggested things related to making money. If you're not getting calls, go to a supermarket, a Wal-Mart, or convenience store and drive around. There are always people looking for cabs at these places, and you can negotiate a price and stay booked in, just in case another call comes in.

Murray implored me to get $20 up front at night to protect myself from being ripped off. This is a two-fold measure of protection. First, if they bolt on a $40 fare, for example, you still get something. If the fare is only $12, you can always give change. I never did this, because my theory was I might lose more in tips because the fare was pissed at the implication of thievery.

He also suggested not taking personals, unless it was more than $30. The theory was that you are committing your time and will be in a particular location. You may have to drive 30 extra miles to fulfill this commitment, and block 60 to 120 minutes of your time, so it should be worth it. This was easier for me to do.

Funnily enough, I had another one of these discussions just a couple of days later. I was at the Mesa cage for a PM. I was chatting with Fred, the driver who looked like former Notre Dame Football Coach Charlie Weis. He, too, provided some interesting insights about Discount Cab.

The first thing he said was what he considered the best piece of advice: DON'T EVER TALK TO ANYONE!! If I had taken this literally, of course, it would have made the continuation of my conversation with him impossible, so I correctly guessed that he meant AFTER we were finished. The reason was immediately obvious: you really can't trust anyone. Now, that's not 100% true, but it's 93% true. Everyone is always looking out for himself or herself, and that generally requires screwing the other guy. More often than not, it's not malicious. It's just the way it is, and you have to be careful.

He next told me that the company keeps a certain percentage of each mile paid on vouchers. While this is underhanded, it doesn't come as a surprise to me. I also learned from Fred that the lease prices have gone up four times in less than four years, and when it does, the company ALWAYS says it hasn't gone up for more than two years. Sure enough, the one time it went up during my tenure, that's exactly what the memo said.

Fred also told me that the two safety guys were the best friends I could have. He said one of them had gotten him out of a spot where an accident wasn't his fault. The safety guy was able to prove it and Fred did not get charged. I didn't really want to burst his bubble, but I'm pretty sure the only reason that kind of effort was made by the company to prove his innocence was so Discount's insurance wasn't charged. Plus, I told him my flat tire story and he seemed to be stunned at the lack of help I received.

Fred is also one of the many drivers that don't like the Prius. They are smaller than the Crown Victoria, but not as much as they may appear. He never really gave me a reason, although I'm pretty sure it was because the leases are quite a bit more. If you are a full time driver, by the time you reach 1000-1200 miles per week, you start saving money. When I told him the reason I like my Prius was that it didn't have a camera, he suggested I don't mention THAT to anyone either. If I say that to the wrong person, they will put one in the car. That is a piece of advice that I did take.

The last driver I really conversed with is someone I expect to see frequently. This guy's name is Zane and he was in the Ohio State University's law school when I was doing my undergrad stuff. He said his father played football there and was the MVP of the 1950 Rose Bowl. In my last six weeks on the job, we had many more discussions about football than the cab industry. He did tell me he got tired of being a lawyer after 22 years, and that's why he's driving a cab. I'm sure we will commiserate Buckeye football a lot.

Smile, You're on Candid Camera ━━━━━━━━━━

The first week I drove, I worked two days, thinking I was going to stay at Jason's Deli and do both. It didn't work out that way, and I started driving full time the following week. I drove 56 of the first 58 days that I was a full time driver (including a run of 35 consecutive days). I started with weekly leases during my second full week. I was assigned cab number 476 as my permanent car. This meant that I could take days off and I would be given the same car back upon my return.

Returning from what were my first days off after my initial consecutive days streak, I came back to the cage and cab number 476 was not there. Anson apologized and gave me cab number 392. I called Roger the driver liaison and my facilitator Dennis to tell them about what happened, but neither one of them answered. Being novice to the industry at the time, and mixing in my personality, I wasn't a happy guy.

I left the cage and 30 minutes later received my first call. As I headed towards the address, the call was cancelled. Fucking great.

I re-booked in and got another call about 15 minutes later. Again, on my way there, the call was cancelled. I was starting to get really mad.

I stayed in Mesa and got a third call to an apartment complex to get a voucher passenger. Unfortunately, no one answered when I called and knocked. What a fucking start.

After two hours, I finally got a call that I actually got paid for. It was a long trip, but anything was acceptable at this point. This led me to another voucher that was a good news/bad news scenario. The good news was that it was worth $35 dollars; the bad news was it took me all the way towards the football stadium in Glendale. Plus, it started to rain heavily outside.

I picked up the kid and drove him home, detouring along the way as required because it had already poured in Glendale. This kid was in one of those programs where a Foster family was taking care of him and several others. I had to sign him back into the house when we got there. It was very dark outside at this point, but it was a nice neighborhood, so it wasn't scary.

After I dropped him off, I tried to call Roger and Dennis again. For a second time, neither of them answered. At that point, I just lost it.

I started yelling and screaming at the top of my lungs in the empty cab as I drove back towards the highway. "WHAT THE FUCK IS GOING ON. I DON'T GET A FUCKING CALL FOR THE FIRST TWO FUCKING HOURS. I'M SUPPOSED TO HAVE MY REGULAR CAR. IT'S NOT FUCKING THERE, WHAT THE FUCK IS GOING ON WITH THIS FUCKING COMPANY. I CALL FUCKING ROGER; HE'S NOT FUCKING THERE. I CALL FUCKING DENNIS; HE'S NOT FUCKING THERE. WHY THE FUCK AM I DOING THIS SHIT." This continued for another five minutes. I wove a tapestry of obscenities that to this day hangs over the Salt River. I only stopped because my head started hurting. I finished my shift and went home.

I really didn't think about it again until three days later when I was in my cab, and I was sent a message to come in to see Roger, the safety guy. I was pretty nervous because the message didn't say what the meeting was about. I wasn't that far away, so I got there and he was free when I walked into his office.

Almost all of the cabs are equipped with cameras that are always on, recording activity from both inside and outside of the car. If there is a sudden stop, caused by either the cab bumping something, crashing into something, something crashing into it, or the driver hitting the brakes too hard, the camera will save both views, 10 seconds before and after the impact or brake. It turns out that when I was having my little meltdown I must have hit the brakes at a stop sign hard enough for it to be recorded.

Roger sat there and explained to me as one would to a child that I should probably pull to the side of the road if I'm going to do that again. He said he understands the frustrations involved with the job, but my safety is much more important than anything, and I need to be extremely careful when my emotions ride high.

Then, he started questioning me about the two guys I mentioned during my tirade. I told him that the stuff I said about them was just said in the heat of the moment and I wasn't really mad at them. I had tried to call them a combined about 10 times since

I started and neither of them had EVER answered the phone or called me back. I said, "If it's their job to help me, they should be available to me when I need them." He thanked me for the input and sent out four e-mails about our conversation.

All of a sudden my satisfaction became a priority, because both Dennis and Roger called me that afternoon. I pretty much had the same chat with both. There didn't seem to be any animosity. I just said that, while I wasn't really angry with them, I had called them each several times and neither had ever been available, nor did they return my calls. The upside to this whole thing was that I never really had a problem with either of them again as far as returning calls was concerned.

But this incident made me angry in another way. I considered it an invasion of privacy that the "Higher Ups" can view my personal business at any time. I don't know whether there are other ways to save what the camera records, but there probably are. They tell us they are concerned with our safety, but to me they are simply interested in keeping an eye on us.

Later on, I moved into a Prius (cab number 732), which was one of the few cabs that didn't have a camera in it. I guarded that car with my life. The C-Book screen was at least 30 seconds behind, but I put up with that and other minor drawbacks. That's how important not having a camera was to me. I never did anything nefarious; I simply considered it was a blatant invasion of my civil rights.

I've been a Cab Driver for 20 Years

I made it a rule not to have a whole lot of interaction with other drivers. This occurred almost immediately. Within two weeks of my orientation, I only came across one person from my training class ever again, so I figured it wasn't a good idea to get too close to anyone. I wasn't going to make a whole lot of friends.

There are other reasons. My experience with cabbies prior to becoming one was not good. I always felt as if they were trying to rip me off, so I didn't have a high level of trust going in. I understand now that their attitudes are most of the times based on, "Get them before they get me", and I completely get it. It doesn't excuse reprehensible actions, but at least it isn't born completely from being a crook.

I had one particular experience with a driver that could have gotten me fired. I was in Chandler and I got a call to the Wal-Mart in zone 363. When I got there, I didn't see the woman, so I called her phone number. It turns out, the address on the dispatch was wrong and she was at her apartment about two miles away.

The reason for the mistake was a technical glitch in the automated order answering system. I have to assume Discount had installed this system to expedite the ordering process. The problems started immediately. Once a phone number was associated with an address, the system presumed that the address would always be the same for that number. The system linked the address to the phone number in its database. But if two (or more) separate orders come in for the same phone number over time – one with say a home address and another with a work address – the system put out whatever it ingested as the original address. Since cell phone use is so prominent, this mistake was doomed to happen a lot.

This was the case for the fare at hand. This woman had been picked up at a Wal-Mart the first time she called Discount, now she was calling for a pick up from her home.

So I went to the address the woman gave me when I phoned her. Just as we were leaving, another cab pulled in. The driver asked me if I had this address and I said I did. I told him he must have gotten a duplicate and I drove off. I brought the woman to her destination and went back towards QT 341. As I got to the intersection of Ray and Arizona, I saw the other driver again and realized that he was following me. I got nervous and started scripting what I was going to say to him when I stopped.

When I got to the QT, he got out of his cab and started walking towards me. I got my hackles up and leaped out of the car, ready to defend myself. He started yelling, telling me that the order wasn't a duplicate. He then said that he followed me just to tell me that he was going to report me for stealing his fare and I was going to be charged back $25. I told him he was wrong and that I legitimately had that order. He claimed that it wasn't any benefit to him and that the company was going to get the money, and that he just was "forced" to do it. He had a smug look on his face as he got into the front of his cab and was going to shut the door. Now I was pissed.

I grabbed the door and I wouldn't let him shut it. I said, "Don't you shut that door, you're not leaving here until you hear what happened." He said, "OK", but I really wasn't giving him a lot of say in the matter. I started yelling at him about how the order was sent to the Wal-Mart and I spoke with the woman who told me where she actually was. Before I finished with that explanation, some dude walked by and said, "Can't we all just get along?" I told him to mind his own business.

When I was done, the other driver said, "See, that's a reasonable explanation. Now I'm not going to report you." I was like, "Are you fucking kidding me, you jackass? The only reason you came over here was to rub it in my face. You're not reporting me because you know you're wrong." He said, "No man, I've been driving for 20 years and I know how tough it is. It is good to know there are some honest guys out there." After hearing that, I actually apologized to this clown for yelling at him when I had every right to punch him in the face. We shook hands and he drove away. I took a deep breath and called the driver liaison and told him what happened, just to cover myself from this guy. Asshole!

"The Apple"

They told us at orientation that among the ways to develop a business plan and, subsequently, a business, was to accumulate a group of "regulars" – people that you pick up and drop off with some regularity – and work from there. One of the facilitators told me that for about a year he had a Monday through Friday customer who paid him $85 a day to drive him to work and back. That paid his entire lease and left him 10-12 hours daily to make more money. Those examples are few and far between.

I came to realize that it was impossible to have 10-20 weekly regulars that would fill my bankbook. The people who pay for their own cabs are generally only in temporary need of a regular driver, like for going out to get shit-hammered and avoid the wrath of the Valley's DUI patrol or in an emergency where a cab is the only solution. Almost always, when people have your number, they never call you back. The one time in twenty that someone does call me back, I'm nowhere near the place I dropped them off. That said; it is possible to have semi-regulars to boost the cash flow. One of my favorites was not a regular for long, but she was enjoyable to have in the cab for one main reason: She was very easy on the eyes.

The first time I got a call to pick up "The Apple" I was not having a great day. Three of four calls had been no shows, and the three previous calls that I did pick up were from supermarkets or some other short drive that didn't earn me any money. So when I got to her place, the fact that it took her about 10 minutes to get out to the cab pissed me off. One of the things I dislike about my "co-workers" is that a lot of drivers would have turned the meter on while waiting. In their defense, it's pretty rude to waste a person's time when that is how they earn a living. I, however, never turned the meter on *until the passenger was in the car, unless they told me to do so.* When she got to the cab, I was like, "Wow, she's hot". She was very exotic looking and she was wearing a nice, light-colored sundress. She told me that she needed to go to an insurance company on Queen Creek and Alma School, which was going to be a $30 trip.

She really didn't say much at first, but opened up when I started talking about car insurance. She looked really young, about 21, to be an insurance agent. It isn't that I didn't believe her. I just thought she just looked really young. She told me that she could give me a better rate on my insurance, but I just ignored that comment for the time being.

She wanted to try to barter me down on the fare as well. She was told by a friend to ask for a flat rate and I said I might do that if she was a regular customer, but I wouldn't do it for this trip. What I was thinking during this time was "What's in it for me?" I have to admit; I'm not a good person for this part of the job, because I have the tendency to hurt myself by feeling bad for someone and cutting them a break, with no benefit to me, other than satisfying my conscience. She was talking about what a pain not having a car was and that she was going to need cabs for a while. That was when I was willing to listen.

The fare ended up being $28. She paid for that and told me she could get me a better rate on my insurance. I told her I would charge her $20 in the future for regular work. "What is regular work?" was her response. Twice a week was what I was thinking, and that's what I told her. She said that was fine, so I gave her my phone number and told her to call me when she got the chance.

I had pretty much forgotten about her when she called me out of the blue about a month and a half later. She had misplaced my number, but she sure as hell remembered that I told her I would give a discount, since it was the first thing out of her mouth. I really didn't care that much, because the way I saw it, $20 puts me that much closer to making my lease.

Anyway, I picked her up several more times. The first time, nothing really happened, except she tried once again to get me to change my insurance. Normally, I would put it off, but I really didn't want to be hassled anymore, so I told her the truth. I don't change services vendors to save $5 a month. It leaves me open to plenty of anxiety, because I would think over and over about it.

I said, "If you could save me $50 a month, I'd consider it. She said no to that, which I knew would be her response.

The second time was much more interesting. I picked her up at her boyfriend's house. She had brought her car, which was messed up, to his house so he could work on it. Whatever he wasn't able to fix (which, in the end, was everything), her brother was going to do. When she walked up the driveway, she was arguing with him. She looked incredible, as usual. He called her a bitch, and she put up her hand and got into the cab. As I turned the car around, he was calling her name. I turned to tell her that, but before I said anything, she told me to ignore him and just go. So I did just that.

After the hellos, she started complaining about him. She wasn't even angry, saying in a calm tone that he was being mean to her for no reason. He apparently wanted her cell phone because his was on the fritz. She told him no. Most women would be shaken, angry, screaming or something. The tone of her voice never changed, it was amazing.

After a few minutes, her cell phone rang and it was her boyfriend. He had walked across the street to use a neighbor's phone. He started yelling at her again (I know this because I could hear him). She just stayed calm, saying "I'm not sure why you think I'm going to do what you want when you're calling me hurtful names like that, but I'm not going to" and "I'm already on my way, so you'll just have to deal with it." She never lost control and just hung up on him. It was tremendous, I was thoroughly impressed and I told her as much. But it didn't end there.

He called back three more times and the same thing happened. He really wanted the phone, because she told me he said he would pay me $20 to go back and give him the phone. She left it up to me, so I said sure. When we got there, he started yelling again. You could tell he was really angry, because he had to pay $20 to get that phone. But, again, she calmly told him to fuck off, gave him the phone and a kiss on the cheek, and she got back in the cab. I love this chick!

Anyway, she handed me the $20 and she started telling me how she wanted to break off the relationship with this dude. She said she was used to older men. I started thinking "Ooh, there might be an in here for me." But then it occurred to me that this woman claims to be 21-22 years old and she works for a major insurance company. That doesn't quite sound right.

We stopped because she wanted a Starbucks. I told her I hate Starbucks because their coffee is awful and I can't figure out how they are as popular as they are. She had a gift certificate card and offered to buy me one of these coffees. I saw they had some Pumpkin flavored something or other, so, even though I was still on the cookie diet, I got one. I now understand why Starbucks does the business it does. It isn't the coffee that sells; it's the other stuff that goes in it.

She then told me that she really enjoys riding with me, because we always have interesting conversations and she feels safe with me. I was very thankful for that, because that is the impression I like to give people. Trustworthiness is a trait I admire and aspire to. People are people and they do what they do, not because they are pre-disposed to be good or bad, but through their experiences, they become what they become.

A couple of minutes went by and then she asked me something that gave me wood. She said, "I hope you don't mind me asking, but I was wondering how old you are"? I was thinking (more like hoping) she was into me. I told her my age and then she nodded and said "Oh". Now, she might have been curious, nosey, making conversation, or trying to work me. Whatever, it gave me hope.

When we got to her office, she said. "Jonathan, are you going to let me sell you an insurance plan?" I responded honestly, saying, "Look, I really don't have interest in changing insurance companies to save $5 a month. If you wrote me a policy that cost me $21 a month, that would be different, but I know you can't do that." She said that she understood, because she felt the same way.

She called me about four more times for rides. Twice I wasn't available; the other two were occasions where, other than having some laughs along the way, nothing eventful happened. I guess she got her car back. She had asked about taking four to five hour blocks of time to drive her to these audits she would do and if I helped her with that, she would pay me 20% of her proceeds. I told her I would be interested in doing that. Unfortunately, nothing ever came of it.

As it turns out, I never really heard from "The Apple" again. About eight months later, I was close to the insurance office where she worked, so I decided to stop in to find out what was going on with her. I walked in and she was not there. I asked a couple of the guys that worked there what had happened to her. One told me she had moved to Seattle. I said, "Yeah, I figured". Then, one guy said, "Why, does she owe you money?" I chuckled and said, "No, she doesn't owe me money?" The other guy said, "Are you sure she doesn't owe you money?" I said, "I had given her rides in my cab and she just disappeared, so I was curious." Then one of them asked if I wanted auto insurance. Based on that conversation, I'm glad she didn't become the "The Apple" of my eye.

Windfalls

If it rains here in the Valley, it might be 20 days a year, at the most. There are a number of occasions when it rains but we never know because the water evaporates before it hits the earth (this is a scientific fact). Last year when I was home in NJ for Thanksgiving, it rained almost every day. I was talking to my dad and I told him, "You know, it's rained more days since I have been here than it does the entire year in Phoenix." That isn't exactly true, but it's close, and when it does rain in Jersey, everyone knows.

A couple of weeks after I started with Discount, I had gotten a couple of no shows, so I was getting annoyed. I chased a call to the Greyhound bus station near the airport, probably four zones over, when the sky opened up and dumped so much rain so fast that half the cars on the road pulled to the side and waited for it to stop. That's the smart thing to do, because as hard as the rain can be, it generally lasts for only a few minutes. It is amazing how quickly it floods out here, but there is no drainage and the ground is as hard as concrete, so there is no place for it to go.

Anyway, I got to the bus station just as the rain was stopping, and the lady I was supposed to pick up was right there. I confirmed her name and grabbed her suitcase. She had a walker, so it took her a while to get in the cab. What made it really difficult was, even though she spoke English, I could barely understand anything she said.

She started telling me about the fact that she just came back from visiting her family in Los Angeles and she was glad to be home. At least that's what I thought she said. She was easily in her 80's, if not older. She seemed to have a speech impediment that sounded like she had been suffered a stroke. She was cheerful enough, so it wasn't an annoying problem.

After a few minutes, I figured out the address she wanted to go to. She lived up in Peoria, so it was going to be a great fare. I decided the best way to go was to travel via Grand Avenue, which goes on a diagonal towards the Northwest part of the city. Looking back, there were three reasons it was NOT the best route. Number one, financially, it wasn't the most lucrative route; Number two, I was right by I-10, so it wasn't the fastest route; and Number three, the road became a problem.

Normally, I would say that Grand Avenue is not a problem. In spite of the traffic signals, it saves a lot of mileage and, often enough, time. However, I wasn't really familiar with it yet. There are a lot of dips in the road, and consequently, after a lot of rain, much of the road floods.

I can't recall exactly where the first water hazard popped up.

But I didn't see it until it was almost too late. I slowed down just enough to wade through this newly formed river. If I had hit it with any velocity, I might have gotten stuck. Of course, I was driving a car that used to be a police car, so it had a powerful engine. Plus, it was a really heavy car, so it wasn't likely that I was going to get stuck. I did have some experience to draw on.

About 15 years earlier, I was driving around Plainsboro, NJ with my friend Mark Schuster. We had been at his pool all day and a storm was starting to roll in. He is really into storms, so he said he wanted to go out and chase a tornado, because the conditions were right for it. We are driving around in a flash flood storm, laughing our Asses off, looking for a funnel cloud. After 15 minutes, the rain stopped and we never saw a tornado. Mark did see a pond of freestanding water and he decided to spray it. Unfortunately, he went in too deep and we got stuck. There were no cell phones at the time, so we really didn't know what to do. He somehow managed to start the car, even though the water had come through the floorboard and we were now up to our chests in water. We just kept laughing because we couldn't move the car. Finally, some local redneck drove up and Mark rolled down the window. As water spilled out of the car, the guy asked us if we needed any help. Sarcastically, Mark said, "Oh no, we're fine, it's another beautiful day." The guy said, "OK" and drove away. We laughed harder than ever.

Getting back to cab stories, the trip got really hard, because I patronized this woman, as I couldn't figure out what she was saying while I was trying not to drive into this ocean that wasn't on the map. I ended up getting behind a Range Rover and every time it went through a patch of water, I just followed through. I never really had to worry about the water from then on.

I was not familiar with Peoria and Glendale, so I now have another problem; my fare couldn't give me directions and I don't where I'm going. She could tell when I went the wrong way, but that was about it. I didn't have my GPS yet, although this might

THE ME SECTION ⤷

have been the last straw to me getting one.

Somehow, we found her home, an assisted living place around Peoria Avenue and 83rd Street. I helped her out and brought her suitcase in. The fare was $46. She handed me $104 and said, "Thank you, you can keep it." I started to say something, but then I realized it was in my best interests to shut up and just leave. I drove straight back to Tempe, but I used the I-10.

Interestingly, I had that woman as a fare six more times, and her total for those fares didn't add up to half of that first huge fare.

One Saturday I drove straight to Scottsdale to start the day. Often enough, I get someone needing to retrieve his or her car from a bar from the night before. The first couple of pickups were decent so I was in a pretty good mood.

I got a call to the Circle K on Indian School and 82nd. It was this older guy that I had picked up at the Casino Arizona on Indian Bend a few times before. This time, he wanted to go to the casino.

He had retired to Phoenix from Detroit about six months earlier, and he was going to this casino at least three times a week. He was a nice enough fellow and he took care of me.

We got to the casino and he gave the exact amount he always gives me, so I was happy. Before I had a chance to pull away, these two guys jumped in the cab and told me they were going to the west side, close to the University of Phoenix Stadium. At this point in my career, I didn't care if I was scooping anyone, because I had been skunked at all of the casinos multiple times. Plus, this was going to be a huge fare. As we got to the 101, I asked if they wanted me to use the freeway or go straight across. The freeway would probably be more expensive, but it would be way faster. They chose speed.

They had been at the casino all night and they had tickets for the Coyotes game that day. They were telling me about the poker tournament they were in, how they should have done this differently and should have done that. They said they each lost a ton of money. I asked them if they had fun, to which they said "Hell yeah." I followed with, "Well, then so what." They agreed.

We were talking about nonsense when it came up that I had broadcasted hockey for Princeton University several years ago. Then they asked what I thought about the Coyotes. Now, I'm really in my element. I told them what I have said since I've been here; Wayne Gretzky should be an ambassador to hockey, and let someone else coach the team. I suggested they figure out a way to get Mike Keenan here, because the level of play is doomed to improve. (I later rethought; Keenan may be "past his prime" as a coach. But they need someone like him. Dave Tippett replaced "the Great One" to start the 2009-10 season, so we'll soon know if he is the answer. Of course, the Coyotes might not stay in Phoenix. That is one fight I hope Gary Bettman wins.)

I asked them why they took a cab from this far away. They both had lost their driver's licenses to the dreaded DUI. They always say that Arizona has the toughest drunk driving laws in the country. Do I think drinking and driving is a good idea? No, I don't. But, as I've said before, this is not simply about safety. It is about money. The more DUI's there are, the more dollars there are.

The meter read $50 by this point, and we weren't even close yet. I was amazed at how lucid these guys were, considering they had been up all night losing their shirts. As if on cue, I had my answer. I looked in the rear view mirror and saw one of them take out a small baggie with some powder in it. Again, as if on cue, the other sniffed a couple of times. I decided to put a lid on that immediately.

I told them, "Guys, look. I like you both. But I have to draw the line with drug use in the car. I don't care what you do. I'm not going to judge you. But, I've never touched that shit in my life. I know there is almost no chance anything will happen, but I'm NOT willing to take that risk. Please, put that away." They were like, "That's cool. We can wait." I was lucky in that it never came up again, as far as I know.

We finally got to the first guy's place and he gave the other guy a wad of cash to pay for his portion. He told me we should all go to Coyote's game. Now the truth is I haven't had the opportunity to hang with these guys. But I would. I still have their number.

We were still a fair distance from the other guy's house and we started to talk some more about how ridiculous the laws are for drinking and driving. I don't know this, but I believe that with a little creativity, you can make statistics say anything you want them to. I don't believe these laws have made the slightest difference in reducing drunk-driving deaths or accidents. I guarantee that money collected has not created a proportionate drop in deaths and accidents.

We soon arrived at the second guy's place and he reiterated the desire to get together at a game. I found it funny that the meter hit exactly $100 when he got out of the car. He gave me that, plus a $25 tip. Now, that fare was tremendous.

The most money I ever got from one group, in one day, came 10 days before I quit the industry. I was in a pretty decent mood, because the last fare I had was this attractive woman who gave me her phone number. I told her I would get in touch in three weeks after I came back from my pending trip to New Jersey. So, I am not only ending this phase of my life, but I might "get some".

I picked up these three Indian guys at a Thai restaurant on Chandler Boulevard. They wanted me to drop one of them off at their hotel and then drive the other two to the Chandler Fashion Square. They were asking me questions about the malls in Phoenix, and I told them the Chandler Fashion Square was as good as any. I dropped off the first guy and that was the last I saw of him. We had gone the opposite way from the mall, so the meter was running up nicely. They really didn't know where they wanted to be dropped off, so I suggested the Cheesecake Factory.

I let them off there, with the understanding that I would be back in about 90 minutes to pick them up.

I took another short fare, driving a couple of sisters (siblings as opposed to nuns) from Bashas' back to their apartment. It ended up being slightly more than the minimum. I decided I would wait for these guys and not take any other calls, because they were going to Fry's Electronics on Baseline and the I-10, and that would be a solid fare. I waited about 45 minutes and they called.

I was in the parking lot of the Fashion Square, so that transition was very quick. They came out and confirmed they wanted to go to Fry's. It was a large fare, and they said they would be about 45 minutes. I decided to go home for a while and eat. I came back at the instant that they walked out of the store.

On the way back to their hotel, they mentioned that wanted to go up to Scottsdale in about 90 minutes and they would need a ride back at around 11 PM. Now, this gave me a really difficult choice. If I agreed to do this, my day would be an 18-hour one. On the other hand, it would be worth another $100-$150 dollars minimum. Since this would put me in a position to have my lease paid for the rest of my career, I made the commitment.

I went back to their hotel right around 6:30 PM, and they told me that they first wished to go buy wine, then to an Indian restaurant to pick up dinner, and finally to their friend's house. It turns out the restaurant was up by Thunderbird and Hayden, so this fare was going to be massive! The difference between these guys and a lot of the other passengers I've driven long distances was these seemed more interested in speaking with each other than to me. There was, however, a shared funny moment. They were talking about their business and I interrupted, saying, "I don't understand Hindi, but I do understand 'he's full of shit'!" Everybody laughed.

We stopped at a Wal-Mart close to the restaurant to get the wine. I was hoping to get to the place we were going quickly so I could take as many fares in between then and the time I had to bring these guys back. They were only in Wal-Mart for five minutes, but we were at the restaurant for well over 30. The upside was that there was a gas station a few yards from the door of the restaurant, and my low fuel light had just come on, so I filled up. Also, the meter was running, and the fare was close to $80. We ended up going even further north to their friend's house and the total was $92. I still hadn't received a tip from either one of these guys.

I probably could have gotten four or five additional fares. But I knew I was in a bad GPS zone. I ended up taking two fares, one of which was two mother-daughter pairs from South Carolina. It was a short trip and the four of them barely fit in the Prius. They were nice enough, and they got my sense of humor, so I had them rolling. I also received a good tip.

The next fare was bringing this whiny bastard to the Indian Bend Casino. He was talking about how unhappy he is with his girlfriend, his siblings, his job, and (seemingly) anything else that crossed his mind. I tried to sympathize with him, but upon arrival he handed me a wad of money that shorted me by two dollars. Dickhead!

At that point, I decided to wait down the street from where these follows were having dinner. It was only 9:30 PM, so I might be waiting another two hours for them, but I figured it was going to be at least $60 to get them back to their hotel, and I could get in a little naptime while I was waiting.

They ended up calling at about 11 PM. They were obviously tired, because they both slept, loudly, for most of the ride back. I just wanted to get back quickly so I could get some sleep as well. The final return fare was $66, so from about 3 PM until midnight, I billed $268; $225 of which came from these guys over five separate fares.

I'm Too Sexy For My Shirt

There are many positives to being a cab driver, not the least of which is that you are constantly meeting new people. You do meet a lot of people you probably don't want to meet as well, but, relatively speaking, it is a positive. I have met a number of women who have been interested in me, and, being a heterosexual male, that is a good thing...for the most part.

One night, I went to pick up a passenger in the part of South Phoenix I was told to avoid, between 16th Street and 19th Avenue after dark. The woman wasn't quite ready when I arrived, so I waited. Delores came out of the house, looking like she was ready for a night on the town. She was a black woman around 50 years old. Her trip was going to take 20 minutes and it was one of those nights where the wind had kicked up to monsoon level. I had to drive slower, so we had plenty of time to talk.

We were making with the small talk, but it was hard to concentrate on the conversation because the wind was making it hard to control the car. The chat was about common subjects, like the price of gas, whether Obama would make a good president, the weather in Phoenix as compared to anywhere else. Then, the wind forced the car sharply to the right, almost causing an accident. The car that I almost bumped into honked at me for about 10 seconds really loudly. I saw that he pulled along side of me and rolled his window down, so I put my hand up to try to indicate I was sorry, because it was my "fault". Before I had the opportunity to see a reaction, Delores rolled down her window and started yelling at the guy. She must have felt the intensity of the wind that pushed the car, because she screamed "That wasn't his fault you jerk, there's a damn hurricane blowing out here". I was amazed, because when I looked over, he had already rolled up his window and turned away. What else could I say but thanks?

We kept going on and she started to talk about her family. It turns out she has six children and seven grand children. I told her I thought that was great and how she must be proud. She was, but since her husband had died, she was feeling a bit lonely. I told her that I understood, because I hadn't really been involved with anyone since my wife and I had split up. She asked me what happened, and I told her my version. She seemed sympathetic and continued to ask me about myself. I wasn't all that comfortable talking about my lack of a sex life over the previous five years, but I don't mind throwing down the "woe is me" card sometimes, so that carried us to her destination. Then something really strange occurred.

Her apartment was down a back alley. It was hard to maneuver the Crown Vic because the alley was so narrow. I got to her door, and she asked me how much it was. She paid the fare, putting her hand on top of mine as I reached for the money. I looked at her, said "Thank you", and took the money. I don't often get stunned into silence, but that was one time that I certainly did. She then asked what time I got off. I wanted to chuckle and say "About 10 minutes after I turn the computer on", but since she's a grandmother, I said "around midnight". She then told me she was going to some club (I forgot the name), and asked if I wanted to meet her there. I don't get propositioned very often, and certainly not by 50 year-old black women. I told her I was going home when I was finished, but I appreciated the invite. I have to admit that I was flattered more than I ever thought I would be. She was very attractive, but I can't have a one-nighter with a grandmother.

I never had sex with a passenger, though I certainly had enough passengers with whom I wanted to have sex. I probably had two-dozen times where I got the feeling the woman wanted me to hit on her or ask her out. Unfortunately, boldness with the opposite sex is not one of my strengths. Generally, I would wait for the action to come to me. Along those lines, I had four situations where a female passenger gave me her number.

The first time was probably the craziest. Not because of what happened before, during or afterward, but because of the circumstances.

I picked up this woman at an apartment complex close to

where I live. I was voucher ride all the way to East Mesa, worth about $32. She was an attractive blond woman that looked to be fairly close to my age.

For the first few minutes, we really didn't say a whole lot to each other, mainly because she was messing around with her purse and I was fiddling around with the MDT. But, after a while we started talking.

She asked me if I watched a lot of TV and I said no, because I really don't, unless it's sports or movies. I told her the only thing I watch with ANY regularity is a rerun of SVU. She said, "Wow, that's amazing, because I was just thinking that you look like Christopher Meloni." I said, "Really, I have never been told that before. I've been told Tom Cruise and Dennis Quaid, but never him."

We kept talking about that show some more, and it came up that I was from New Jersey. She said she was as well, so I asked her where in New Jersey lived. She told me she was born in Bayonne (just across the river from New York City), but she lived in Somerset. I said, "Wait, where did you go to high school?" and she said "Franklin Township". So I said the only thing I could. "Your kidding, so did I, what year did you graduate?" Before she answered, she said, "Get the fuck out of here. I graduated in 1978." I said, "That's the year my sister graduated, I graduated the year after that." Wow, what a small world.

Her name is Jillian, but she went by Jill in high school. She asked me what my sister's name was and I told her it is Nancy. She didn't remember her, but, as you can expect, we started exchanging names of people we knew back then. We each recognized a series of people. One sad thing was we both remembered the name of a chick that died in a car crash right before the start of the 1976-77 school year.

At the destination, I told her I would be hanging around in the area to see if I could find a return trip. It was way out there, and having a voucher pay for me to go back was certainly advantageous. I ended up taking another passenger first in between, but I did get the return trip from Jillian.

On the way back, we continued to talk about high school. She brought up a guy who was called Turdo (I never knew why), and she asked if I knew him. Now, this guy was the king of the school when he was a senior. He was the captain of the football team and he wrestled heavyweight (I don't remember exactly, but he may have won the state title). *Everybody* knew this guy. I didn't know him personally, but I had a gym class that he showed up for occasionally, when we played indoor hockey. He and another football player used to check me through swinging doors all the time. At the end, they both told me it was nothing personal. It sure felt like it was personal.

After a while, Jillian asked me if I was married. I told her I was at one time, but no longer, and I don't have any children. She told me about herself, that she had been married four times and had five children, one of who was living with her. She said she was still looking for her soul mate. I hate that phrase! What does it even mean? Anyway, she started hinting at the fact that she would like to get together, so I figured, why not.

I already had her number from the dispatch, and I suggested we go to a Mexican place nearby call Arriba's. We did that two days later, and had a very nice time. But, I started seeing "chinks in the armor" pretty quickly. She got annoyed at me for not allowing her to order first. She also mentioned the soul mate thing again, and I was starting to wonder. Plus, when I dropped her off, she really didn't let me kiss her goodnight. Maybe she was just being cautious.

I called her a couple of days later but only got the machine. When I finally spoke with her 10 days later, she told me one of her ex-husbands was giving her a hard time and she needed to concentrate on dealing with that. Talk about a blow off! I told her to call me when that gets straightened out. More than a year later, I haven't heard from her.

About a month after that, I got a call to this nursing home in Scottsdale. I walked into the lobby area, and there was nobody at the front desk. I looked around and I couldn't even find anyone to talk to for the first five minutes. Finally, some old lady came back to the reception desk and asked me for whom I was looking. As if I should be surprised, I gave her the name and she had no idea who she was. Fuck!

I explained I was from Discount Cab and was supposed to pick up this woman at 8:30 AM. While she was looking around doing nothing, I started searching for her myself. Nobody could tell me who this patient was, until someone mentioned that she might be a nurse. Eventually, I saw this tall woman in scrubs walking towards me. I said, "Are you Nurse Betty?" Fortunately, she *was* Nurse Betty. I walked her out to the Crown Vic, refraining from cursing the receptionist, and opened the door for her. She was amazed by that, and said, "I guess chivalry isn't dead."

We started rolling towards the 101, because her voucher was all the way to the 17 and the 101, 27 miles away. She explained to me that the hospital really needed someone because of call outs, so they paid her extra AND paid for her transportation. She was a nursing student who generally worked two long weekend shifts and went to school during the week. That's cool.

I seemed to have the Midas touch with her. Every time I said something that was meant to be funny, she laughed. I have a pretty dry, tongue-in-cheek sense of humor, and she kept up with it pretty well. I also told her about why I moved to Phoenix, my recent disappointments and failures, and she seemed to be eager to help, as opposed to just being sympathetic.

She was making a lot of suggestions, and asking a number of pretty bold questions. I was a little uncomfortable with some of it, but I went along. I definitely realized how attractive I thought she was. She also reminded me of the woman that introduced me to my ex-wife. I mentioned that to her and she said she was sorry. I told her not to be sorry, because I don't regret the marriage at all.

That's when she started to tell me about her marriage. Her husband apparently had been cheating on her with a much younger woman (don't they all). She got primary custody of their two kids and she was trying to make a go of nursing. She said she could not understand why a man would want a woman that young. I thought, "These fucking women don't know shit about men". Then she asked me for a pen.

We were getting closer to her apartment and she went back to telling me what I ought to do. I just kept making jokes, and she kept laughing. When we got to her place, she handed me a piece of paper and said, "Look, I usually don't do this, but here is my phone number. I've been dating this other guy, but that's coming to an end. I'd like to get together with you sometime." I told her I would call her tomorrow. I was thinking about Ohio State football: "WOODY".

We arranged to have dinner a few nights later. In the meanwhile, I was given the go-ahead on driving a Prius. It took me a while to get used to some things, like it doesn't start with a key. You put a computer chip into a slot and hit a power button. The yard dog that gave me the car couldn't tell me how to start it! Plus, there was a gear called "Battery (B)" and I didn't know its use until one month before I left the job. Obviously, some trade secrets are on a need to know basis.

Anyway, I had told her that I would be coming straight from work, and I would call as I was on my way. Fortunately, things timed out perfectly. I should have gathered something was up when she told me she would be waiting outside the gate by the leasing office, instead of me picking her up at her door.

I decided we should go to the Macaroni Grill, because it's good, and I was sure she would like it. She was dressed very nicely and was showing a lot of cleavage, my favorite thing. When we sat down, she became very conscious of her boobs, saying, "I shouldn't have worn something so revealing." I thought, "Yeah, you should have."

We were having a good time and I suggested an entrée for her, which she really liked. She kept telling me how funny I was, but then something happened, and to this day I still don't know what it was for sure. It was like someone had flipped a switch. She told me she was in a relationship with someone else and she was "very sexually active." I didn't react, because I don't know why she said that to me. Dinner was over, so I paid and we left.

As we were leaving, a couple came up to us and asked if I was on duty. I asked Nurse Ratched – I mean Nurse Betty – if she wanted to take the fare, but then I said we really couldn't (if I had only known then what I know now, I would have taken that fare). Sweet me, I let them use my cell to call the cab company, which cost me a pound of my ass in the end, as they ditched the Discount call and the driver called me on it.

Anyway, I drove Nurse Betty home, and when I parked, she told me she wasn't going to "tongue kiss" me, which was kind of a rude thing to say. Right then, the Discount driver called, and she bolted on me. I tried to call a couple of times after that but she never responded. When she eventually did call me back, I was on another call. I tried getting back to her four times in the next three hours, but again, no answer. Oh well.

Nothing happened again until nine months later. I went to a house in the Foothills in a gated community. This dude and woman came out of the house, and she told me to run some errands with this guy, and then bring him back and pick her up. I said, "Fine."

On the way, as we were bouncing from place to place, the guy was telling me what he did and that he was basically this woman's "Guy Friday". This day, he had a ton of laundry to do. I was trying to keep a straight face, as this toothless bastard is explaining his life to me. After three stops, he told me to head back to get the woman (for the sake of ease, let's call her Sally). He really must have misunderstood the plan, because when we got back, she told him to stay at the house and that she was going with me.

I never caught his name, but it might as well have been Fido or Rover.

When she got in the cab, Sally and I talked about nothing important. She told me she needed to go to this woman's house to find her son. I thought that was strange, and then she started berating the woman. She told me this woman was an asshole and treated her son badly. When we got to the house, Sally stood in the doorway for about 30 seconds, said a couple of things, and came back to the cab rolling her eyes.

She got back in and again told me what an asshole this woman was, and said she wanted to go to a convenience store for a drink. At this point, I'm thinking, "This bitch is going to hose me." After a couple of minutes, she came back and accidentally did something that scared the shit out of me. She dropped a hunting knife that was clipped on her belt loop. She saw my face and said, "Don't worry, I throw knives as a hobby, I'm not going to do anything." THAT SURE PUT MY MIND AT EASE. She said she wanted to go out towards Tempe, so we did.

In spite of everything so far, I was beginning to realize how much I think with my cock. She was pretty sexy. Half way towards Tempe, she asked me if I played pool. I told her "not very well". She said she wanted to go to this place where we could play for free. I said, "Now, this isn't in lieu of payment. I want to make sure we understand each other." She said, "I know, I'll pay you." That really didn't make me feel better, but I decided to hang with this woman. One never knows.

We played pool for 90 minutes, and she beat me two out of three. I sank the eight ball twice when I wasn't supposed to. It pissed me off, because if I were any good, I would've won all three games. Even with billiards, when I know I suck at it, I hate losing.

She then told me to drive her to this apartment complex near Rio Salado Avenue. On the way, she told me about how her ex-husband got custody of her kids and they just moved to California.

And then she started crying. I held her hand for a few moments and she calmed down.

When we got there, the meter said $100 (it had been running the whole time). She said, "What the fuck, I'll give you $40." Now, I could have called the cops, or said the meter was at $55 when we got to the pool hall (which it was), but, instead, I said "Alright". She then wrote down my phone number and gave me hers, saying she will talk to me soon. I would have called her, except for one thing: SHE SCARED THE SHIT OUT OF ME!!

As it turns out, she called me twice. The first time she called was about a week later, although I never found out why. The second time she wanted a ride to Tempe and it was during the final week of my cabbie career. I was laughing hysterically, because she was wearing a bright yellow smock. She looked like a Russian Cossack. She was hauling an entourage around with her, so I squeezed five people and a bike into the Prius for a three-mile trip. We dropped off one guy, and then we drove to a bank on Mill Avenue. She originally wanted to go further, but then changed her mind, and they all got out and she told me to call her. Yeah, right.

Lastly, I picked up a gal named Deborah 10 days before my last day on the job. I noticed immediately the deliberate manner in which she spoke and that she was quite attractive. I was hired to drive her from her house to a school to pick up her daughter, then over to a Circle K and take them home.

She started telling me about what a drag it was to not have a car, but she couldn't afford it right now, because she was trying to start a real estate business. I was telling her I wasn't going to be doing this much longer, but I was writing a book about the experiences I have had. She thought that was fun.

We got her daughter and Deborah started haranguing her about missing the bus, although more sarcastically than angrily. The kid was really quiet, so I tried to cheer her up. It didn't really work though. We stopped at the store, and traveled a specific way back to their house so that the daughter could see the easiest way to get home.

When we got to their house, Deborah waited for her daughter to get out of the car and then said, "I know you probably have the girlfriend of your dreams, but if you would like to get together for a coffee or a soda, please call me." I told her, "I was going to be driving almost all the time over the next 10 days, then going to New Jersey for 10 days, but that would call her when I got back. She said that was cool.

I was driving in Princeton, NJ, near the University the day before I flew back to Phoenix, and I called her and reminded her who I was, saying I would call again to make plans when I returned. She said, "Wow, that's interesting." I thought this was a very odd response.

After I got back, we made plans and I picked her up and we went out for a drink. We had a fun conversation and, after we left the bar, spent the next 30-45 minutes making out in the cab, but I sensed a little reluctance on her part. I took her home and we said goodnight and I told her that I would call in a couple of days.

A week later, I called her and asked if she'd like to go to a movie. She said she had a bit of a conundrum (I wonder what that could that be). While I was in NJ, her "childhood sweetheart" contacted her and she felt she "owed it" to him to try again. I was diplomatic while talking to her, but I was pissed.

It turned out that the old sweetheart deal didn't do the trick for her, because she called me three weeks later. I thought about calling her back, but I decided I didn't want to be someone's back-up plan.

I'm sure there are plenty of cabbies that had sex in their cabs. I was not one of them.

I'm Going to Call You

I have developed a number of unmarketable skills in my adult life. I know more trivial facts than anyone I know. My brother teases me every time I state a fact that won't win me a Pulitzer Prize, which it pretty often. That doesn't stop him from calling me when he has a question. One of my better-known unmarketable skills is giving people nicknames.

During one of my bartending jobs, the owner had a serious problem in that his hands shook uncontrollably all the time. It could be that he drank a lot of coffee, or alcohol, or both. Finally, I started calling him "The Diamond Cutter." The name stuck so well that when he would call me, he would say, "JZ, DC here," and then he would crack up.

Anyway, I have given many passengers nicknames. Here are some of them:

Beavis and Butthead: This was a mother and daughter team from South Phoenix who I brought to dialysis a dozen times. The daughter spoke with a really high voice and it was difficult to hear exactly what she was saying. But she was always cheerful. Every time she would say something, her mother would look straight at me and laugh the same monotone laugh. Huh-huh. Huh-huh. Huh-huh. Huh-huh.

Tee Time Charlie: This regular worked at a company near my apartment. Each time, he was wearing golf clothes, a Callaway hat and windbreaker, and he had a golf tee behind his ear. We always talked about golf. Jack Nicklaus is my hero and he likes Arnold Palmer and Tiger Woods. I once took him to play at the Legacy golf course. We also goofed on George W. Bush all the time. He was a solid tipper and a lot of fun. I never asked why he didn't drive, but since he had three cars in his driveway, I made an educated guess.

Candace Many Names: She worked as a cocktail waitress in one of the Scottsdale clubs. I picked her up eight times from her home. A few times, I dropped her off at a shopping center and watched her walk in an alley behind store, thinking something

illegal was going on. I called her this because she used a different last name almost every time I picked her up.

<u>Mr. Phlegm Ball:</u> I only picked this guy up once, but he stands out because not only was he from New Jersey, but I thought for sure I would find his esophagus lying on the floor of my cab. He hacked up his lungs the entire trip to and from the pharmacy.

<u>Curious George:</u> This was a woman I had as a voucher customer about 10 times. The only thing she was really curious about was whether I went to church. But she had the fat cheeks with freckles all over them and a quizzical look on her face.

<u>Jessica Super Rack:</u> Anyone who knows me knows how much I enjoy the boobs. I really don't care for the fake ones. If you have them great, if not, no problem, just don't mutilate your body. This woman, who I picked up just once, was perfect. They were real, and they were spectacular.

<u>Sammy Double D:</u> See above. She was a regular for about a month, while her car was being fixed. I enjoyed her company as well as her D's. Also, she was very upbeat and being around positive people is something I strive for, because they tend to improve my mood.

<u>Super T:</u> I only picked this woman up one time, but I really dug her. She worked at a Super Pumper gas station and her name began with a T, hence the name. She wasn't a bikini chick, but she was so pretty and confident and she smiled all the time. I kept going to that store, but I never saw her again.

<u>The Three Amigos:</u> There is a senior citizen home in Scottsdale, just north of McDowell Road. I have been there dozens of times. There are three women who always travel together, pooling there HHV's. They always sit in the back seat, criticizing everybody that lives there.

<u>The Iron Greek:</u> This was a guy I took to the airport at the same time every Monday for five straight weeks. He gave me his number because I was on time the first time I picked him up. I was on time every subsequent time as well. I thought it was going

to last forever, but he just stopped calling. There was a wrestler named Spiros Arion, who was called the Iron Greek and that is where I got the name for this guy.

Budd Light: I drove this guy on a voucher to his daily session about 15 times. He is from the area in New Jersey where I lived right before I moved to Phoenix. In fact, the library his sister works at is yards from my old apartment. He lives in a home with two other special needs people, one of whom I had also given several rides.

C-Note Bonnie: I brought this woman to the Wild Horse Pass Casino. She was in her 70's, if not her 80's. She was from New York and when I told her I was writing a book, she told me I was wasting my time. When she got out of the car, the fare was $26. She handed me a pile of bills and told me to have a party. I saw the twenty on top and stuffed them into my shirt pocket. I looked about 30 minutes later, thinking she had given me a twenty and six singles. The last bill was actually a $100 bill.

Heart Attack Tracy: I only had her as a fare once, driving her back to her car at Va Bene, two miles from my home. She told me she moonlighted as a waitress at the Heart Attack Grill. I'm pretty sure that the women that work there are in there early 20's. She looked older than that, but looks really good in their outfit.

Zone 69: I drove this guy to a strip club four times. The first time, I informed him he was located in zone 79. He said he was hoping to find zone 69 that night. I told him that would be a great name for a strip club and he thought that was funny. So, from then on, that was his name.

Picasso Back: Shortly after I began driving the cab I got this flag while waiting in a parking lot. She had on a top that exposed her back, and there wasn't an inch of her body that DIDN'T have tattoos on it. She also had dozens of piercing, including horns in her forehead.

Three Cackling Yentas: I brought four pharmaceutical reps to the airport, three attractive women and a guy. The women sat in the back and NEVER stopped talking. I finally leaned over to the guy and said, "How do you put up with these three cackling yentas. You're a better man than I am." Everyone laughed; then the yentas immediately resumed cackling.

Million Dollar Bus Boy: I picked up this kid way out east in Mesa. He would take $30 cab rides to San Tan Village where he would work six to eight hour shifts at two different restaurants across the driveway from each other. I said, "You must be a million dollar bus boy for them to accommodate you." He really wasn't a bus boy, but it made me laugh.

Radio Voice: I picked up this stunningly beautiful young black woman named Nadia at a What-a-Burger in Phoenix at least five times. She would walk from her work office to that spot. Her voice was the perfect combination of clarity and depth for radio. I told her so and she liked the idea. A "face for radio" isn't a compliment, but a "voice for radio" sure is.

The Butcher: This woman was fabulous. I had her as a passenger three times and she had an interesting, unique look that I found very attractive. She was probably 23-26 years old and had a seven-year-old daughter who was extremely cute. I call her "the Butcher" because she cut meat in a Safeway.

Deena on Javelina: This woman was a waitress from a Mesa bar. I gave her rides four times. Her name was Deena and she lived on Javelina Avenue.

There are others throughout the book. They will pop up when the story is about the person to whom I gave a nickname. My ability to give nicknames may be due, in part, to the myriad of nicknames I've been given over the course of time. Most are name related, but some are situational. Here are the ones I recall:

Prince Valiant
The Big JZ
J-Meister

Jiggy J
J
Zittelman from Accounting
JZ
Jo Nathan
JTZ
Jon of Thain
Jon the Thing
J-Bird
Z-Dog
ZPW
Zisspotaweenie
Weezer
Boozer
John Boy
Bird
Sone-tee
Fabio
Jitz
Hippie
Vincent Vega
Simba
Milk and Pepsi
Klunky
Toddler
Uncle Johnny
Stealth Z
Juan
Ziggy
Yanny
Jersey Jon
Johnny Z

My favorite One-liners ━━━━━━━━━━━━━━━━━━━━━━━

There are so many things I found entertaining while doing this job. It is hard to tell an entertaining story, based on one funny line. Have you ever seen the skit "The Sinatra Group" on *Saturday Night Live*. I read that the writers wrote that entire skit around one line, where Sinatra (as played by Phil Hartman) says, "I've got chunks of guys like you in my stool." Now, I'm not that creative, so I will tell you some of the one-liners I have found funny. Maybe I said them or perhaps, a passenger did.

I was waiting at QT 85 for a call. I noticed there were a couple of kids standing next to a garbage can. Convenience stores like QT are notorious for panhandlers, and those people generally stand by garbage cans. But these were kids; they couldn't have been more than 15. After about 20 minutes, I needed to go to the bathroom. I went in, took care of business and got a drink. As I came out, the kids were still there. The heavier one asked me if I had any spare change. I just looked at him for a second, and I finally said, **"You know, I bet it's a comfort to your parents to know you're well on your way to becoming a bum."** He said, "Fuck you," and I laughed at myself.

Another time, I had these two guys in the cab and we were driving towards Gilbert. I saw a car go by with a license plate "TUPACCC." One of the dudes in the back saw it as well. He told the other guy to look at it. I said, **"That stands for Tupac Community College. It is a rap school."** As far as I know, they still believe there is such a thing.

I picked up this guy in Scottsdale who was entertaining two beautiful women. They were all very open and cheerful, and when he found out I was from NJ, he was that much happier to talk to me. We were entertaining each other on the way to the bar to which they were going, when we came to a traffic signal. We all looked as four guys walked right in front of the cab. Three of them looked exactly the same, wearing white sleeveless T-shirts, blue jeans and Beatles like, dark hair. The fourth guy had short blond hair, a jacket, tan pants and sunglasses. One of the women said, "What the hell is that?" Without missing a beat, I said, **"That's Bingo, Bango, Bongo and Irving."** We all laughed hysterically. I'm not sure they knew it was a reference a *Gilligan's Island* episode (the one with the faux Beatles group "The Mosquitoes"), but it was funny. They called me at 2 AM to pick them up, but I was already asleep.

On another Saturday night, I picked up this group of four that were going to a nightclub down in the Foothills. They had been drinking for a while when I got there, so they were in a good mood. After we got going, one of the men said they needed to stop and get cigarettes. We were passing an AM/PM and I said, "Do you want me to stop there." He said, "No way, I'm not giving any business to that Iranian Nazi". I said, **"Iranian Nazis? They must really hate Jews!"** All four of them thought that was hysterical. They, too, asked if I would pick them up later. Having a good sense of humor can be helpful. I gave them my number, but they called at 3 AM, long after I had called it a night.

I was down in the Sun City part of Chandler, and got a call. Sun City is almost all older people. When I got to the house, it took the guy 10 minutes to open the garage and get to the car. The dispatch said his name was Gordon. That was his last name. I finally got him in the car, and asked his name. He said, "Marvin Gordon." I said the first thing that popped into my head, **"Oh good, all I need is Ventnor, and I'll have the yellow Monopoly."** I don't think he heard or understood me, but I thought it was a great line.

I picked up this sexy chick at a house in Chandler on a Sunday morning. She was wearing a bikini top and denim shorts. She had great boobs, so I was happy. She seemed a little out of it, so I guessed she might have had a fun night of debauchery. At first, she didn't say anything, but then she started talking about her evening after her boyfriend sent her a text message. She told me they are not absolutely committed to each other and that's why she was where I picked her up.

The guy she spent the night with was a "Friend with Benefits". Then she said, "You know, sometimes I feel guilty." Then she got a shit-eating grin on her face and said, **"But how can it be wrong when it was SO beautiful."** Then it looked like she had an orgasm. I cracked up and she winked at me.

One of my favorite female passengers was this chick that worked at a Hair Cuttery in Tempe. It was the end of her shift and I drove her to the other end of Tempe. She was very animated and friendly. She said we needed to stop at a Circle K to get some beer. Before we stopped she was talking about "really wanting a beer right now". She also asked if I needed anything when we got there, a rare showing of consideration. When she came back, she talked about how much she loved beer. I agreed and said I don't know a lot of woman that like beer. She said, **"Are you kidding, beer is the new White Wine."** I really liked her.

I brought these two dudes in their mid-40s into Old Town Scottsdale on a Friday night. They were going to Loco Patron, and they were talking about the last time they had been there. Apparently, they were able to pick up these women and were recalling how they did it. They were telling me how charming they were and the ladies bought right into it. I said it couldn't have been that simple. One of them said, "Well, we were flashing around a lot of cash." The other guy started laughing and said, **"She also liked me because I can lick my eyebrows."** That was a keeper.

I haven't had a lot of people that have been annoying for no reason. This one time, I picked up three people who were angry about something and they started in on me immediately. The loudest of them was wearing a University of Michigan t-shirt and hat. Anyway, I went five miles and they were complaining about the air-conditioning, the radio, the traffic and the cost of the fare. The Michigan guy wouldn't shut up. We finally got there, and they reluctantly paid. I got no tip. I was pretty aggravated, so I said, **"As soon as I saw all the Michigan shit, I should have known you were a prick."** He said he was going to call my supervisor, but he never did as far as I know.

The Great Epiphany of My Life

I think every one, presuming they live long enough, goes through a mid-life crisis. It can be really freighting, because you don't know whether it is a mid-life crisis or an end of your life crisis. The only time you know is when it's too late.

I would say that my crisis was a large part of the reason I left my family and friends in New Jersey to start again in the Valley. I was feeling bad about myself when I got here and, in all honesty, after almost three years I don't feel a whole lot better.

I was at the end of a really bad moneymaking week, sitting in my cab just before going to the cage to do my reconciliation. Out of the blue, I received a call from my friend Mark Schuster. He and I worked together at TRC, and have kept in touch since he moved back to Pittsburgh in 1990. He and my father are particularly close. Mark's dad died really young, and I am of the impression he thinks of my father as his surrogate father, which is nice.

Mark had just visited my father in New Jersey, and he called to tell me about this, as well as about his receiving a chance phone call from another TRC crony, Nick Tortorello. Nick was Mark's boss, and Mark was mine.

As we usually do, we rehashed all of the things that we used to laugh about, the beer drinking, the softball team, the goofs that we worked with, etc. Mark also told me Nick was patting him on the back for managing such a large group of people, which included data processing, word processing, and systems. That was a pool of about 50 total people, all with their own personal and professional interests, plus all the interaction with project directors

and account executives. Being the conduit had to be tough.

It's always fun chatting with Mark, but this particular conversation added intrinsic value to my ability to move forward in life. I've thought about it long and hard, and many things popped into my mind.

First, TRC was one of the great experiences of my life. I worked there for seven years, first as a spec writer, then managing two of the data processing departments. During that time, TRC saw its biggest growth period. There were about 30-40 people between the ages of 25-35 in that firm, and we all worked in concert with one another. We partied together. We stayed until midnight finishing projects together. We went on vacations together. Some people even slept together. Mark and I were the unofficial "cruise directors" as well, planning company functions like "Movie Nights," "Chili Cook-offs," along with golf outings, the softball team, football games with the MCI office downstairs, International food days, bowling, etc.

But it was the people that made it work. Lori Clark, Donna White, Paul Neifert, Eric Widmaier, Matt Campion, Trent Liakris, Anne Groom, Terri Flanagan, Irene Lang, Bob Trulio and Lisa Kreutle were among the great people the fueled the engine of that company. Our hard work enabled TRC to grow to the point that my dad retired with a great nest egg.

Thinking about that reminded me about other experiences I have had. I worked at many different restaurants as a bartender. It is a great training ground for dealing with people. I met great people at all of them, although the Rocky Hill Inn was the best of them all, despite my fuck-up there. I went to Baltimore twice for New Year's Eve with a group from there, including the Kerneys, Dr. Mooth, Howard Best and the future mayor of Princeton, NJ, Pepper Taylor. I also worked there with the most stunningly beautiful staff of waitresses ever. And, the guys in the kitchen were great. It was awesome.

Through my brother, I became friends with Dan Lankford, Bill

Metzger, John Guhl and Jim Billow. We played street hockey to-gether and partied as well. For about eight years we would gather in Levittown, PA on Sunday and play hockey until we couldn't stand it anymore. It was great.

My first radio station was WTTM. Dan got me involved there, too. Patrick Daily became part of that circle of friends after join-ing the radio station, which also led to the trips to Dewey Beach, where I made many more new life-long friends.

While working at WTTM, I broadcasted hundreds of games for Princeton University, Rider University, Drexel, and the College of New Jersey (aka Trenton State College). I did a ton of traveling, and made a lot of friends with the coaches, players and their fami-lies. I keep in touch with a lot of those people today. That doesn't include all of the high school stuff I did. I was the program direc-tor and created a bunch of programs for the station through trial and error. It was the time of my life.

Three years later, I worked for another radio station, WBUD in Trenton. I was working with another great group of people, and enjoyed my three years there as well. I also got married during this time. Now, while that didn't end well, I don't regret it, be-cause it introduced me to another great family, in addition to the joys of Phoenix.

So, I was thinking about all of that, and that made think about all the fun I've had aside from those experiences. Then, I thought about all the success I've had at the jobs at which I've worked. Those things made me realize something very important. *I've had a really good life up to this point. People care about me, I'm healthy and I think have managed to leave a positive impression on almost everyone I know. What do I have to be unhappy about? There is no reason for me to be so sad all the time.* Almost instan-taneously, I felt a lot better. And that is the great epiphany of my life, and I had it while driving a Discount Cab.

CHAPTER 10

My Favorite Stories

Leggo My Eggo

Voucher customers quite often become repeat fares. They go to their appointments at the same times on the same days, pretty much every week. Chasing fares can be risky during the week, because there are plenty of trips that are one or two miles, and you only get $1.45 or $1.80 per mile.

I chased zone 381 every time, because it was a straight shot down I-10 and the chances of a $20-$40 fare were always strong because it is so far south. I had gotten Rebecca a couple of times as a fare and we had always had pleasant conversations. The thing is that she is a Magellan patient and is not quite right. She is about 50 years old and speaks like she had a stroke. I never ask these people what happened to them for two reasons: 1) it's none of my business and 2) I don't think I really want to know. Besides, I can have a conversation with a broomstick, so I try to avoid making people uncomfortable.

Rebecca walked to the car very slowly, and I held the door for her when she got to the car. She looked like she just got out of bed, which was, in fact, the case. She muttered something about it being too early and that she didn't want to go. At that point, I would have been paid the fare whether we went or not, so I didn't care. But we pressed on.

She asked me if I had slept well, and I told her "No", because I never sleep well, which is also true. Then we started talking about the weather, because it was going to be warmer than normal for November. She was also talking about California, because she was from a town just outside of Los Angeles and she really missed it. I was talking about New Jersey, because I was getting ready to travel back for Thanksgiving. Then I remembered that the other times I had given her a ride, we talked about breakfast. And that's when the fun began.

I had been early getting to her house, so I stopped at a Burger King to buy breakfast for myself. I got a French toast sticks meal. I ate the tater tots before I got to Rebecca's, but I hadn't touched the French toast yet. On our way, I asked Rebecca whether she had eaten breakfast yet, and she said no. So, being the wonderful human being I am, I offered her one of the French toast sticks. Or at least I thought I offered her one.

She opened up the container of syrup and I decided I better pay attention to what I was doing on the road. Every now and again, I would hear her mumble, "I like the French toast" or see her dipping the toast in the syrup. I'm thinking, "No way is she going to eat the whole thing." There were five in the package, so if she ate two or three, no big deal. Well, you really have to follow the road, because half the drivers in Phoenix might as well be blindfolded, so I wasn't watching Rebecca too closely. After five minutes or so, she tapped me on the shoulder and handed me the container. There wasn't even any syrup left. She ate the whole thing. I sort of stared at her, thinking "What the fuck," but I said "Did that work for you". She said, "Yes, thank you". I looked up just in time to stop myself from bumping the car in front of me. I had stopped at a light, but while I was reaching back, my foot came off the brake. Fortunately, I saw what was going to happen, and I said "Whoa, that was close." But Rebecca just sat there with a content look on her face and didn't even notice.

You would think this would have been the end of this misadventure, but NO-O-O-O-O. I went back to the cage a couple of days later because I wanted to cash in some of my receipts. Adrian asked me if I had taken this fare, and I said yes. It turns out that Rebecca was supposed to be getting a blood test that day and she was supposed to fast for eight hours prior to it. Of course, she was oblivious to the whole thing, but they chewed me out because she told them I gave her the food. I really wasn't in the mood to be yelled at for being a nice person. So I said, "How was I supposed to know she wasn't supposed to eat? You're giving me a hard time for being considerate?" Alejandro just kind of shrugged and said, "They told me to tell you." I asked who "they" were. No response. Sometimes, being a benevolent soul is the wrong choice.

Life's a Bitch, And So Are You ━━━━━━━━━━

Probably the nastiest passenger I've ever had in the cab was this chick I picked up at a hair salon in Scottsdale. I called to tell her that I was on my way, but I didn't know exactly where the salon was. She was mumbling so badly it took me four tries to understand what she said. She got indignant with me, but I defy anyone to tell me they could understand what she saying. She finally gave me an address that showed up on my GPS, but I couldn't find it from the street. She then snapped at me and told me to hurry up because she was late. My first thought was *"You're at the salon; whose fault is that?"* But I gritted my teeth and was finally able to find the place. There wasn't an obvious sign out front and the main entrance was not on the main street. This bitch couldn't have been less helpful.

She power walked to the car when I arrived. She was wearing a tight white top, which showed off her fabulous fake boobs (she wasn't fooling anyone with those babies), cleavage and flat stomach, and tight jeans, which barely topped her crotch. She also had long blonde hair and full beautiful lips. She may have been trying to look like Pamela Anderson, and brother, let me tell you, she was succeeding! (There are plenty of Hollywood chicks I would fuck in a heartbeat, just to be able to say I did, but Pamela Anderson is NOT one of them.)

She continued mumbling, telling me where she wanted to go, but luckily for me this time I could name that tune in only two tries. I took her to the place; it had an alleyway back entrance. The fare was $8 and she said the dude inside was going to cash her check and give her the money for the fare. Waiting outside, I thought she was going to try to beat me on the fare, but they both came out within minutes. I looked at the dude and I thought, "This fucking guy is a pimp". He was short, wearing a vested suit with an unbuttoned shirt and a ton of bling. He looked like the pimp from *Bachelor Party*.

Boobarella then told me that her plans had changed. Fortunately, I hadn't turned off the meter. Mr. Pimp handed her some money and she got back in the cab. So now we're off to Walgreen's and then back to her apartment in Scottsdale. I really wasn't that familiar with Scottsdale at that point, so she directed me. The street was backed up by construction, so the ride started to drag a little. She starts complaining about the traffic, in a tone that blamed it on me. I don't think she really was, in retrospect, but at the time I was really annoyed with her. I chose not to say anything.

When we finally got moving again, she continued to speak to me in a rude tone. She told me three times to "make a turn" and got mad because I didn't magically know street what she meant. She said "No, not there, the next one, jeez," but she never told me a street name. And, all the while, she was calling me "Sweetie"! I was ready to cold cock her. Could a person be any more condescending? I wanted this bitch out of my cab, instantly!

The shit really hit the fan when I thought there was a back entrance to the Walgreen's. She asked if there was an entrance there (probably knowing full well there wasn't), and I said, "I think so". But there wasn't, so she screamed, "I told you not to go that way!" I though to myself "She didn't really just say that", but instead of defending myself, I just said, "I'm sorry", nearly biting a hole in my lip. She yelled again, but I couldn't make out what she said. Why was she so angry?

Fortunately her cell phone rang and she said, "Keep your shirt on, or don't", and she started giggling. This had a two-fold positive effect on me. First, she seemed to forget about chewing me out, but more importantly, I realized that this piece of crap WAS a hooker. Now I don't have anything against hookers, but she was such an incredible bitch that the mere fact that had to rely on sloppy sex to survive somehow made me feel better.

After spending ten minutes in the Walgreen's, it was a quick quarter-mile to her apartment, and the meter read $19.60. As a final insult, she gave me a twenty and told me to keep the change. I made a mental note, logging her name deep within my mind: I don't care how hot she is; I will NEVER pick that asshole again.

Interestingly enough, about a year later, I picked up a woman named Maura to bring her to pick up her car at a Scottsdale Bar. We started talking and during the conversation, she told me she worked at that same salon and that it was really hard because the customers were so bitchy all the time. I asked her how long she worked there and she told me up until last August. I mentioned the foul slut's name and her Pamela Anderson features. Maura remembered her very well, and described her as "well known" on the Old Town nightclub circuit, always trying to whore her way into free drinks and free admissions. She was so obnoxious that people just gave her what she wanted so they didn't have to deal with her. Amen to that!

I'm Doing Wonderfully Well ━━━━━━━━━━━━━━━

This ranks right up there as one of the weirdest moments any-one could ever have experienced. I was parked at LA Fitness, and I had decided to take an hour off to work out. Just as I was get-ting ready to book off, I got a call in the condo complex that was adjacent to the parking lot in which I was waiting. I decided to take the call and do the workout later. I went to the nearby Shell station, took care of some personal business and went back to get the fare.

I called the passenger (Brenda) when I pulled along side her building, but I got her answering machine. Then, I tried to walk in and knock on her door, but there was security that required a key. I went back to my car and called her again. Fortunately (or un-fortunately) she answered and I told her I was outside of her back porch. She opened the porch door while still on the phone with me, and asked if I was in the red car. I should have known some-thing was up with her, based on that question alone. She was 10 feet from the car, and there isn't a speck of red on my cab. But, I said, "No, the car is green, purple and black." I was looking right at her, waving, and she finally appeared to see me. As she walked over, I got out and opened the door. She commented how clean the cab was and got in. That's where the fun began.

She told me she wanted to go to the South Mountain MVD and I asked where that was and she said, "I don't know". That was helpful! I looked it up on the GPS but it didn't pop up. OK. Then I thought it's probably in the map book. It was, but it was at Baseline and Third Street. I asked her if she was sure that was where she wanted to go, because it was probably going to be $50-$60 one-way. She said that's where she wanted to go, because she needed to get her driver's license (she had lived very close to there before she moved to Scottsdale). I thought it was strange she didn't know where it was, but the thought of a huge fare was more important. I thought I was taking a chance not getting the money up front, but this woman was not very imposing.

We started talking and she said she was getting a new car, because her son had "thrown away" her old one. I said, "He doesn't sound like a very good son". She didn't answer, but instead started asking me personal questions. "Are you married?" I started to answer, but then she started talking as though she hadn't even asked that the question, saying she had been married twice before but neither one had worked out. I asked her a question, but she continued to speak out of turn again, so I just shut up.

Before I knew it, she had lipstick on her teeth. You know what I'm talking about. The lipstick is caked on and it just finds its way to the teeth. I laughed out loud, so she did the logical thing: she asked me if I was married again. I thought "What the fuck", but I said, "I was, but I am not anymore." She next asked me what happened, so just to fuck with her I told her I found my wife in bed with another woman, to which she said, "That's weird". I looked right at her and said, "Not nearly as weird as some of the shit I've seen in this cab". Fortunately, she didn't seem to make the connection.

Then she started talking about the car she had picked out and how beautiful it was. She couldn't tell me what model it was, or who the manufacturer was, just that it was a lovely red car and she was picking it up tomorrow. She continued on about what a bastard her son was for getting rid of her old car. I tried to be sympathetic, but she would not let me get a word in edgewise. She said she worked in the mortgage industry for 25 years and she was looking forward to working again, and that she was going to enjoy driving to work every day.

Well, we got to the MVD and I let her out. She said that she needed me to wait for her. I said I would and that I would park over there (pointing to the spot). I walked her in and found where she needed to go, got her a "waiting in line" ticket, and went out to the cab. After couple of minutes, I thought to myself that I'd better go in and help her.

As it turns out, she needed more than my help. She had just finished filling out the paper work when I walked up, and she was telling the clerk how she was going to be getting this brand new, beautiful red car. The clerk was saying how nice that sounded and then asked who I was. "I'm Brenda's driver," I said. The clerk said there was a problem with Brenda's paperwork and that she needed to call the supervisor. Brenda just smiled pleasantly and said OK. I saw she had an old driver's license with a hole punched through it and that means one of two things: It was expired or it was suspended. Brenda said again "I can't wait to get my new car."

The supervisor told Brenda that she needed to have a medical clearance to get her license and that the form for this was missing. Brenda said, "Oh no, let me tell you what happened. The doctor told me I was doing wonderfully well and I don't need the form". The supervisor (Ann) said "Well, that's sweet of him to tell you that, but we need to have it in writing to be able to give you a license." Brenda calmly responded, "That's ridiculous, the doctor said I'm doing wonderfully well." Ann repeated her statement and told Brenda that she was unable to authorize a license without the medical clearance. Again, Brenda said, "This is insane. My doctor said I'm doing wonderfully well." We did that a few more times. Finally Ann said, "Ma'am, I done with this, you can't get your license without the medical clearance." They went back and forth again for a while, as Ann decided she wasn't going to let this go after all. Finally, Ann reached over to pick up one of the forms Brenda had, but Brenda snatched it angrily from her. Ann threw up her hands and walked away. I said to Brenda, "Let's go".

We got in the cab and started back. The meter was at $70 and I was wondering whether I was going to be paid. She kept muttering to herself and then to me "I don't understand this, I'm doing wonderfully well". She still had that same blank, contented look on her face. Then she started plotting out loud how she was going to get her license. Eventually, she asked me if I would lend her my license or sign something for her so she could get her license. I told her I would like to help her, but that I could get into trouble if I helped her fraudulently get a driver's license. She was offended that I wouldn't help her. Sorry, tough shit lady. As she kept scheming over what to do, I realized why her son had "thrown away" her car. This woman was certifiably nuts, and she would be a danger to herself and the rest of Phoenix if she was on the road.

When we got back to her condo, the meter said $103. She was very disheartened by the experience; for that, I couldn't blame her. She handed me a hundred dollar bill and said something about being short on money, so I charged her $95 (that's pretty good for 90 minutes of work). She moped out of the cab. I thought, maybe I should call the authorities, since she wasn't through trying to get a license to drive. I asked my sister-in-law and another woman I know what they thought and they both told me to forget about it.

In Lieu of Payment

When you deal as frequently as cab drivers do with cash, there is a very good chance that people will try to negotiate with you, or just flat out steal from you. I most certainly had my share of these experiences. On my first Saturday night, I got a call to a Circle K in Scottsdale. It was pretty suspicious-looking from the word go. I got to the store and started asking around for Craig. No one knew who I was looking for, including a security guy who was outside. A guy who was walking by asked me if he could borrow some money. The security guy told him that he couldn't hang around the store and ask people for money. After a couple more questions, I realized that this panhandler was the person I was there to pick up.

In hindsight, I should have known that taking this dude was a mistake, but I went along with it to see what would happen (we are all naïve or in search of troublesome entertainment sometimes). He told me to drive to his friend's house, where he was going to pick up some money, and then to drive him back to his home. We went to this other guy's house and I waited for 10 minutes. He came back out and said his friend wasn't there, but his roommate was at his apartment, and he would pay for the fare. By the time we got to his home, I was pretty sure I was screwed.

The biggest problem was that he was stoned. He was talking to me, but he might as well have been speaking Cantonese. I tried to have a conversation with him, but I was just lost. When he got out, he said he was going to go in and have his roommate give him the money. I waited outside and realized I had to take a piss. Fortunately, I was parked next to a park and it was dark, so I locked the door, ran over to a tree and took care of business. I went back to the car, told a couple of 15 year-olds to mind there own business, and waited for my man to come back. When he finally did, he told me that his roommate wasn't there and he didn't have any money, nor did he have a credit or debit card. He then asked me if I like movies, so I asked him why he would ask this. He handed me a VHS copy of the movie "Nothing to Lose" with Martin Lawrence and said I could have it. He asked me to give him my phone number and he swore that he would pay me back. I gave him my number, knowing I would never hear from him, but I had nothing to lose at that point. He then walked away and fell flat on his face. I had to laugh, but I was still out $19. I have since discovered that calls at night from Circle Ks are almost guaranteed to be no shows or total wastes of time.

Another time, I got a call to pick up a girl at Fry's in Mesa. I knew where it was because this Fry's is where I ordered my SRP meter (Salt River Project is one of the two power companies in Phoenix). When I got there, the girl came up to the cab and asked me if Discount still did deposits. She said a passenger could leave an item of value with the driver and pay for the fare at a later date, although I doubted that any cab company had ever done that.

She offered me her watch as collateral. The way she offered it up really made me laugh, and reminded me of *"Planes, Trains and Automobiles"*, when, after Steve Martin gave the hotel clerk his $2000 watch in exchange for a room, John Candy modeled his $10 Casio watch to try and get a room as well. She said, "Well, you can have this really nice watch". Firstly, if it really were a valuable watch, why would anyone offer it as collateral for a $10 cab ride? Secondly, I was sure nobody would ever accept merchandise as collateral (or as payment). Although this is a cash-based industry, for the most part, the administrators don't know what the drivers are accepting for payment. Drivers can pretty much accept anything, as long as they don't charge more than what the meter says.

But in this case, for some reason, I said OK. It probably had something to do with her sweat pants being rolled down to where her thong and part of her cute little ass were visible. So she and her male friend got in and I drove them a few miles. The fare ended up being about $10. When they got out, they didn't say anything, not even thank you. I guess they didn't want to hang around, since they got away without paying for the ride. I drove around the parking lot in which I dropped them off and I saw them in the rear view mirror pointing and laughing at me. The real humor of me getting a watch "In lieu of payment" was that I never wear a watch. My father has been trying to get me to wear one for 35 years, and he pesters me mercilessly, asking me "What time is it?" or "When are you going to get a watch?"

Sometimes, he will offer to give me one of his hundreds of watches. My brother harangues me about it almost as much as dad. My sister and her husband Rob got me this really expensive watch a couple of years ago under the guise of "the chicks will really love it". I probably should wear this piece-of-shit watch that little bitch gave me, but I just can't stand wearing a watch.

Sometimes, I can't believe the gall of people. I stopped at a place one Saturday night called "The Well" to pick up a fare.

When he waddled his ass out to the cab, his first words were "Didn't they tell you I need to sit in the front seat?" Funny question, considering the probability of dispatch giving me important information is so low. His request wasn't a problem, though, and I just put my stuff in the trunk. I shoehorned him into the front seat and we left. We started talking and it turns out that he was from Northern New Jersey. We discussed accents, places, how much we like Jersey, etc., and that was enjoyable. After a while, however, he said he only had about $10 dollars. I was fairly new to the job, so I wasn't sure what the final fare was going to be, so I said if he were a little short it would be OK. Sometimes, if you give an inch, some jackass will take five miles.

He asked me to stop at a Mexican restaurant, some hole in the wall that the name of which I don't remember. It was closed, so I thought I'd get the full fare. WRONG AGAIN, GOPHER HOLE BREATH. He saw a Burger King and asked to stop there because he was starving. He ordered two burgers, which left him with about $2, (he had given me $5), but instead of saving that to pay the rest of his fare, this jerk orders a large bag of fries! I couldn't believe it! What a prick. I'm just shaking my head, watching him shove fries into his pie hole as we get close to his apartment. When we get there, the fare was $8.50. He hands me some coins – change from the fries – and starts making small talk: How we should go hang out and talk some more about Jersey. I said "sure" but I was thinking "Are you out of your fucking mind?" The guy never even offered me any of his fries!

I had another similar situation. I picked up a woman and her two daughters at their apartment. The trip had two stops; first bringing the girls to a babysitter, and then the woman to work. Fortunately, the girls were fairly well behaved, and they were cute. They kept saying, "Mommy, are we there yet?" or "What does that sign say?" I was thoroughly amused.

Since she was heading to work, mom decided that we stop at Taco Bell and get some dinner. She also got the girls a snack and, to her credit, offered to get me something, which I declined. I mean, I had a bucket filled with bottles of water and grapefruit in the cab, so what else did I need? She ended up spending around $20 at Taco Bell, and I started thinking, is she going to have enough money for the fare?

We get to the babysitter's house and drop off the girls. The meter is nearing $20 by now, and she directs me to her place of work at a gentleman's club. It took 10 minutes to get there and along the way she started questioning me about the fare, wondering whether she was going to have enough to pay it. I knew it! Here we go again!

A half a mile out and the meter hits $27 and she said, "I don't have enough, can I pay $25". I rolled my eyes and said "All right". In one of the most incredible displays of nerve I've ever experienced, she hands me $30 and said, "Can I have a five back?" I said, "Are you kidding? You just told me you only have $25". Her reply was "No, I asked if I could pay only $25." I should have slapped her silly, but I told her that not only was this never going to happen again, but I was going to let every cab driver I know in Phoenix about her so she doesn't pull this stunt on anyone else. Her answer was "Like I care!"

My favorite (and perhaps worst) story where I get something short the full fare happened in my first or second week driving. I was in Mesa, having just dropped off an elderly man from a trip to the bank. I was at a light and I glanced in the rear view mirror. I saw a woman waving and I assumed that she was trying to flag me down. I turned around and pulled up to her. She said, "Thank god you saw me". She asked me to "hold on" as she needed to talk to some woman across the street. So I looked across the street and saw this hideous hag; she was missing a bunch of teeth but what really stood out was she was wearing a pair of shorts that were pulled up so far that a large chunk of her ass was exposed.

So the fare (call her Carol) came back to the cab and started berating this street urchin, calling her a nut, a loser, and a pain in the ass. So I asked Carol why she was talking to her. She explained that the woman was holding on to her wallet and wanted to arrange with her to meet at a bar across the street in about 20 minutes. If I had been a bit more experienced, I would have asked to see some money right then and there.

Carol gets back in the cab and starts negotiating. She wasn't really very clear about what she wanted me to do, but she said she only had $6. Again, I rolled my eyes, but I went along with it. She asked me to take her about a mile down the street, to the apartment of some dude who had things that belonged to her. We pulled into the driveway, and we reached $7. She told me she had to go inside and asked me to wait. In my mind, I was stuck, so I said sure. She went inside and eventually came back with the resident dirt bag in tow. She threw a few things in the back seat and then started to talk with the guy (yelling at him, actually), when a big white pick up truck came flying into the driveway. The dirt bag went running off, leaping over a fence and into the back yard, possibly for good reason, because the guy in the truck leaps out holding a handgun and starts talking to Carol. Turns out she knew him; he was an INS agent looking for illegal aliens. The dirt bag was not the guy the agent was looking for, but the reason he ran was because the cops were looking for him on a drug possession warrant.

What really concerned me was the fact that the meter was now at $15. Carol finally got in the cab and asked me to bring her to some other apartment, because she now had to check on some other person (creature) who had other stuff of hers. Even though I was really annoyed, I remained calm and conversed with her. The more I talked, the more she laughed. I don't know whether she was bullshitting me or not. As I looked at her, I realized she was pretty attractive. She was really thin and she was wearing a tank top, so you could see she had muscular arms with a bunch of tattoos (not my thing). She kept telling me how funny I was, laughing at everything I said. I admit that she turned me on, which I'm sure was part of her plan. However, any attractiveness I saw in her quickly disappeared when she said she recently been in jail. Like I need that baggage!

We got to friend number two's house and the meter was now at $22. She went up a staircase and came back down pretty quickly. She then said she needed to go to McDonalds's because she was getting hungry. I told she was going to have to give me more than $6. She said she would and handed me a five as a down payment. We went to the drive-thru and she asked for three of the dollar sandwiches and a cup of water. At the window, she tried to get away with only paying for two of the sandwiches. Sure enough, the clerk only charged her $2.16. She offered me one of the sandwiches. Since I was sure I wasn't going to be paid in full, I took one. I told Carol that I was taking her back to the bar we started out from. She asked me if I was mad at her and I told her I wouldn't have agreed to a fee of $6 if I had known she was going to take advantage of my kindness the way she had. She got annoyed but I didn't care. I was the one losing money.

We got back to the bar and that toothless sea hag street urchin friend of hers was waiting outside. Carol told me to wait there so she could get me more money. I waited for five minutes and she returned, asking me for my phone number. She said she was definitely going to use me again. I said "Well that's an appropriate choice of words!" I gave her my number, knowing that I would never pick her up again. She gave me a whole dollar and said she'll pay me $5 more the next time. I chalked it all up experience – call it "Learning To Drive A Cab 101".

About five months after that, I got a call for this Hispanic chick near Chase Field. She came stumbling out of the house, holding a paper shopping bag and a huge cup full of beer. She said, "Oh, I'm going to be respectful and not bring this cup of beer in the cab, and she dumped it on the ground. I asked her what was in the paper bag and she said a couple of cans of beer.

About a mile into the trip, she hands me $5 and says, "This should cover it, right?" I made a face and said, "Are you kidding me?" Then she said, "Well, I haven't taken a cab in a long time." I was pissed. *"How can you possibly imagine that a cab ride would cost only $5?"* She continue to tell me how she didn't know she was going to need a cab, and her friend offered her money but she didn't think she would need it. Then it was "Oh man, its $7.55 already!" *What did you think, sister? That the meter was going magically start moving in reverse?*

In the end, the fare was $9. I could have, and probably should have, threatened to call the police. That might have improved her level of effort to pay me in full. She apologized. That was useless, so I told her to give me the beers. She said, "You aren't allowed to drink". I said, "Yeah, well you're not allowed to take a cab and not pay for it! I'm not going to drink your beer until I get home!" Her response was, "Can I keep one beer for myself?" I retorted, "Hey, you owe me money. Give me both beers." And she did. She also kept saying she was going to be alone all night. I would have gone in and happily fucked her if I didn't want to strangle her.

Police Involvement ━━━━━━━━━━━━━━━━━━━━━━━━

Just when you thought it couldn't get any weirder, it does. I had been to this apartment complex many times before, so I didn't need to use my GPS. I drove into the gated area and saw him walking towards me. The dispatch said the name of the person was Robin, so I was surprised to see that it was a guy.

He was very effeminate looking in the way he walked (not that there is anything wrong with that). He got into the cab and I said hello, and he sort of grunted hello back at me. I thought, "OK, this could be interesting" and I headed out. He was wearing sunglasses and a baseball cap to the point where it looked like he was hiding from the paparazzi or something. I asked where he wanted to go and he said "McDowell and 38ᵗʰ". I knew this was going to be a pretty good fare, so I smiled to myself and took off.

I tried to start conversations a couple of times, but he ignored me. The only time he spoke was when he was on his cell, and even then, he only spoke Spanish (I have thought many times to myself in the time I've been in Phoenix that I really need to learn Spanish. It was never more apparent than this day). I noticed that he looked like Freddy Mercury, and for the rest of the ride, I kept singing "Somebody to Love" to myself.

We got to his apartment complex pretty quickly and the fare was $31. As we drove in the 38ᵗʰ Street gate entrance, he asked to stop as this huge woman was walking by. She had long frizzy blond hair, was about six-foot-three and looked like she lifted weights, a lot of weights. She was wearing a white tank top and a very short white skirt. I thought, "How many transsexuals can I see in a one week?" She handed Robin $10, which he gave to me. I was starting to feel uneasy about this, because Robin didn't seem to have any money. When we got to the apartment and he asked me if I wanted to come up, and I originally said no, but then I thought a second and said I would. When we got to the top of the stairs, he held up a finger saying to, "Hold on a minute". Then he shut the door in my face. This was looking worse.

I stood there for about five minutes without doing anything. Finally, I knocked on the door. About two more minutes went by with no answer, so I knocked again. Still no answer, so by now, I'm muttering "oh, come on." and "for Christ sakes". The third time (another two minutes later), I pounded on the door. Then, I called the number on the dispatch. No answer. I pounded harder on the door and looked through a crack in the blinds. I saw a little dog running around and I thought I saw someone walking to the right. Now, I'm thinking about this story a passenger had told me. The guy said that the driver had taken him all over the place and run up a $30 fare for a trip that should have cost $7, and the cops sided with the driver. In this case, I'm in the right, so a police officer would certainly help me. I debated to myself, and finally decided, I'm calling the police.

I had the number for the Phoenix Police on my cell phone, because I thought it would be a good idea for just such an emergency. They sent a patrol car over in about 15 minutes. The two officers got out and walked over to me. They were both about 5'10" or 5'11" and real stocky, solid looking guys. One was black, one Hispanic. I told them what had happened. We started walking to the stairs and they told me that I should wait by my cab. They were both wearing bulletproof vests, so I guessed that was probably a good idea.

I heard them knocking on the door, saying "Open up, the Phoenix Police." After a little while, I heard them talking to someone. While I was waiting, the brutish looking woman in the short white skirt walked by and didn't even look at me. I thought this was weird, because she was the one that was supposed to be giving me the rest of my money.

The policeman called me upstairs. There were two other people standing in the doorway, and both of them were fairly large, but they seemed to be wearing woman's outfits. The one officer asked me if one of these people was my fare. I told them no. They then asked if I was sure this was the correct apartment. I told them I followed the guy up these stairs to the door, and that he had shut the door in my face. Now, in mind my, I'm going, "Son of a bitch, this prick is going to get away with ripping me off." Ah, not so fast, show a little faith, my friends.

The black cop then asked if there was anyone else in the apartment and they both said no. I told the officers I thought I had seen someone walk in the area to the right when I looked through the window. They then told the two guys they wanted to look around and one of them said it was OK. They looked around for a few moments and the black cop yelled from the back room, "Hey, there is someone in the bathroom".

The Hispanic cop said, "Why do you have to lie to me?" (I have confirmed this with other officers, lying to the police is not a good idea.) One of them said, "I didn't know he was in there." This infuriated the cop. "YOU DIDN'T KNOW HE WAS IN THERE? HOW DO YOU LIVE HERE AND NOT KNOW THERE IS SOMEONE IN YOUR BATHROOM? YOU'RE LYING TO ME AGAIN! The guy insisted he didn't know he was there. "YOU BETTER STOP LYING TO ME RIGHT FUCKING NOW." Then from the back, I heard, "You better come out of there right fucking now." Another voice said, "I'm in the shower." "YOU HAD BETTER COME OUT RIGHT NOW OR I'M GOING TO FUCKING TAZER YOU." Then I heard him turn the tazer on, either to get ready to zap the guy or simply to make a point. As disturbing as this was on many levels, I was getting a big kick out of watching these guys work. This wasn't really funny, but it was, kind of.

They brought Robin out of the bathroom, and I told the police he was the guy who was in my cab. He looked completely different though, because he was only wearing a t-shirt and a towel. His hair was all the way down past his shoulders. It made him look like Unfrozen Caveman Lawyer. Then I looked into his face, and he still looked like Freddy Mercury. He was fighting the cops all the way. They made him sit down in one specific chair, facing away from me. He looked back towards me and said, "I told you I was going to give you the money. I said, "When, next month?" The cops told Robin that he needs to give me the money that he owes me. Robin pretty much kept saying he would give me the money if they would let him call that woman. He said, "How am I supposed to pay if you won't let me call the person who has the money. The other two people were standing there and Robin looked to them for help, but apparently, neither of them had any money. One cop then stood Robin up and put handcuffs on him. I just stood there with my mouth open and shaking my head in disbelief. I was thinking, "How did I get myself into this?

Robin resisted the attempts to put the cuffs on, but his "friends" weren't helping, so they cuffed him pretty quickly. Robin started screaming at me, "I told you that woman was going to give you the money." Now, at least three other things contradicted that statement, but I said, "Hey, she walked right past me just now and didn't even look at me." Robin said something back at me, but the one policeman told me to go back downstairs, which I did. I walked down to my cab and just buried my face in my hands. I kept thinking that these guys might try to seek retribution, so I was pretty unnerved. (Over the next week or so, I realized that nothing was going to happen. I think I caught them off guard by calling the police.)

After another five minutes or so, the two officers came down the stairs, with Robin in handcuffs and the other two in tow, trying to talk the cops into letting him go. One ran around the corner and disappeared. Robin was yelling and screaming, then crying, and he was drawing a crowd. He still had on only a t-shirt and a towel. After (apparently) all else had failed, Robin pulled his towel off, trying to get a sexual harassment charge or something against these two cops. They made the other guys go back upstairs and get a pair of jeans to put on Robin. When they tried to put them on him, he fought it all the way. It took about five tries to get them on.

Something happened then that I guess only I saw. This dude who had come out of one of the nearby apartments was trying to signal to one of the officers to come over. I'm not sure what the guy wanted, but I think he was going to rat Robin out for something else. I don't know for sure, because he was being very secretive, sort of waving him over with one finger. It also appeared that he changed his mind, because he left without speaking to them.

The black cop put Robin in the car and read him his rights, and the other guy came to talk to me. He said that it sucks that I didn't get my fare, but that for me to prosecute him probably wouldn't be worth it. I would lose a day of work, and wouldn't get my money. But then I found out that Robin already had a misdemeanor warrant out for his arrest and they were going to be able to book him anyway. I found out about five months later that he actually had four total warrants. He said they could use this report as evidence if I wanted to put my name on it, so I said sure.

Finally, one of the other guys brought back the woman in the short white skirt, and she gave me the other $21, and said, in her deep Spanish accent "I don't know why he just didn't ask me for the money". I couldn't have agreed more. Plus she gave me a tip on top of that. The officer said to me, "Plus, you got a pretty good story out of this". I said to him, "It's funny you would say that, because I've decided that I'm going to write a book about this job, and this incident will certainly be in it." He got a big smile on his face and said, "I know I'll buy it." Let's hope about 12 million people feel the same way.

I would name the police officers, to give them credit for being good officers. In the end, I decided it wouldn't help the story and I wouldn't want them on the hook for anything that could come back to haunt them later. I thought they did a tremendous job, but sometimes justice is a little odd and I don't want anything said in this book to come back and haunt them.

While that was a pretty nutty story, it is not the only one that involved the police. I got this call to an apartment complex on the west side, and it was an electronic voucher. I don't remember the passenger's name, but I drove to the place, thinking I was going to be late, and needing to take a piss real bad. I snuck around the side of the building and found a tree I could hide behind, as I maneuvered my cab to provide even better camouflage.

Later, I walked up to the door and heard the television on and I saw that the door was opened a little, so I thought, "Good, someone is home". I knocked on the door and nobody answered. I knocked two more times with no response. I had been given a phone number, so I dialed it, again no response. The thing was that I could hear the phone ringing standing outside the door. I tried knocking again and then I tried calling the number again, but still no answer. I started thinking that something was wrong, and I noticed a woman speaking with a pool guy and I presumed she was the superintendent.

I waited about five minutes before I approached her, because I didn't want to interrupt, even though I'm thinking it could be a life-threatening situation. Finally, she was done with the pool guy and I told her that I thought something was wrong in this apartment. Her response was not what I expected. She didn't do anything and told me I had to call the police myself. I was pretty annoyed that a landlord didn't give a shit about a tenant. Well, now I had to decide how much I was going to get involved. After I thought about, I decided to call the police, because who knew whether this woman was even alive.

I waited 20 minutes for the police to show up and I was starting to get really pissed off. The fare, which I wasn't going to get, wasn't going to be very much. Plus, I couldn't find her and now I was losing time trying to be a Good Samaritan. The first officer showed up, and it was a female (and an attractive one at that). I told her what had happened and I did it in an apologetic tone, because I was feeling like it was going to be a colossal waste of their time.

She asked me if I wanted to wait and I said no, and started to leave. Just then, the second officer pulled up, so I decided to wait, because I figured it would be over soon. I stood back at my cab and the officers came back after only a few minutes. I asked them what the deal was and it turns out the lady was asleep. I was pretty embarrassed, but I kind of thought something like this was what happened. I could rest in good conscience.

I had another call once while I was in downtown Phoenix, having just gotten a no-show, which, of course, put me in a shitty mood. Then, I drove to the given address. Unfortunately, the given address did not exist. I had the phone number and I called the woman. It turns out they were at a liquor store two miles away, where their car had broken down. Or, so the woman told me. I told her I was about five minutes away and I would be there as soon as I could. She was fine with that, so I continued to curse dispatch and drove towards Central and Mohave.

When I got there, she waved me down, and I pulled into the lot. What I didn't expect to see was two police officers, a tow truck with a female operator (you don't see many women driving tow trucks) and the people I was to pick up. It turns out the cops were impounding the vehicle and towing it away. It had one of those Historic Vehicle plates on it, but pre-historic would have been a better description.

There was a bunch of personal belongings sitting on the ground and the woman told me I needed to put that stuff in the trunk. A fan, a stereo, some clothes, etc. were among the things they were taking. I didn't think all of it was going to fit. They were fairly large people and there was still a bunch of stuff in the trunk of the impounded car. The guy made one final, agonizingly slow sweep of the car to make sure he didn't leave anything he needed. As a matter of fact, it looked as if he was trying to antagonize the officer, he was moving so slowly.

The fun didn't end there. They started bickering as soon as I asked where they wanted to go. He said 36th and Thomas, and she said 38th and Broadway. She was getting on him about the fact that some dude at the address she wanted to go to would help them, but he said he didn't think the guy was there. They went back and forth about this, and she called him just about every name that meant stupid I had ever heard. He finally won out, so we headed north. Then he started tapping the cord of the stereo on top of something hard, so it made a noise. She soon got pissed and asked him to stop, so, of course, he kept doing it. She asked him again to stop, so he started tapping her in the head with the cord. She yelled, "Didn't I ask nicely for you to stop?" He said "no". That really pissed her off. (I grinned to myself, because when I was married, I would have stopped immediately when my wife said to stop, or more likely, would never have done that in the first place. *In my opinion*, this let her know that he wasn't going to let himself be bossed around).

She then tried to retaliate by hitting him in the head with her hand. She called him a fool and told him to stop when he put his hand up to block the hits. She continued to hurl insults at him, while he continued to mutter to himself about what is he going to do without a car. We were at about McDowell and 24th when we must have passed a Wendy's. I say we must have passed a Wendy's because he said, "Sir, I just asked you if we could stop at Wendy's". I said, "Sorry, I didn't hear you", because I hadn't.

After a while, I really wanted them out of the cab. I wasn't afraid anything was going to happen as much as I just was tired of listening to them. She just kept nagging him. He asked me if I would stop at a Burger King on the next corner and she started bickering at him before I had a chance to answer. He said, "I'm hungry." She said he could eat when they got home. They went back and forth about that for a couple of minutes, when he finally said "Stop nagging me about the damn car, and I'm getting Burger King."

Finally, I couldn't take it anymore. I said, "Look, we're almost there. I'm not stopping at Burger King. I will drop you off at your apartment and help you take your stuff into the house, and then I'm leaving. I thought to myself, I wonder if they think that means they don't have to pay me.

Well, when we got there, she told me he's going to bring everything into the apartment. As we were unloading the car, they were laughing out loud, so I guess all was forgotten. She didn't give me much of a tip, but it was a good fare, so that was good enough.

I got my first call on a Sunday in a condominium complex around the corner from my old place of employment. It said to meet the person at the leasing office. When I got there, there were two police cruisers, two officers and two other people.

One officer asked me if I was there to pick up Devon (da-VON), and I said, "I was the cab driver for Devon." The two guys were standing there yelling at each other. Devon had a bunch of stuff in one of the police cruisers, including two suitcases and a huge duffle bag.

I really didn't do anything for the first five minutes I was there. The one cop told me this was going to take a few minutes and I would be taking Devon to the Greyhound station on 24th and Buckeye, adjacent to the airport. I was thinking, cool, that will be great fare.

The other guy (Tom) was saying how Devon was crazy and how he was trying to get out of paying him for the rent that he owed him. Devon retorted by saying he wanted to pay the rent, but Tom expected him to pay the whole thing. Tom started swearing and the one officer told him not to speak that way.

Tom then accused Devon of stealing his (hair salon) clippers and they were worth almost $200. Tom's voice got a little higher at that point. Devon denied it, but Tom insisted that he had them in his suitcase. When they opened one of the suitcases, there was a clipper, wrapped in a plastic wrapper. The weird thing was nobody really reacted. Devon said he didn't know how that got in there. The police didn't act as though it was anything strange and even Tom didn't say anything. It was almost as if they knew all along the clippers were in the suitcase.

In the end, it seemed as if the officers were there to get Devon out without a physical incident. Tom kept yelling about rent money, Devon told him to fuck off, and the officers kept threatening to bring Tom to the station. The officer told me to get Devon and his stuff in the cab and get going.

Devon got on his cell phone and was speaking with someone for quite a while. He was telling the guy on the phone that Tom was going to pay for the cab ride and any other expenses he might incur. I started to worry, because I thought this meant he wasn't going to pay me.

Then, something totally unexpected happened. We were just past where the I-10 and 60 meet, when I noticed a police car right behind me. After about 10 seconds, on go the lights. I was thinking, "What the fuck?" I pulled over and it was the same officer from the apartment complex. He walked up to the cab and asked me to roll down the back seat window. He handed Devon the same clippers and told him they weren't Tom's after all and they had brought him to the station for questioning. Devon said "serves him right, you can put him in jail for all I care."

The rest of the trip, I listened to Devon bad mouth Tom to his friend on the cell. When we got to the bus station, Devon said he needed a receipt, "Because that mother fucker is going to pay me back!" He didn't tip me, but the fare was good, so that was fine.

Danger is my Middle Name

One of the biggest surprises for me in taking this job was the fact that no member of my family expressed any kind of fear about the dangers involved. I thought my father was a guarantee to tell me he didn't want me doing this, and that he would have a laundry list of reasons for me not to drive a cab. In fact, I'm sure if we hadn't cremated my mother when she died, she would be turning over in her grave knowing that I was a cabbie. But nobody said a word, other than asking questions about the details surrounding what I would be doing, the rules, the amount of money I could make, etc. That doesn't mean that other people haven't offered their thoughts on my career decision though.

One of my first days on the job, I was waiting at a Circle K by the airport for a call. I have used that particular store many times as a rest stop and call waiting place. On that day, I stopped for gas and a guy walked up to me and asked about the job. I told him I really didn't know a whole lot yet, because I just started, but I hadn't had a lot of problems so far. He told me how much respect he had for cabbies because of the dangers involved. Before

I could get a word in, he told me about a driver that was in the news because he had been robbed at gunpoint, and was eventually shot. He didn't tell me was whether the guy lived or not. I really didn't want to talk to this guy anymore, but he just kept yammering on. "Boy, you guys are always getting ripped off, shot at and yelled at by people. I sure respect what you do. I would never be a cab driver. Your job is fucked up." Wow, thanks for that!

Another time, I was checking out with Angelo at the cage when another driver told me a story about how he was over in South Phoenix for a pick-up. The woman walked up to his window and asked him if he had a lighter so she could have a smoke before she got in. He reached down for it and turned back to find a 9 MM pistol stuck in his ear. The engine was running and there was nothing in front of him, so he floored the gas pedal and got out of there, but not before she took a couple of shots at him. Fortunately, she missed him, although the car got clipped. This woman was, apparently, a major crack head and her boyfriend had just broken up with her. What's that phrase, "Hell hath no fury, like a woman scorned?"

I got a call to pick up a guy in Tempe, south west of the Arizona State campus. Sometimes, you just know what kind of a call you are going to get, but this wasn't one of them. I pulled up to the apartment complex and the guy was walking towards me, saw me, and held up a finger to let me know he would be right out. Sometimes, a passenger will do that and take 10 minutes to come back. That is one of the things I truly dislike. If I'm 14 seconds late, people will get bent out of shape, but it's OK for them to keep me waiting forever. If I have the nerve to turn the meter on, that makes them even madder. Most people don't get that I only make money if someone is in the cab. My time truly is money.

Anyway, this guy came right out. I was driving a mini van at the time, and he threw a duffel bag in the back hatch and slid open the door, telling me "You're going to make some money with me today; I need you to take me on some errands." I was thinking, "Cool". I always almost notice clothing, hats and other ancillary things about passengers and this guy was no different. He had a Seattle Seahawks hat; his head was shaved, had a goatee, and wore blue jeans and a black t-shirt under his windbreaker. And, of course, he was wearing shades. He asked me if he could smoke. Normally, I would say yes, but because we were in a van and the front seat windows were the only ones that would open, I told him he could move to the front seat. He said that wasn't necessary, he would acquiesce to the rules of my cab.

We went on our way and he told me the first place he wanted to go was a Fry's supermarket on Southern and Mill. He went in and asked me to wait out front. I had a hard time negotiating the area in front of the store, because of the size of the van, but I was able to turn and park right in front. I had been there for about ten minutes when a clerk came and asked me why I was there. I said I was waiting for a guy and he should be out soon. Sure enough, 20 seconds later, there he was. He got in and told me that the Western Union was closed and he needed to go to a different store. For a second, I thought, "It took 10 minutes to find out that Western Union wasn't open?" I forgot about that just as quickly, and on we went.

The next stop was a Fry's on the next block, Southern and Rural. We pulled in and he pointed to a small cactus towards the farthest back part of the store and told me I should park there, so I did. I waited for about 10 minutes, and he came out, got in and said, "OK, I guess the next place should be this smoke shop in Mesa."

We headed towards Mesa on Southern and he decided to stop at a Circle K on the way. He said he needed some cigarettes and a drink. We stopped pretty quickly, since there are four million Circle Ks in Phoenix. That didn't take long, so we went towards the smoke shop. Again, I was thinking, "why are we going to a smoke shop *and* stopping for cigarettes?" But, whatever, I guess.

We were having a series of conversations of interest, like sports, the cab industry, racial prejudice, etc. and I really was enjoying this trip. I'm thinking, "Boy, this is one of the great things about this job. You're helping and meeting people, making money, maybe I will do this for a while".

We got to the smoke shop and he went in. I flipped on the radio and the song "Carry on Wayward Son" by Kansas was playing. It just so happens this is one of my favorite songs. It reminds me of my mother, partly because I have come to realize that I am her "Wayward Son". He came back to the cab and we got going, this time headed back towards Tempe.

After a couple of minutes, he changed his mind and had me double back towards Mesa. "Flip a bitch" was the term he used. I know it means make a U-Turn, but I can't figure out where that phrase comes from. He said he wanted me to drop him off at the Fiesta Mall. He gave me his cell phone number and said, "Drop me off over here, than I would like you to come back in about two hours and drive me to Tucson." Well, Tucson is about a $150-200 fare, so I was really excited. He gave me $75 (the fare plus a $40 deposit to come back) and gathered his things. Excellent.

I chased another call about five miles, which turned out to be a voucher that took me 15 miles from the Fiesta Mall, into South Gilbert. I had plenty of time to get back, so it was no big deal. This woman was nice enough during the trip, although she really didn't express much of a desire to talk. As I got to her house, a universal message came out on the MDT saying, "Any driver that was in the area of Southern and Rural at 10:30 AM, please call dispatch." I knew that call was for me.

I called the main number and was transferred to dispatch. They really didn't tell me anything, but asked me to stand by. Ten seconds later, I received a call from Roger, the safety guy. He told me I was the person they wanted. Like I said, I was sure that message was for me. He also asked me to come back to the cage and didn't say another word. I was thinking some company safety patrol guy saw me make a u-turn or something like that, and I was going to be suspended. So, I was pretty nervous when I finally got back there at about noon. I would never have guessed why I had been called in.

Roger said, "Your passenger robbed the Fry's at Southern and Rural when you were there." I just stared at him and thought, "Wow, I could have been hurt." He also told me the guy had a gun in his waistband. I guess that's why he didn't want to sit in the front seat. He didn't want me to see the gun.

Just then, the detective assigned to the case called Roger to see about getting the van to use as a decoy. Roger gave me the option of going over to the Fiesta Mall, where the police were conducting a stake out. I really didn't feel like getting another car and relinquishing the van. Actually, I really didn't want to drive at all. So I told Roger I would go. By the way, he also told me the detective asked him whether he thought I might have been involved. My first reaction was to be offended, but I quickly realized that it was a pretty reasonable question. Roger said, "I told him I thought it was possible *some* guys could be involved, but not you." That was nice of him. He could have really thrown me under the bus.

Anyway, I drove over to the Fiesta Mall, and they had a central location for this operation on the under side of a parking structure. I met the detective and two others, and described what I knew and remember about this guy. I told them everything I thought they needed to know about the van itself. They showed me a mug shot of the guy, and he looked the same, except he didn't have a goatee in the picture. They put the fellow that looked the most like me (although neither of them really did) in the driver's seat and they left.

For the next 90 minutes, the lead detective and I stood and talked about a bunch of stuff when he wasn't on the phone coordinating things. He got one phone call that was for his wife, and it produced a funny moment. He was constantly interrupted on that call by police business. Finally, he had to explain to the person, "Look, I'm at a shopping mall on police business, can I have you call my wife?" He got off of that call, and his wife called two minutes later. I had to laugh.

They called off the search around 2 PM, and that's when I realized how serious this was. A couple of the other detectives came back, and they thanked me and shook my hand for helping. I never felt like I was in any danger, but they certainly acknowledged the risk I took. But then, 10 other detectives made their way back to "headquarters", and every one of them was wearing a bulletproof vest, as were the guys already there. That's when it hit me just *how* dangerous this was. They told me that this guy had been released only six months earlier after doing an eight-year stretch for armed robbery.

I started thinking about the movie "The Shawshank Redemption" when Red (Morgan Freeman) is talking about being institutionalized. I came to the conclusion that this guy got out, couldn't cope, and went right back to robbery because he wanted to go back to jail. Who is going to hire a man who robbed banks? I was thinking he was in a no-lose situation. If he gets away with it, he's free. If he gets caught, he goes back to a familiar life. Some choice!

Nothing really changed for me, outside of the fact that people heard about the incident. When the driver liaison saw me, he told me I have *Titanium Testicles* and that what I did was very brave. The safety guy told me I was a "true company man". Months later, Dorothy (she works the cage) said, "That was you?" She was in training and knew about this incident. So, I guess I earned a bit of celebrity within Discount Cab.

One thing I find humorous about this story is a part of the conversation I was having with the guy while I was driving him around. At one point, I thought about the fact that I had picked up an inordinate amount of blind passengers recently. He and I talked about that, and I told him, "You know, if I EVER saw a driver take advantage of a blind person, I would punch them right in the face." He then said, "Yeah, I agree, what a terrible thing to take advantage of someone for your own gain." Five minutes later, he robbed a supermarket. That just strikes me funny.

One final note: I called the detective eight months afterwards to find out if they caught the guy. He told me that they got him that night. He apparently used cabs two more times to commit two more robberies, but they weren't Discount cabs.

The Dumbest Idea Ever

One of the reasons I moved to Phoenix was to find myself. I had a series on negative things happen to me between 2002 and 2006, and I felt really lousy about life. I had invested in a candy machine business that led me to bankruptcy. That is probably the dumbest thing I've ever done, considering the end result. As dumb as that might have been, however, I didn't have to work 133 days in row while doing it.

During my time with Discount, I have had plenty of highs and lows. At least a dozen people told me I should write a book about my experience. Finally, I thought, "Yeah, I am going to write a book." I started writing in a notebook what I though was going to be the body of the book; some stories, some introductions, etc. As time went along, my vision of what this was really going to be turned into something different, more than once.

I was on vacation the week of my birthday (April 25) when I came to the conclusion I didn't want to drive a cab anymore. I was tired of the 80-hour workweeks. I gained back a lot of the weight I had lost, mainly because of the sedentary nature of the job. I lost money anytime a mistake was made, regardless of whether I was at fault or not. I found myself getting really angry with a lot of really small things. I could make decent money, but there were no guarantees.

I looked at a calendar, and realized that a schedule of four weeks on and one week off would lead me right into my annual trip to Dewey Beach, Delaware. That seemed to be perfect. Then, I had an incredible brainstorm a couple of days later. Since I'm leaving anyway, why don't I just work everyday until Dewey? I'm going to be taking "x" many weeks off afterward to finish writing the book, so I will need to back up some money for bills. It will be 19 weeks, 4½ months. I can do that. Damn, I'm a genius.

Around the Valley in 133 days

When I first decided to drive everyday for the final 19 weeks of my cab career, part of my reasoning was that I wanted to write a diary for this period of time. That is what I did when I wrote this section initially. After I reviewed it, I decided it was not a good idea to keep the text the way I originally wrote it. It was fairly tedious and I thought I could make this part of the book a lot more concise and keep your interest by discussing strategies, a typical day, my mood swings, etc. I have also included additional, less-detailed stories that I hadn't written about in the previous chapters.

It took me a long time to devise the quasi-formula I would use to succeed as a driver. I'm pretty sure no template would work for everyone. I don't necessarily think my strategy would work for *anybody* else. One of the biggest problems in devising any strategy for this job is that many factors have to be taken into account and those things often change.

For example, the price of the lease alone makes you think quite a bit. It is less expensive to lease a cab by the week as opposed to 12 or 24-hour leases. Leasing weekly made me feel like I needed to drive as many hours as I possibly could to get as much value out of the lease. For that reason, many drivers *don't* lease weekly.

The company was very particular to whom they would lease the Prius. From their perspective, they needed to know those cabs will be on the road as much as possible, so they demanded a commitment from the drivers that wanted to lease the Prius. I had my first Prius taken away from me, because I would take a week off after driving 21 days in a row. That wasn't good enough.

I eventually got a different Prius, cab 732, which was the car I drove for the most part, for the final nine months I worked for Discount. I loved this cab because it didn't have a camera. I protected that cab, seemingly with my life. I would go either four or five weeks before taking time off. There were no complaints, except maybe from Abner at the cage, who had to make sure my cab was there when I would come back.

There are other leasing issues. There is a colossal difference in price between the Crown Victoria and the Prius. The weekly lease price is $100 a week more for the Prius. There is an even greater disparity on the shorter lease prices. That is another reason many of the drivers preferred the Crown Vic. I think it's fairly shortsighted, because if you were a full-time driver (which means 70-90 hours per week) you would generally make up the difference and then some. However, most guys still don't want the Prius.

The constant fluctuation of gas prices made it hard to know whether the Prius was worth it or not. When I first got a Prius, gas was more than $4 per gallon, so I would save about $50-$150 per week in gas. Shortly afterwards, the prices went all the way down to $1.40 per gallon, so I would have to drive 1500 miles in a week to break even. By my last day, the prices leveled off to around $2.50 per gallon, so I would save some money if I drove the entire week. Who wants to do all of those calculations?

As it turns out, the ideal cab to get was a mini-van. The lease was the same as the Crown Vic, but the vans would get as much as 10 miles more per gallon. Plus, many passengers would request vans and there were only about 10 available. I had a van for three weeks and I wanted to keep it, but I was not permitted to do so.

The vehicle I had also was a determining factor for how far I would chase a call. If I was in a Crown Victoria and getting 12 miles per gallon, I was less likely to be willing to take a risk on a call 15 miles away than if I'm driving the Prius and getting 44 miles per gallon. The risk was much less of a risk if the trip there only cost 80 cents, as opposed to $2.50.

The expense involved is a small part of the plan to maximize potential income. I spent a lot of time trying to figure out which are the more lucrative areas. I am sure of only two things: One, zones 251 and 261 were almost always airport runs (worth $25-$35) and aside from that, it isn't obvious which zones are more valuable.

There were some rules of thumb I would use to decide where I wanted to be. First, since I leased my cab weekly, I was able to take it home at night. This enabled me to start the day in Ahwatukee instead of having to drive 15 miles to the Mesa cage and then doing a check-in every morning. This easily saved me 90 minutes and almost 30 miles a day.

Since I was usually awake between 4:30 and 6 AM, I could book-in to the number one spot in zone 81 almost all the time. I found this to be advantageous, because I would frequently get an airport run to start the day, and they were generally worth $20-$35.

A second part of my strategy was repeat electronic vouchers. There were a series of fares that went every weekday, every other day, every Monday, Wednesday and Friday, whatever the case might be. Vouchers were usually worth anywhere from $6 to $81. Most frequently, they were worth less than $20, but if you paid attention, the more valuable ones were there for the taking.

My thinking changed during the last three months, because there was a location near me that had two huge vouchers Monday through Friday. One was a guy named Don and the other was John. Both of their vouchers were worth more than $30, so I would try to get them. I couldn't get them everyday, because about four other drivers knew about them. If I got up early enough, I could take another call first and then get back to try to get in position for their fares. There is a park one and a half miles from their house. There were two reasons I waited in this park: it had a bathroom and it was right on the edge of two zones. If I was sent a different call, the chances were it would be just as valuable. The exact locations in which I waited were almost always determined by the availability of a bathroom.

Another factor, which I used to determine where I drove, was the day, and the time of the day. I think it's pretty obvious Friday and Saturday nights were prime driving times. I did not, however, drive these shifts often. My prime driving times were on weekdays between 5 AM and 7 PM. The main money making times for me were between 5-10 AM and 3-7 PM. There are always plenty of trips to the airport during either rush hour. Plus, the vouchers and their return trips would come during these times.

Sometimes in midday, I would luck out and a get a long trip or two. I would often go to Scottsdale during this time of the day to get the myriad of 80 year-olds with HHVs or to kill an hour or so at the gym. A lot of my time was spent gnashing my teeth, because I would go three hours and bill $20. The key to success was not to get too caught up in worrying about slow periods. You have to look at days, not hours. And really, you have to look at weeks, not days or hours.

I generally did not drive at night at all. I think the main reason for this was that I needed some semblance of normalcy to my life. Working during the day and sleeping at night was the only way to do that in this job. During the rare occasions I drove late or overnight during the week, I did OK. I also did well on weekend nights. There are plenty of drivers that do very well driving overnight. I just didn't want to drive at night.

Saturdays and Sundays were hit or miss. There were tons of calls for people who wanted to be brought back to their cars the morning after. I would also get fares taking people shopping or to the airport. By the same token, there were a lot of occasions when I would wait two or more hours to get a fare.

Yet another consideration while strategizing was return trips. Generally speaking, I would wait for my next call in the zone I dropped off the previous passenger. In most zones, a call would come quickly, especially if when I booked back in, I got position number one. I realized after a while, that if a passenger wanted a return trip after a $30 plus fare, it was usually worth it for me to wait for them. If they were going to be 30-45 minutes, it was certainly worth it. My goal was to bill at least $20 per hour. If I did that, I would make a decent amount for myself for the day. Any and all consideration for strategy was based on that notion.

Moving right along, for the last two months of this time period, I concentrated on getting the aforementioned Don or John. If I got in my cab after 5:30 AM, I would go directly to the park in zone 80. The call for Don would come at exactly 7:00 o'clock. It was a no-lose situation, because if another call came in, it was almost always as valuable or more valuable than Don's fare. Plus, on some occasions, I had time to go back and get Don or John's fare. If the first call I got was Don, it was worth $35. John's was $40.

Next, I would spend the rest of the morning in Mesa. There are plenty of vouchers with decent value in Mesa. The key is to have as little down time as possible. Five $10 fares in a two-hour period is better than two $20 fares.

In the last two weeks, I realized there was a $63 fare in a zone 10 miles directly south of where I would drop off Don. Now, it was tricky to get because my C-Book screen was 30 seconds behind. The fare would automatically come up at exactly 8:30 AM. So I had to time it almost perfectly, and I did manage to get that call four times in nine days.

As I mentioned earlier, most of the time I would spend the mid-day in Scottsdale, generally between McKellips and Indian School. There were plenty of constant small fares, especially during the week. Things would change if I were able to chase what I viewed as potential big fares.

Now, I knew drivers who would tell me they wouldn't leave a five-mile radius, they wouldn't chase credit card calls or fares in out-lying zones. I felt exactly the opposite way, especially when it came to credit card calls.

I'm sure the main reason the other drivers didn't like credit card calls was that the company kept five percent. The fact that they did was lousy. I also realized that the reason the passenger would use a credit card was because it was usually a long trip and they didn't want to use their cash for a cab ride. The minimum for a credit card was $10, and a credit card call was more than $20 three-quarters of the time. It was a simple bottom line question in the end: What would you rather have; two $10 fares where you clear $20 or one $40 fare where you clear $38?

Getting back to the average day, once you got into the evening rush hour period chasing credit card calls seemed even smarter to me. People were always catching flights or going back to their hotels. Making $75-$150 in a four hour stretch was easily within the realm of possibility.

I was also able to arrange a few personals for myself during this time, "The Iron Greek" being the most memorable one. I gave him that name because his given name was so Greek, you couldn't possibly think he was any other nationality. He asked me to be his regular driver to the airport every Monday for about two months. Apparently, I was the first driver he had in a six-week period that showed up on time. He would spend almost the entire trip to the airport conducting business via cell phone or laptop computer. I would run a credit card for the same amount every trip before we left his house. It was a solid, easy fare.

Another lucrative personal for me was a pair of visiting computer techs, whom I will call "The Two Indians". For a two-week period I drove them to and from their hotel, which was a $30 fare. It was a good news/bad news situation.

In reality, the only good thing was the money. They were late by 10-30 minutes almost every time I picked them up. On two occasions, I waited 45 minutes during evening rush hour to bring them home, only to have them *finally* call to tell me they couldn't leave for at least another hour. I wouldn't wait anymore for them, just on principal.

One time I charged them $31 when the meter said $30.25 and they complained. Another time, I was 200 yards from their hotel right at 9 AM. The pickup was scheduled for 9 AM, and they called wondering, "How much longer THEY would have to wait." Plus, I NEVER got a tip. In the end, I made enough total money to make their bullshit worth it, but they frustrated the hell out of me.

I was on autopilot a lot of the time. For the first four weeks of this period of time, I was OK, because I was making decent money. I really started to feel my mood shift to a bad place during the month of June.

The summer is a bad time of the year for the cab industry. A good chunk of the reason for the downturn was the fact that a lot of the older people go to a cooler climate for the summer. This takes away a lot of vouchers, both electronic and hand held. During the summer of 2009, the company seemed to be hiring more and more drivers, which also took fares away. Between Memorial Day and the middle of August, I considered myself fortunate to clear $200 in a week.

This really brought my temper to the surface. I never got mad at a passenger, but I would get so angry at blunders by dispatch, traffic, traffic signals or $6 vouchers. By the time the summer was coming to an end, I felt like my heart was going to explode. I would give myself a headache from yelling at my MDT. Even during the final three weeks, I was pretty miserable.

What was kind of interesting was how quickly those 19 weeks seemed to go. I remember thinking after 10 days, "How am I going to drive 123 more consecutive days?" The next I knew, it was September.

Now, here are some additional, interesting passenger stories from these 19 weeks that haven't already been told. They are in chronological order.

WEEK 1: One trip that stood out for me was a fellow that I brought to the airport who was in the military. This guy looked like a football player and he was on his way to Atlanta to report to Fort Benning. He had just come back from North Korea and was being reassigned. After I thanked him for his service, he told me something that was startling, but only at first. He said, "No offense to anyone, but I don't want to die for my country." I thought that was a pretty courageous thing to admit that to a stranger. Then it occurred to me, I would feel the same way.

I also got the opportunity to meet a couple of former NFL players. I went to a Scottsdale Bike Shop where I met former all-pro lineman Fred Smerlas of the Bills and Patriots. I also drove Sean Mcnanie, who played in the NFL and at Arizona State, and his friend to the airport.

WEEK 2: I had an interesting pick-up on Monday. This fellow had a New Jersey area code on his cell phone so we started talking about the Garden State. It turns out, not only had he been to New Jersey, but also he had ridden on the bike path that was adjacent to the Griggstown Canal about one mile from the house I grew up in. He was asking me about where I lived, and I couldn't believe he had actually heard of Griggstown, much less biked there.

The only other unusual thing that happened this week was I needed to swap out cars. I had a PM and they found a coolant leak for the second consecutive month. I was given a temporary cab that had a cracked windshield, but when I did my reconciliation on Sunday, Alfred told me cab 732 still wasn't ready. They gave me a choice between two new Priuses, 791 or 1002. I chose 791, because it had a back up camera.

These types of exchanges are a constant necessity, especially when your permanent car is an older Crown Victoria. As far as the Prius is concerned, relying on the reverse camera isn't a good idea, because the view is distorted. When you get used to having it, though, you want to have it. Plus, the passengers love it.

One of the passengers this week made me laugh. I know quite a bit about the history of sports. I also know the sports themselves and how they should be played. People here in the west have way more of a bias then in the east, but the fans here have convinced themselves there is a bias against the west.

I bring this up is because of this bonehead I picked up. He told me no one cares about the Cubs here, the Southeast Conference is overrated, and the Pac 10 is underrated, blah, blah, and blah. The Diamondbacks, the Suns got screwed, etc. Shit head. I didn't bother dusting off facts.

WEEK 3: This week started off horribly. I didn't get a call for the first two hours. Then, I chased a call six miles for a no-show. By noon, I had gotten two minimum vouchers, an airport run that was less than $10 (that is virtually impossible), another no-show and a small credit card trip. I was fuming.

It got better, though. I picked up a series of attractive women, plus I got a couple of decent vouchers, then a couple of good credit card fares and a reimbursement of close to $80 for the days I had the Crown Vic. I ended up making a decent amount for the day. It just goes to show you can't panic when a three-hour period of time doesn't go well.

On Wednesday, I had three fares that are examples of how to use your brains and experience to maximize the ability to make money. The first was a call I chased eight miles to zone 251. As I stated earlier, calls in this zone are almost always trips to the airport. This one was indeed an airport run. As an added bonus, she was a beautiful AND a doctor. We had an interesting conversation about health insurance. She was of the opinion that, while the current system is flawed, it makes the physician's lives quite a bit easier. Fair enough.

I had made my way back to Chandler and got a fare that needed to go to Phoenix to get his social security card. I had been to that office a year ago, so I knew it was a really long trip. I told him I would wait for him, because the return trip would be worth it. It certainly was, especially since he was only there for 30 minutes. Again, that was smart. And, I'll say this: If I could average that amount every 90 minutes, *I would still be a cab driver.*

The third trip was similar to that one. I brought this woman and her son to a medical building in North Phoenix from Scottsdale. Again, I saw an opportunity for a return trip and told them I would wait. I even went shopping while they were with the doctor. I also ended up driving them around to get prescriptions. By the end of the safari, I had billed nearly $100.

I have to tell you that on Friday this week, I heard the best classic rock set with 20 songs commercial free I have ever heard. It went as follows:

- You May Be Right, Billy Joel
- Blinded By The Light, Manfred Mann
- Down On The Corner, Creedence
- Stairway To Heaven, Led Zeppelin
- Show Me The Way, Peter Frampton
- Wonderful Tonight, Eric Clapton
- For What It's Worth, Buffalo Springfield
- Renegade, Styx
- Maybe I'm Amazed, Paul McCartney
- Legs, ZZ Top
- American Woman, The Guess Who
- Making Love, Bad Company
- Mama Told Me, Three Dog Night
- Never Been Any Reason, Head East
- Edge Of Seventeen, Stevie Nicks
- School's Out, Alice Cooper

- Jainie's Got A Gun, Aero Smith
- Long Cool Woman, The Hollies
- Cold As Ice, Foreigner
- Island Girl, Elton John

Now, I'm not saying every song was a Hall of Fame song. But that 20 song set, without interruption, was tremendous.

<u>WEEK 4:</u> On Wednesday, I was very busy. I had 20 calls and only one no-show, including seven vouchers, three airport trips and three repeat customers. One of the passengers was a marine who was going to pick up a truck at a friend's house. He was really angry about a lot of things about the military. He told me that a Navy SEAL told him, after they had been drinking for a while, that he hasn't done a legitimate *military mission* in ten years. The marine also told me the Bush family backed a bank that funded Nazi Germany and Pat Tillman's death wasn't an accident. I looked up the Bush thing. According to Wikipedia, that association was rumored but wasn't true. As for the Pat Tillman thing, I really hope that isn't true.

I had an interesting weekend. I was having a bad morning on Saturday when I chased a call pretty close to Sun Lakes in Chandler. I brought this woman in her 70s or 80s to the Wild Horse Pass Casino. She was from New York City, so we talked about the east coast. When I told her I was writing this book, she told me what a waste of time it was and I should go back to school. I bit my tongue, because I thought that was incredibly rude. She kept talking about how important it is to get a good education. I agree with that, but until formal education ceases to be big business, my Master's Degree is on hold. When we got there, the fare was $26. She handed me a pile of bills. Then she said, "Have a party" and got out. I saw the twenty and figured it was the exact amount. I stuffed the bills in my shirt pocket and left. Twenty minutes later, I looked and saw one of the bills I thought was a one *was actually a $100 bill*. Excellent.

I also found out on this particular Saturday that some people are very protective of their stuff. I took this whiny little bastard to a party. When I got to his apartment, I asked if I could use his bathroom. He acted as if I had killed his parents. Then, when I dropped him off, the fare was $14.80. He gave me $15 and asked for the 20 cents. Prick.

Sunday started like it was going to be a disaster. I got up and was putting in my contact lenses. Unfortunately, one popped out and went into the overflow drain. Thinking quickly, I turned off the water. I took the drain apart and amazingly found the lens stuck in the u-bend.

WEEK 5: I got a repeat fare from a guy who was a shining example of how certain types of people can really be jackasses. He called me, asking me to run some errands. I had done this for him two other times. He asked for a flat rate, but he lied to me about where we were going, so he ran up a $120 fare, for which I only got half. His argument was I agreed to a certain fare so I had to stick with it. I really didn't have to, because he lied about the destination. The only reason I didn't punch him in the face was because $32 an hour is pretty good. I have never been good at sticking up for myself. The truly amazing thing is this fuck face had the balls to call me again, expecting another discount.

Sunday, I waited almost three hours for my first call. The only good fare I got all day came towards the end of the afternoon. It was from this dude who worked at the airport. He played basketball at Bridgewater West High School in New Jersey against my high school, Franklin Township. He was in the class of 1977. He remembered players from Franklin that I mentioned, especially Roy Hinson, who later had a solid NBA career. It is a small world.

When I went in to do my reconciliation, Amare told me I had gotten a photo enforcement camera ticket. This particular camera is half a mile after the speed limit drops from 65 to 55. The substitute safety guy told me I had to take an on-line safety course within four weeks to keep my cab. He also told me it would be $35. It turned out to be $165. I decided to not do it. I was pretty sure they don't have the right to order me to do anything like that. Since it never came up again, I have to presume I was correct.

WEEK 6: No matter how well or poorly my day would go I could rely on odd things happening. I was waiting for a call at QT 317 when a woman opened her car door and hit my cab. She looked at it, saw me looking at her, and started to walk away. I got out and said, "Hey, I think an apology is in order." She said, "For what?" What do you mean, for what, you hit my car with your door. She denied it. I said, "Are you kidding me? Of course you did." She harrumphed and walked into the store. When I finally got my next call, I got a flat tire on my way there. I was lucky, in that it was near the cage, so they came and fixed it quickly.

I also had a funny incident at a MARC center when I picked up this fellow. I told the woman at the desk I was there to pick up Bill Murray. She said, "What time is his appointment?" I said, "I don't know, I'm supposed to pick him up at 10:30." Then she asked, "What's his date of birth?" I DON'T KNOW, I'M FROM DISCOUNT CAB AND I'M HERE TO PICK HIM UP. She snapped out of it and said, "He'll be out in 5-10 minutes." What the hell?

As I'm waiting, an attractive woman walks up and asks me, "What have you got for me?" I know what the normal heterosexual answer was, but before I said anything, a dude in a white PT Cruiser yelled to her. He had supplies for the office. As she walked by, she said we had the same car and that confused her. I thought, "Let's see, I have a lime green Toyota Prius and he has a white PT Cruiser that doesn't have a speck of green. Whatever.

WEEK 7: I had a couple of strange thing happen this week. I was at QT 84. This woman with three kids and a bike begged me to bring them to the 17 and Northern. She yammered on with her really young kids about adult things, which I thought was weird. When we got to the destination, I realized she was the woman that bolted on a $10 fare about six months earlier. She sent her daughter to the apartment to get the money. I was ready to make one person stay with the bike, but they did that voluntarily. The girl brought back the fare and she also tipped me $6. Why did she rip me off for $10, but pay $45?

Another female passenger told me a disturbing tale. She said she spent three months in Tent City, despite the fact that she had problems with her legs to the point that a doctor was recommending to her that she amputate her right leg. As much as I detest the sheriff, I wondered how much of the truth she was omitting. It didn't keep me from feeling bad for her.

WEEK 8: On Monday, I had a seemingly stupid moment. I got a call to an Applebee's and the woman was loaded, AT 1:30 IN THE AFTERNOON. When I got her back to her hotel, she asked me to come up with her. I still don't know why I didn't.

On Tuesday, I had an opportunity to guarantee myself almost $30 per hour every Tuesday morning from 8:30 to 12:30. I got a fare, bringing this Ugandan from South Phoenix practically to Cave Creek, to a Huntington Learning Center. Since I was so far north, I decided to wait for his return call 90 minutes later. I was going to write as much of this book as I could, but another driver came by and we talked for more than an hour. His name pronounced my-ROOF (he pointed to the top of his car, and I laughed). We were discussing all kinds of driver issues. It was weird for me. It was probably the first at-length discussion I've had with another Discount driver, and despite his cordial nature, I didn't fully trust his motives.

Anyway, the return call came, and this guy told me his brother was involved with engineering on Air Force planes. He seemed to know a lot, although I found it hard to believe a lot of what he was telling me. It would have been great money had I been to have him as a regular. I was, unfortunately, never able to get his voucher again, no matter how hard I tried.

I also had one real disappointment occur later in the day. I just had a real good fare to the airport, and this French Canadian walks up to my cab and asks if I could take him to Mesa. I figured out it would have been a $55+ fare. Nobody would take him, because he needed two child seats. I still had three months to go and didn't want to create a problem for myself, so I turned him down.

On Friday, I picked up this young woman (Jackie) that worked at a homeless shelter. It would appear these well-intentioned places are no less prone to politics than any other business. She first went off on her boss who, according to her story, allows this chick to do her work and then would blame her if there were mistakes.

Ten minutes into the trip Jackie called her roommate. The roommate didn't put her base makeup in Jackie's purse, like she said she would. Jackie screamed at her for 10 minutes about a lack of reliability and loyalty. The roommate finally remembered she put the makeup in Jackie's backpack instead. Jackie must have realized she called her "best friend" every expletive known to mankind, because she didn't say one more word about the makeup.

Instead, she chose to read me a letter she wrote to her boss's supervisor, complaining about the way she is treated. She kept stammering over her words and I thought, "If you wrote that as poorly as you read it, YOU SHOULD BE FIRED." I also suggested she not put her co-workers on the spot to corroborate her story, but I got the impression she didn't understand what I was talking about.

I also picked up my hero midday on Sunday. I was in Scottsdale, and I got a call to a house in a gated community. The house was damn near impossible to find. When I did, my boy comes out with this beautiful blonde and he stands there making out with her. You could tell she was into him. After about five minutes, he finally starts walking towards the car. She runs after him and hugs him, wraps her leg around him and starts kissing him again. When she let him go, you could see the longing in her eyes. She blew a kiss at him as he got in and kept waving.

The first words out of his mouth were, "Do you believe how hot that chick was?" He had a shit-eating grin on his face and waved goodbye as we pulled away. He told me the story I expected to hear. She just got divorced, her husband was nasty, she took him for the house, etc. I said, "And you were there to comfort her, what a humanitarian you are." And we both cracked up.

His exploits were just beginning. We drove farther northeast, to this house to pick up another friend. She was staying at her friend's house; only she hates her friend's parents, so she needed to get out of there. We had trouble finding this house as well, but eventually, you can find a needle in the ocean if necessary.

After a few minutes, they came out. She looked completely different then the other woman, but she was smoking hot also. She was shorter, had red hair and a slim body with big fake boobs, which she was showing off prominently. She looked fabulous.

He remembered that his ex-wife misplaced the keys to his SUV, and we had to go back to his condo to look for them. We ended up making three stops for various supplies before heading back to Southern Scottsdale. Eventually, I would end up dropping them off at the Mondrian Hotel.

The three of us were laughing the whole time. They were talking about what they were going to do, and she said oral sex was out. He said, "Actually, that would be a good start." I laughed so hard I nearly drove off the road. They were even laughing at the fare. By the time we got to his condo, it was $60.

He couldn't find the keys, so he looked underneath the truck. No luck. He was so pissed he said, "Man there has to be a way to lock her (his ex-wife) out of the house," and I laughed again.

They ended up giving me $75 and as we pulled up to the hotel, we saw a sign for a bikini contest. Three of the contestants were standing outside the gate, looking fantastic. Then, one of them bent over and vomited into a garbage can. What a trip.

WEEK 9: This story is part of the reason drivers end up being anti-company. On Wednesday, I was way out in Avondale and saw this kid waving me down. He wanted a ride half a mile up the street, during which he told me his car was at the airport. Since I didn't want to stay in Avondale, I made a deal with him. I said I would take him to the airport for $15. It would have been $45. So he said sure. When we got to I-17, he changed his mind and asked to go to I-17 and Peoria.

After all the nonsense he told me about what a bad person he was, I figured he was up to no good. I told him he would have to pay $10 more to go to the new destination. He said OK. In the end, I charged his credit card three times. Of course, because they were within an hour of each other, the office wouldn't pay them until they confirmed them. And the lazy asses in the office didn't get to it for almost two weeks, so I lost $25 in the end. And, when I asked them about it, the response was: It was TOO BAD.

I also picked up a woman who used the name Pam Greer. She looked more like Rosey Greer, unfortunately. Plus, the dummy left her cell phone in the car, so I lost another hour returning it to her.

WEEK 10: This was the worst week financially and other-wise I had experienced to this point. Besides making almost no money, one of the most depressing things for me is to see a kid with Down's syndrome. I picked up two of those kids today, and I cried both times. They just never have a chance. I know there are plenty of kids that make something of their lives in spite of it, but that doesn't make it any less sad to me.

I also had two things scare me over the weekend.

Saturday, I took this guy to his bartending job in Scottsdale. Practically the first words out of his mouth are "Obama is the Antichrist." He yammered on about how SOUTH Korea was going to attack Hawaii. This guy was crazy. I decided it was in my best interests not to mention that I'm Jewish.

On Sunday, I was dropping a passenger off on a neighborhood street that wound around the Camelback Country Club. I got kind of lost within the confusing streets and found myself behind the green of one of the holes. I slowed down to watch the group play their shots. The guy hitting to the green over-clubbed so badly, his ball came right at me. It was coming RIGHT IN MY WINDOW. I put up my hand and hit it back towards the green. My hand stung for a long time, but I didn't hear anyone yell, so I just kept going.

WEEK 11: Tuesday was a strange day in a couple of ways. First, I was delayed three times for funeral processions. In Phoenix, a hearse is like an emergency vehicle, and you have to pull to the side of the road. I think they can ticket you if you don't. Motorcycle cops block intersections to allow the procession through. After the second one, I was like, "What the fuck." When the third one showed up, I had to laugh.

Among my last four fares, I took a guy to his "I'm an asshole because I got a DUI" class and back. Then I got a voucher bringing this couple home from the movies (I need to get one of those). Finally, I brought a deaf-mute home. This woman tried to communicate with me, so I handed her a pen and paper. I couldn't even understand her handwriting. When we got there, of course, the fucking guy wasn't there to pay me. She apologized over and over and over. I had to wait 25 minutes, but I wasn't leaving without my money.

She decided to show me pictures of her wedding. It was sweet, she looked so happy and she was so proud of the pictures. BUT YOU'RE NOT GETTING THIS RIDE FOR FREE. When the guy showed up, of course, he was $6 short. If I had run the meter the whole time, he would have been about $20 short.

WEEK 12: Just to give you an idea of how bad things were getting, I'm making no money and the fares are becoming boring. One interesting thing happened the whole week. On Wednesday, I was way the hell out there in Peoria near the complex the Padres and Mariners share and I got a call to the hotel across the street. I kept thinking an airport call would be great. I was at least 30 miles from home, and a paid trip home is the best.

Sure enough, I got the airport run. I brought two guys from a group of four to Southwest Airlines. One of the others was going to pay for the trip. He said to me, "How much is that, $25?" I looked at him like he was nuts. "Twenty Five Dollars, it will be at least $50, probably $60." He started complaining, but I stopped him. "Look, it's at least 25 miles, which means $55-$60." He said, "All right," and he paid me.

We got about five miles from the hotel, when one of the guys realized he had the keys of the fellow who paid. They decided the best thing to do was for the others to drive to where we were, so I pulled off the road. During the 15 minutes we waited, these two fellows told me why they were in Phoenix.

The other two people that were there were brother and sister. Her husband had apparently had some sort of a nervous break-down and gone berserk. He was even threatening suicide. The two fellows I was bringing to the airport were detectives brought in to find him and help with an intervention. I really don't know what happened, but that story was bizarre.

WEEK 13: This week seemed to be picking up where the last one left off. Finally on Friday, I was all over, but I had a solid day. I had fares in Mesa, Chandler, Phoenix, Glendale, Avondale and Peoria. Late in the day I ended up at a Goodwill store north of the 101, around Deer Valley. The person I picked up was a military guy from Ohio (I recognized the Cincinnati area code). I figured he would be an Ohio State fan, and he was, so we had that to talk about. After a while we started talking about the military.

I have learned that military people have very strong opinions, especially about military issues. This fellow was adamant about not wanting homosexuals or women in the military. He felt they create an unhealthy distraction. When one considers the primary function of any branch of the military, it's a fair point. I think it is possible that political correctness could undermine the effectiveness of the armed forces as it pertains to gender or sexual orientation. I think *that* element is completely ignored, but it shouldn't be. I have nothing but respect for the people that risk their lives for our country. Perhaps their input should count for something.

This pickup was particularly lucrative. After we got to his apartment, he asked me if I would be available to drive him to a bar in North Scottsdale in about 30 minutes. When he told me where he was going, I told him I would wait for him right there. He accommodated me by changing in half the time he said originally. I'm no genius, but this is another example of how being smart can make you some good money.

There was one fare that my odd mind gave me something at which to laugh. I saw this really old man's name was Ninfa. I asked him if his last name was Maniac. I'm not sure he got it.

WEEK 14: I thought this week was going to be better. In fact, it was until the weekend. On Monday, I brought a guy to the airport. After we got there and I told him about my book, compared me the author of the book "Fight Club." We have kept in touch, although I haven't bought the book like I said I would. Many books have been helpful to me in constructing this book.

On Thursday, I had the biggest disappointment, as fares go, of my career. I got a voucher sent to me worth $240 dollars. I was going to bring this kid home from the hospital, all the way to near Pine Top. The trip was 165 miles one way.

It turns out this guy wasn't ready to go. I actually spoke directly to him and he said he wanted to go now. The hospital wasn't ready to release him. I didn't know when this was going to happen, so I no-showed the call. If he had gone then, it would have taken about seven hours round trip, and I would driven 330 miles. During the rest of the day, I was about $50 short of the $240, but I only drove another 120 miles, so it might have been a wash. Man, I really can't wait to be finished with this shit.

WEEK 15: This was the worst week of my career. I cleared $45 dollars for the entire week. Now, I only drove for three hours on Thursday and, aside from doing my reconciliation, not at all on Sunday. I was ready to drive into the Tempe Town Lake I was so depressed.

On Wednesday, I had five consecutive passengers whose average age was 88 YEARS OLD. I also picked up this couple that loved the idea of this book. I drove them to a liquor store and back so they could get drunk. They asked me to join them. I thought that was nice of them.

The only satisfying thing about the entire week was when I helped a family move into a public assistance hotel. There were six of them, so I had two more people in the car than I should have, but they were so grateful, they tipped me $20.

WEEK 16: I was hoping the last four weeks would be a bit better, and it certainly started out that way. Monday's first fare was a couple going to the airport. I have brought them to the airport three other times. Then, I found my way to Gilbert and picked up this sexy-as-hell chick from San Diego. She made no bones about the fact that she wished she were back in San Diego. She looked pretty tacky, the first sign of a stripper. I was bringing her to traffic court, the second sign of a stripper.

I got an odd fare after that one. I picked up this fellow from

Thailand. He graduated from the University of Arkansas with a degree in mechanical engineering. So he did the logical thing and moved to Phoenix and opened a Thai Restaurant. I bet that doesn't happen very often.

By the day's end, I had made my way out to Glendale and then all the way back to Mesa and then to Chandler. I got a great call to end the day, but it wasn't without problems. Dispatch gave me the wrong address. It was for an Albertson's at Ray and McClintock. They gave me an address for the one at 48th and Ray, THAT DOESN'T EXIST ANYMORE. Anyway, I brought this woman from the Albertson's at which I found her and took her to her hotel and back. I got nearly $30 for it. Plus, she was fun.

Friday would have been my mother's 73rd birthday. This day is always tough for me. I really miss her. Plus, reverting to almost no money made ruined it some more. Three weeks to go.

WEEK 17: I came into this week again hoping that my fortunes would improve. They really didn't, at least until Friday.

I like hearing people's opinion on health care, because I really need an explanation as to why everyone doesn't feel that every American is entitled to proper health care. Around 2:30 PM on Thursday, I got a call, taking this hot redhead to the airport. She had a Philadelphia area code on her cell, so we talked about that for a while. She lived in New Hope, PA, which is across the river from Lambertville, NJ. I told her how I twice almost moved to Lambertville. Man, she was fabulous. Then we were talking about health care. I think she was saying that "socialized health care" wouldn't work "because the government would screw it up", although, in theory, it is a good idea. That, as a reason not to do it, is way better than "socialized medicine is the first step towards socialism as a political system", which is what Republicans try to make people think is the actual agenda of those in favor of "socialized medicine". Anyway, it was a good fare and a decent tip. She was hot too; did I mention that?

Friday was the best day for me in about two months. My first call was solid. It was taking a blind woman to a doctor. What was interesting, to me anyway, was she had a seeing-eye dog from "The Seeing Eye" in Morristown, NJ, the premier seeing-eye dog company in the United States, if not the world. She told me the difference between this place and others is that "Seeing Eye" places emphasis on the fact that the dog is a resource, more than just a pet. Her dog was beautiful and very efficient. She doubled the fare in a tip and asked for my card.

After that call, I started to have a bad feeling about the day. I didn't get a call for 90 minutes, and then that one was cancelled soon afterward. It turns out I shouldn't have worried. The call that was just cancelled was resent 20 minutes later. Thank god it was. I brought this woman that looked like Allyson Hannigan to a sleep clinic in Peoria. She complained about how much it was going to cost her and asked if I would give her a Medicare discount. Since it would come out of my pocket, the answer was no. She was interesting to talk to, although she was clearly sleepy and forgetful. She was very interested in hearing the stories I could tell her about prostitutes. I really don't have a lot of weird stories; I have just had prostitutes as fares many times. Plus, she gave me a sizable tip for someone who complained about money. This was among my top 20 highest payoffs.

Over the next couple of hours, I got a couple of vouchers, but nothing big. I chased a call to Surprise, approximately seven miles to zone 34. Trust me, this was WAY OUT THERE. It turned out to be a Holiday Inn, so I'm thinking airport run. It was better than that, all the way to Scottsdale. It was two guys from Pittsburgh, and they were snake hunters, meaning, they hunt rattlesnakes. After a while, I could hear the Pittsburgh accent on the one fellow. When I said it was a long haul, they asked me for an estimate. I told them between $80 and $100. The same guy said, "Jeez, cabs are getting expensive." One thing about Pittsburghers, they complain a lot about how things are expensive anywhere outside of Pittsburgh.

You can probably imagine the various subjects we talked about with that long of a trip. Gun control, healthcare, Obama, illegal immigrants, the Steelers, etc. When we got there, the meter said $94, so, as per our agreement, I charged them $80. They gave me $90. That worked out great.

I went home with the intention of going back out by about 4-5 PM. I didn't get out until 7, but at least I made it for a change. I ended up taking five fares in three hours, and all but one was very good money-wise.

One of the calls bothered me. It was this guy that bragged endlessly about his karaoke ability. I found it amusing when he told me his favorite song was "Baby Got Back". I'm pretty sure I've seen a better version of that by my buddies Patrick and Todd at Patrick's wedding.

He also told me about his ex-fiancé, who was in the hospital after having, in a three-month period, appendicitis, breast cancer and a disease that caused the removal of her uterus. I'm not sure of his circumstances, but he broke up with her, so I don't get the impression he is a very compassionate person. That's not a judgment, just an observation.

Saturday started in disastrous fashion. I couldn't book in, so I unplugged and re-plugged the fuse in the back. That didn't work after a couple of tries, so I went to the cage.

Imagine the logic of a 24-7-365 transportation company not having mechanics on site on weekends. I would maybe understand Sundays. They will do ANYTHING not to spend money that doesn't directly benefit them. Finally, the yard dog on duty told me to reconfigure the thing (in fairness, I should have thought of that) and that worked. Anyway, the fallout was I lost 90 minutes of time. I would have been position 1 in zone 81.

I was going to drive to Scottsdale to start, but then I changed my mind and went towards home. I got a call at an airport Radisson, taking a woman from Virginia to Old Town Scottsdale.

We talked about the military the whole time. Her husband was in the military, as were her brother and father. One of the reasons she wanted to go to Old Town was amazing.

She told me her father was killed in Scottsdale when she was very young. At first I thought it was a Wild West sort-of story, but it wasn't. Her father and another soldier were doing rounds and the other guy fell asleep at the wheel of the vehicle. He crashed into a utility pole, killing her father. Sadly, the driver has felt obligated to try to make it up to this woman's mother ever since, even though the mother isn't angry. Guilt is a horrible thing.

<u>WEEK 18:</u> I was lucky in that I got a lot more lucrative fares over last few weeks, so I started making more money.

On Tuesday, two sad cases found their way into my life. I brought this 16-year girl to counseling. Apparently, she's a cutter, one of those new-fangled disorders where she cuts herself as a form of self-punishment. It's really sad. Right after her, I picked up a couple at a trailer park to go to a Rotary Club for bingo. What was odd about this fare was the story the woman told me. She was in her 80s and she managed to get a DUI *when she wasn't driving*. At least she didn't go to Tent City.

On Friday, I picked up this young dude at the AM/PM near my home. He told me he wanted to go to North Phoenix to a friend's house, up at Union Hills and the 17. Again, it was a good news/bad news situation. It would be around $50, but I would end up 25 miles from home.

After 10 minutes, the girl called him and told him not to come over. Now what? He says, "Fuck her," and decides he wants to go to Scottsdale.

We reached the Fashion Square area and he told me he wanted to go to one particular bar. Unfortunately, it was closed. He told me to go to another bar, and that one was also closed. This was pretty strange. At that point, he just said he wanted to go home.

From that point, he started talking about sea scrolls and the bible and he completely lost me. I really was trying to keep up, but I couldn't. I don't know that anything he said was true. But, lucky me, it turned out he lives at Broadstone, which a two-iron from my front door. The fare was $75 and he gave me $90. I finished the journey a quarter of mile from where it started. YES.

On Saturday, I decided to drive at night, which turned out to be the right decision. At about 6 PM I picked up four extremely attractive blondes. The thing that really stuck in my mind was how polite they were. They wanted to know when my book was coming out, so I gave them my phone number and said to call around New Year's.

I got calls like this the rest of the night, and I kept getting solid payoffs. The last two fares were funny. The first fare was a couple at a bar on Southern in Mesa. He dragged her out of the bar and threw her into the back seat. After we got going, I heard her slur, "I want to suck your cock." I was thinking, cool. She started to go down on him, but he whispered something to her and she stopped. Then I heard her say, "We better get home soon." Shit. It was a short trip.

I picked up my last fare at the same place I dropped off the four hot chicks four hours ago. I ended up taking a couple down to Chandler, near Pecos and Dobson. Fortunately, the girl decided to vomit BEFORE she got in the cab. That saved me the cost of cleaning the cab. I brought them home without much incident, but she had to keep rolling down the window, because she thought she was going to puke again. It was a good fare, so I had another really good day.

On Sunday, late in the morning, I got a call at a hotel near my apartment. It was this Asian woman. She gave me an address close to the hotel and I dropped her off at a house and she said the guy there would pay for it. I thought, "She's a hooker." I never got her name, so on my log, for her name, I wrote, "Some Asian Hooker". She asked me to pick her up later, and asked for my number. I said OK and forgot about it.

I took two more short fares, and then I chased a call in zone 80. It was a guy that played football at Appalachian State. He needed to go to a Bashas' 10 miles away to buy some things and return home. By the time we got back, it was nearly a $50 fare.

Thirty seconds after I dropped him off, that hooker called me to bring her to Scottsdale. She kept asking me for discounts. I finally said, "Why, what's in it for me?" I was hoping she would try to bluff me, because I would have pulled off the road right there. But, she played dumb and said, "What do you mean?" I just said, "Look, if I give you a discount, it comes out of my pocket." That was the end of it. I didn't get a tip, but the last two fares ended up being 65% of my billing for the day. After she got out, as I was filling out my log, in the name column, I wrote, "Same Asian Hooker".

WEEK 19: The last week of 133 straight days started off with a $50 voucher. I wanted to cry about seven hours later, because I only billed about $50 during that time period. I had four no-shows and a bunch of small fares.

The afternoon bailed me out with six solid fares, including the last two, both of which went to the airport. I increased my output by 160% in the last seven hours. What a fucked-up job.

The rest of the week leading up to my last day was pretty mundane. I had some good fares, but nothing really interesting happened until the last day.

On Saturday, I decided to take it easy. I didn't even make my lease. In the morning, I drove a chick around so she could get her meth addiction medication. She had three kids; it was sad. Later, I took three Welsh disc jockeys to their hotel. They were a lot of fun and gave me a really good tip. I went home to watch the Ohio State football opener, than I went to the Harry Potter meet-up group and quit for the day.

My Last Day as a Cab Driver ━━━━━━━━━

The greatest fear I had, as my career as a cab driver was ending, was something stupid happening to me, like a robbery, accident or traffic violation. I kept thinking that this type of thing would happen on my last day. Not only didn't anything bad happen, but things couldn't have gone better.

I chose not to drive Saturday night, so I needed $150 to clear $500 for the week. I got in the cab around 6:30 AM. My first call came about 25 minutes later, to the Lone Butte Casino. I almost turned down the call, since Lone Butte is the only thing in zone 392, and 50% of the calls end up being no-shows. I took it, and the person was there, a woman who barely spoke English who wanted to go to the Yaqui Indian reservation in Guadalupe. She didn't tip me (because she "only had $20"), but it was a decent fare.

I went back to zone 81 and got another fare shortly afterward. I brought a woman from Georgia to a hotel from some dude's condo. She didn't say much, which was fine because her accent annoyed me. It was another decent fare, with a good tip.

As I said, I was paranoid about the way things were going to go, but it was like I took Felix Felicis (The liquid luck potion from Harry Potter). I saw a fare 20 miles away, which I took after a slight hesitation. They were out in East Gilbert at Power and the 202, a good-looking couple, a sexy blonde and her boyfriend. They wanted to go retrieve her truck, which was over by the stadium where the Diamondbacks play.

If you know Phoenix, you know this trip was quite a haul, which was great for me. Not only was the fare enormous, but also she gave me a phenomenal tip. They got a kick out of the stories I told them about my experiences on the job. When we finally got there, she was afraid her truck was not going to be there, because they didn't park in a "nice area". That wasn't a problem, because it was right where they left it.

I ended up in a zone in which I sure I would get another fare pretty quickly and I did. But not before I nearly lived out a self-fulfilling prophecy.

I turned onto First Avenue and into a massive construction zone. That street is odd anyway, because it merges and separates with Central, but with the barriers it was that much more confusing. I went the wrong way on a one-way street. It took me about five seconds to realize it, when I saw the truck COMING RIGHT AT ME. There was a left-hand turn right there, so I was able to get out of harm's way. But I made another left, turning up a street where a cop was sitting at an intersection. I thought this officer saw me going the wrong way. I decided not to do anything suspicious, and drove right towards him. Either he didn't see it, or he decided no harm, no foul, because he didn't move. After I drove through that intersection, he left his spot. Incredibly, I was making my way to the Circle K on Seventh Street and Buckeye, and I ran into the SAME POLICE CAR. Again, nothing happened, but I sure as hell thought something would.

I was at the Circle K, and I chased a fare two zones over. That was another smart move, because it was a couple of women going to the airport. They were intrigued when I told them A) this was my last day and B) I was writing a book about my experiences. They were going to New York, so that was another topic of conversation. It was a short fare as airport trips go; they gave me a $20 and said keep the change.

I was only $20 from my final day's goal at 10 AM. After waiting at QT 85 for about 45 minutes, I decided to go back to home base. One thing that always seemed to happen when I received calls while moving was that the calls came to me just late enough that I'd miss the turn-off that I needed to use. I always ended up driving two to four miles further than I needed to. That didn't happen today because I had the Midas touch. This call came just as I approached the turn-off for Baseline Road, 500 yards from the hotel to which I was sent.

The woman wanted to go to Tatum and Bell, another huge fare. This trip might have been a tough call, because the freeway was certainly faster but slightly more expensive. I decided to use the freeway and she didn't object. She wasn't sure of where the apartment complex was located, so I dropped her off at a McDonald's, which turned out to be 400 yards from where she wanted to go. The fare was great and I got a 15% tip. What a day!

I waited at the McDonald's for 20 minutes and saw a call a couple of zones over, but when I realized it was 10 miles away, I declined it. When I didn't get a call for another hour, it appeared that I had made the much-anticipated blunder.

Not really. I decided to move to South Scottsdale, where I got two HHVs within the first hour. Generally, these will be old people going to the supermarket or the pharmacy, which end up being the minimum or a dollar more. But not this day! There was a $10 maximum pay out, and they both were far enough to reach it.

I waited about 30 minutes for the next call. It was a charming young woman, probably 19-21, who was going to work at the Scottsdale Fashion Square. She had a very distinctive, high-pitched voice, so I remembered that I had her as a fare once before. She was just adorable and she reminded me of someone, but I couldn't figure out exactly who. She still had a Michigan area code on her cell and she told me she was going back there, because she really had had enough of Phoenix, and the "Scottsdale Attitude" in particular. I couldn't blame her, as there are certainly a lot of "entitled" people living in Scottsdale. I congratulated her on the decision to go where she will feel more comfortable. At least she won't regret not trying something different. It was a decent fare with a good tip.

That shopping mall is in a bad channel spot, so running credit or debit cards is difficult. I gave her a manual copy of the transaction, with the understanding I would run the card when I got to the better spot. It came up declined three times. I just shook my head and thought, "I can't believe that sweet kid would screw me". I still had her cell phone number, so I sent her a text message explaining what happened. She responded quickly, and then called me when she noticed one of the numbers I had written was incorrect. I sent her a return text, thanking her "for putting up with my stupidity". Hey, in this situation, my being wrong was WAY better than being right. This girl was just too nice to be shady.

It was about 3 PM when I got that straightened out. My friend was picking me up at the cage at around 5 PM, so I thought, "I will wait until 3:45. If I get a call by then, I'll take it. Otherwise, I'll turn the car in, about $84 past my goal. I win either way.

But I got what would prove to be my final fare at 3:40 PM, less than a half a mile from where I was. I got to the house, and of course, it was a phenomenal looking woman, who bartended at an Irish pub in Tempe. She was from Boston, which is almost always obvious in the first 15 seconds because of the accent. She also seemed to be interested in the book. I ended up driving her less than two miles from the cage, and she gave me $22 on a $12 fare. What a goof.

As always, Alistair and Dorothy were at the cage, checking people out. I really liked checking out with Archie, because he gets through it so fast. His ears must have been burning, because he said, "When are you coming back, if ever?" I lied and said "in three weeks".

I also had one last little positive surprise. I had a voucher from the previous week that was 10 miles short of what it should have been. Incredibly, I was paid the difference! I'M THE GREATEST CAB DRIVER, EVER!

CHAPTER **11**

Other Stuff

Downtime ━━━━━━━━━━━━━━━━━━━━━━━━━━━━

One of unique things about the driving a cab is that you do a whole lot of nothing as much, if not more, than the time you are doing your job. Sitting in a car 12-16 hours per day can wreak havoc on both your body and your mind. You really don't have a lot of control over that, especially in Phoenix. In New York, most fares are people waving down cabs on the street. You can drive around and you will probably get a fare every five minutes. Out of every hundred fares I took, maybe two were people flagging me down New York City style. In Phoenix, almost every call came from dispatch, so you have to play the waiting game.

Most drivers have their own way of dealing with the boredom. I'm pretty sure I did the common things. I did a lot of reading, and I'm not that much of a reader. There are only four types of books I read. Fact-based books, like textbooks are the only books I like to read that don't have anything to do with entertainment. For example, I read the dictionary a lot. I also have a ton of biographies written by former and current professional wrestlers. I love reading about the history of the mat sport, especially from wrestlers before the 1990's. In fact, I will read anything about sports, college or professional.

I am especially interested in sports history. I know as much as anyone could, and at 47, my memory is still outstanding.

The only fiction I care for is Harry Potter. I'm trying to figure out why it struck such a nerve with me, but I have read all seven books over and over. I am in a Harry Potter meet-up group, just to give you an idea of how serious I am about it.

More than anything else, I would say that the way I passed the time most often was to look up trivia. Having a device that allows you to play around on the Internet when you're not on your regular computer is a very handy thing to have when you have a lot of time to kill. I love trivia, and I am constantly looking up information about people, history, etc. The following pages will give you an idea of some of the things I would do to pass the time while waiting for calls.

Photo Enforcement Cameras ━━━━━━━━━━━━━

The most obvious example of "creative taxation" that I've ever seen is the use of photo enforcement cameras located all over the Valley. Under the guise of safety, these cameras take pictures of people going "faster than the posted speed limit." As a public service, I have listed all of the cameras of which I became aware as a cab driver, starting with the list of stationery camera locations.

- Tempe at the intersection of Broadway and 48th
- Tempe at the intersection of Broadway and Rural
- Tempe at the intersection of Elliot and Kyrene
- Tempe at the intersection of Southern and McClintock
- Tempe at the intersection of Guadalupe and McClintock
- Tempe at the intersection of Rio Salado and McClintock
- Tempe at the intersection of Mill and Southern

- Tempe at the intersection of Ray and Rural
- Tempe at the intersection of University and Rural
- Tempe at the intersection of Warner and Rural
- Tempe at the intersection of University and McClintock
- Tempe at the intersection of Southern and Rural
- Gilbert at the intersection of Pecos and South Santan Village Parkway
- Gilbert at the intersection of Guadalupe and Val Vista
- Gilbert at the intersection of Baseline and Gilbert
- Avondale at the intersection of Van Buren and Dysart
- Avondale at the intersection of McDowell and Dysart
- Glendale at the intersection of Union Hills and Loop 101
- Glendale at the intersection of Peoria and 59th Avenue
- Peoria at the intersection of Thunderbird and 75th Avenue
- Peoria at the intersection of Thunderbird and 83rd Avenue
- Peoria at the intersection of Union Hills and 83rd Avenue
- Peoria at the intersection of Bell and 91st Avenue
- Paradise Valley at the intersection of Lincoln and Mockingbird
- Paradise Valley at the intersection of Lincoln and Tatum
- Paradise Valley at the intersection of McDonald and Tatum
- Phoenix at the intersection of Northern and 19th Avenue
- Phoenix at the intersection of Thunderbird and 19th Avenue
- Phoenix at the intersection of McDowell and 32nd Street
- Phoenix at the intersection of McDowell and 35th Avenue
- Phoenix at the intersection of Dunlap and 35th Avenue
- Phoenix at the intersection of Pecos and 40th Street
- Phoenix at the intersection of McDowell and 67th Avenue
- Phoenix at the intersection of Glendale and Seventh Avenue
- Phoenix at the intersection of Bell and Seventh Street
- Phoenix at the intersection of Northern and Seventh Street

- Phoenix at the intersection of Greenway and Cave Creek
- Phoenix at the intersection of Dunlap and I-17
- Phoenix at the intersection of Dunlap and 21st Street
- Phoenix at the intersection of Glendale and 27th Avenue
- Scottsdale at the intersection of McDonald and Hayden
- Scottsdale at the intersection of McDowell and Hayden
- Scottsdale at the intersection of Shea and Hayden
- Scottsdale at the intersection of Indian School and Hayden
- Scottsdale at the intersection of McCormick Parkway and Hayden
- Scottsdale at the intersection of Shea and Scottsdale
- Scottsdale at the intersection of McDowell and Scottsdale
- Scottsdale at the intersection of Frank Lloyd Wright and Scottsdale
- Scottsdale at the intersection of Cactus and Scottsdale
- Scottsdale at the intersection of Thomas and Scottsdale
- Scottsdale at the intersection of Doubletree and Scottsdale
- Scottsdale at the intersection of Shea and 90th Street
- Scottsdale at the intersection of Shea and 92nd Street
- Scottsdale at the intersection of Camelback and 68th Street
- Mesa at the intersection of Guadalupe and Alma School
- Mesa at the intersection of Southern and Alma School
- Mesa at the intersection of Broadway and Mesa
- Mesa at the intersection of Broadway and Stapley
- Mesa at the intersection of Southern and Country Club
- Mesa at the intersection of University and Country Club
- Mesa at the intersection of Broadway and Dobson
- Mesa at the intersection of Southern and Dobson
- Mesa at the intersection of McKellips and Gilbert
- Mesa at the intersection of Southern and Gilbert
- Mesa at the intersection of Brown and Higley

- Mesa at the intersection of Main and Power
- Mesa at the intersection of Main and Stapley
- Mesa at the intersection of Southern and Power
- Mesa at the intersection of Southern and Longmore
- Mesa at the intersection of Southern and Mesa
- Mesa at the intersection of Southern and Stapley
- Mesa at the intersection of University and Lindsey
- Mesa at the intersection of University and Mesa
- Mesa at the intersection of University and Stapley
- Mesa at the intersection of Baseline and Power
- Mesa at the intersection of Hampton and Power
- Mesa at the intersection of Baseline and Ellsworth
- Mesa at the intersection of McDowell and 202 Loop
- I-10 east bound at mile 117 at Watson
- I-10 east bound at mile 114 at Miller
- I-10 east bound at mile 109 at 287th
- I-10 east bound at mile 146 at 16th Street
- I-10 east bound at mile 144 at 15th Avenue
- I-10 east bound at mile 142 at 31st Avenue
- I-10 east bound at mile 140 at 43rd Avenue
- I-10 east bound at mile 138 at 59th Avenue
- I-10 west bound at mile 134 at 91st Avenue
- I-10 west bound at mile 136 at 75th Avenue
- I-10 west bound at mile 138 at 59th Avenue
- I-10 west bound at mile 144 at 15th Avenue
- I-10 west bound at mile 146 at 16th Street
- I-10 west bound at mile 149 at Buckeye Road
- I-10 west bound at mile 150 at 24th Street
- I-10 west bound at mile 152 at 40th Street
- State Route 51 south bound at Mile Two at Thomas
- State Route 51 south bound at Mile Three at Highland
- State Route 51 south bound at Mile Five at Bethany Home
- I-17 south bound at Bethany Home

- I-17 south bound at Indian School
- I-17 south bound at 12th Street
- I-17 south bound at 15th Avenue
- I-17 north bound at Thunderbird
- I-17 north bound at Bell
- US 60-west bound at Alma School
- US 60-west bound at Mesa
- US 60-west bound at Gilbert Road
- Loop 101 east bound at 75th Avenue
- Loop 101 east bound at 59th Avenue
- Loop 101 east bound at 35th Avenue
- Loop 101 south bound at McDowell
- Loop 101 south bound at Indian School
- Loop 101 south bound at Bethany Home
- Loop 101 south bound at Olive
- Loop 101 north bound at Glendale

The following are locations of the mobile enforcement cameras that I have seen during my time as a cab driver. Some locations are used at least every month and others are used less frequently.

- I-10 east bound under overpass at Ray Road
- I-10 east bound under overpass at Warner Road
- I-10 east bound under overpass at Chandler Road
- I-10 east bound under HOV lane off ramp at US 60
- I-10 westbound under overpass at Ray Road
- I-10 westbound under overpass at Warner Road
- I-10 westbound under overpass at Chandler Road
- I-10 west bound under HOV lane off ramp at US 60
- I-10 westbound under overpass at Elliot Road
- Loop 202 east bound under overpass at Kyrene Road
- North of intersection Indian School and 15th Avenue
- South of intersection at Chandler and Alma School

- East of intersection at Warner and Rural
- Loop 101 North at the top of the on ramp from US 60
- East of intersection at Indian School and Scottsdale
- East of intersection at Thomas and 19th Avenue
- West of intersection at University and Stapley
- West of intersection at University and Extension
- South of intersection at 91st avenue and Indian School
- South of intersection at 48th street and Broadway
- West of intersection at Rural and Broadway
- 51 South of Cactus
- 51 South of 32nd Street

Looking for Stars

A fun game to play while drinking at a bar is called "Looking for Stars". There is always at least five people at a crowded bar who looks like someone who is famous. I have been able to play this game many times with passengers.

Quite often, I would get calls to pick people up from the supermarket. It never occurred to me that so many people would do this, but, hey, you have to eat. I was called to a Safeway to pick up a guy named Greg. When I pulled up, this hulking dude was waiting. I helped him put the stuff in the car, and noticed a lot of frozen dinners, two cases of tonic water and six half gallons of Wolfschmidt's Gin. I guess I know what he does for fun.

We started talking on the way. But when he started talking, I thought it was King Ralph. He had that big, bellowing laugh and a very deep voice. I was thinking maybe if I said something to make him happy, he might go "Yabba Dabba Doo." That's how much he sounded like John Goodman. When I looked at him, I realized that he looked like John Goodman, too. I thought about telling him that, but then I'm not sure he would have considered that a compliment, so I kept it to myself. Of course, all kinds of John Goodman things started popping in my head, like Coach

Harris from "Revenge of the Nerds", being married to Roseanne Barr, etc.

The follow is a list of other known people whose twin (or at least a reasonable facsimile) has been passenger of mine. If there is a "@" next to consecutive names, that means the same person looked like both famous people:

Herschel Walker
Forest Whitaker
Billy Blanks (the Tai Bo guy)
Terry Funk
Orlando Pace
Lisa Bonet
James Laurinaitis
Chris Chelios
Bill Cartwright
Holly Robinson
Judge Reinhold
Eric Byrnes
Pat Buchanan
Al Franken
Jenny Garth
Bonnie Raitt
Wendy Malik
Brett Favre
Tammy Faye Baker
Monica Lewinsky
Pete Carroll
Truman Capote (a Discount Cab driver)
George Stephanopoulos
George Carlin
Candice Bergen
The Marlboro Man (cab driver)
A. Wilfred Brimley

The Brooklyn Brawler, Steve Lombardi
Rosie Perez (thankfully, she didn't sound like Rosie Perez)
Stephanie McMahon
Chi Chi Rodriguez
Jeff Van Gundy
Jerome Bettis
Meryl Streep
Hilary Duff
Jason Biggs
The Cruiser from Stripes
Bob Denver
Don Beard (the drummer from ZZ Top)
Jon Gruden
Richard Dysart (LA Law)
Russell Crowe
Pink
Amy Smart
Vivica A. Fox
Adam West
Jamie Pressley @
Jessica Simpson @
Sara Gilbert
James Van Der Beek
Diana Taurasi
Iman @
Holly Robinson @
Fred Couples
Zelda Rubenstein
Chris Spielman
John Clayton
Mark Messier
Sarah Jessica Parker@
Jennifer Aniston @
Jerry O'Connell

Brooke Hogan
Stephon Marbury
Bernie Williams
Rush Limbaugh
Carla Gugino
John Wayne Bobbitt

As an addendum to this list, I am listing passengers who had the same name as a famous person, and rode in my cab. They include:

Spencer Davis
Gil Hodges
Peter Boyle
Pam Greer
Gisele McKenzie
Michael Geffen
Bill Murray
Cindy Williams
Jesse Helm
Sam Elliot
Joe Thornton
Cindy Brady
Reggie Jackson

Milestones

Most Consecutive days driven: 125
Most QT stops in one day: 9
Lowest Fare: $4
Biggest Fare: $148
Most fares in a day: 22
Most hours worked in a Day: 18
Most money billed in a day (at least 8 hours): $550.75

Least money billed in a day (at least 8 hours): $67.70
Most bathroom trips in a day: 12
Most deuces in a day: 5
Most miles driven in a day: 364
Most miles driven in a week: 1658
Most consecutive No-Shows: 4
Most no-shows in one day: 7
Most consecutive fares of $20+: 8
Most consecutive minimum fares: 6
Longest trip one-way: 75 miles
Most stops during one fare: 6
Biggest Fare I didn't get: $240
Biggest tip: $50
Biggest percentage tip (of at least $10): 200%
Highest average fare in a day: $43.00
Lowest average fare in a day: $8.46
Most passengers who vomited in a day: 2
Most times a stripper has been a fare in a day: 3
Most strippers total in a day: 5
Most $80+ fares in a day: 3
Longest wait during a fare: 32 minutes
Most airport runs in a day: 5
Earliest I woke up to pickup fare: 2:48 AM
Longest wait between fares: 3 hours and 14 minutes
Longest wait for first fare of the day: 2 hours and 23 minutes
Most times transporting same person: 26
Most people in a cab at one time: 8
Total shifts driven: 360
Total fares received: 4716
Total % of fares that paid cash: 44.7 (2108)
Total % of fares that paid with a credit card: 18.6 (877)
Total % of fares that paid with a HHV: 7.8 (368)
Total % of fares that paid with Electronic voucher: 16.7 (788)
Total % of fares that no-showed: 12.2 (575)

Total % of fares that were flags: 1.1 (52)
Average Miles in a day: 158
Accidents I saw: 4
Accidents I was involved in: 0
Subpoenas given to testify from an accident: 1
Flat Tires: 2
Radar tickets: 2
Fights with passengers: 0
Fights with other drivers: 1 (sort of)
Total number of cabs driven: 14
Total airport drop offs: 276
Total airport pick-ups: 1
Number of times I helped passengers move: 17
Number of times I washed a cab: 243
Number of countries from which I had fares: 42
Number of times I had an equipment failure: 6

Top Ten Lists

I love Top Ten lists! This chapter is a series of them, related mainly to things about my experiences with, and opinions of, the cab industry, the city of Phoenix and its suburbs, and my own thoughts and personality.

Top Ten Topics Of Discussion With Passengers

10. <u>Construction:</u> There is so much construction going on ALL THE TIME. It is incredibly frustrating to me, and it has slowed down passengers of mine on many occasions.

9. <u>Religion:</u> I had at least 20 passengers ask me if I have "Taken the Lord Jesus Christ as my savior." I haven't, but if they have, good for them. I freely discuss that my family is of the Jewish faith, although I do not practice it. Ohio State football is my religion.

8. <u>Politics:</u> Another taboo of conversation, I have no trouble debating political opinions or affiliation with passengers. In Phoenix, gun control is always a lively topic, along with the president and health care. I generally change the subject if the discussion gets too heated.

7. <u>Being A Cab Driver:</u> A lot of people are interested in this job. I don't think it's because they really want to drive a cab but more out of curiosity. I think people just like to show off how "smart" they are about the business by asking me questions about the cost of my lease.

6. <u>From Where The Passenger Comes:</u> It seems like at least 95% of the people that live here are NOT from here.

5. <u>The Toyota Prius:</u> Plenty of people asked me how I liked driving the Prius. It was a little different than a normal car, but I acclimated to it quickly. It is NOT as ecologically friendly as the car companies would have you believe. The battery is so big and toxic that disposing of it pollutes the earth as much as a regular engine.

4. <u>This Book:</u> The inspiration for writing this book came mostly from people telling me that I should write a book about my experiences driving a cab.

3. <u>Gas Prices:</u> The price of gas went from $3 to $4.25 to $1.45 to $2.65 during my 15 months as a cab driver. What a load of crap!

2. <u>Joe Arpaio:</u> Since anywhere from 5%-25% of my passengers are people who lost their licenses to DUI's, it shouldn't surprise you to know "The Sheriff" is in the news all the time out here. Plus, he wants to be in the news. He does have his share of supporters.

And my number one topic of discussion with passengers:

1. <u>Their Illnesses:</u> I have carted around hundreds of people with every imaginable disease, injury and/or mental illness. Insurance pays for the transportation most of time. The shear number of people and their myriad of afflictions were so over-

whelming that I cried almost every day for the first two months I drove.

Top Ten Things I Say When I'm In The Cab Alone ━━━━━━

10. <u>Could I PLEASE Get A Call:</u> I'm pretty impatient, generally speaking, but if I were forced to wait for more than 30 minutes, I would yell at the MDT. Three hours and 14 minutes is the longest I ever waited without a fare.

9. <u>Can I Go Two Miles without Construction?</u> The entire region is perpetually under construction, and Gilbert, Mesa and Central Phoenix always seemed to be the worst areas.

8. <u>Look At That Little Hooker:</u> There are so many beautiful women of all shapes and sizes in Phoenix. Since I have a lot of downtime, girl watching was a fun pastime.

7. <u>Hey Roger, Could You Please Fix The Signal:</u> There are so many spots where I lose the GPS. This is one of my main problems with Discount Cab; they won't improve what they have, because it doesn't directly benefit them.

6. <u>Get Out Of My Way:</u> As I said, I am very impatient, especially when going to a fare. So many people drive slowly on the surface roads, some at a snail-like pace.

5. <u>My God, These Fucking Lights:</u> My dad used to get really frustrated at the traffic signals in Philadelphia. Well, Philly has nothing on the Valley. I timed a two-mile trip at 11:47 one day, and it wasn't even rush hour!

4. <u>I Will Kill Myself Now:</u> I have little control over many things that cost me money. Those types of things anger me to the point that I fear for my physical health. My reactions can appear to be a little overdramatic, but that's just me.

3. <u>Oh Sure, But You Can Send Me Five Miles For A $6 Voucher:</u> Part of my strategy was to chase calls to certain zones and chase credit card calls. Since my C-Book screen was about 30 seconds behind, I wouldn't get 90% of my C-Book attempts. One day, I

got six consecutive minimum vouchers and I didn't C-Book any of them.

2. <u>Look At Those Tits. That's Awesome:</u> What can I tell you? I love boobs.

And the number one thing I say when I am in the car alone is:

1. <u>FUCK YOU</u>

Top Ten Things I Say When Someone Is In The Cab ━━━━

I do not only talk to myself. I am a great conversationalist. I am positive half the people who get into my cab are looking for someone to talk to, and I am only too happy to oblige.

10. <u>I Would Prefer It If You Didn't:</u> I didn't get a lot of smokers in my cab. If someone asked if they could light up, I made them aware I don't like smoking in my cab. 95% respected my wishes.

9. <u>Where Are You Headed?</u> Unless it's a voucher, drivers are almost never informed about passengers' destinations by dispatch. For whatever reason, this really puzzles some people.

8. <u>Which Airline Are You Going To?</u> After a while, I learned which airlines were at which terminal. That made it a lot easier for me, because passengers don't always know the terminals either.

7. <u>I'm Used To Smaller Cars Anyway:</u> I was asked almost every day whether I liked the Prius, because so many people are considering buying it. I have always driven sedans.

6. <u>Cash Or Credit:</u> Taking credit cards is a smart move. But, the signal is weak in certain places. For example, I learned to always pull to the side and run a credit card before dropping a passenger off at Terminal Four, where the drop-off area is enclosed. It was important to know this; I would run the credit card and get paid *before* going into the enclosed area.

5. <u>It's Not As Ecologically Friendly As You Might Think:</u> The battery in the Prius, aside from costing more than $6000, is an

environmental hazard. It is very toxic. In my opinion, it's just another way to sell a car.

4. <u>Where Are You From?</u> Almost nobody that lives here is from here, so this is a great question to start a conversation.

3. <u>New Jersey, About 10 Miles North Of Princeton University:</u> People can almost always tell I'm not from here, and the presumption is that I'm from the east coast. Most people associate a Jersey accent with the Sopranos, so in that respect, I don't have a Jersey accent. However, at least 40 people asked me if I was from New Jersey before I told them I was, so there must be something to the way I speak. Among other things, I've been told I speak really fast and that I am really blunt. I even had a fare tell me I LOOKED like I was from New Jersey. *What the hell does that mean?*

2. <u>You Must Get (???) All Of The Time:</u> I loved playing "Looking for Stars", and I said this to passengers all of the time. I had many look-alike passengers. One woman even looked like Sarah Jessica Parker from one profile and Jennifer Aniston from the other.

And the number one thing I say with someone in the cab is:

1. <u>How Are You?</u> Being polite can go a long way. This question would sometimes open up a can of worms that I regretted opening.

Top Ten Ways That Passengers Aggravated Me

I would be the first to admit to a low level of tolerance for certain people. For example, I was watching a Jets game at a particular bar. There was a guy sitting next to me, and when he realized I was a Jets fan, he wouldn't stop talking to me. I tried to "tell" him to leave me alone, but he clearly couldn't take a hint. I was very close to slugging him. This list is the reasonable and (perhaps) unreasonable things that would bother me.

10. <u>Literally Asking For Change:</u> I almost always had a lot of coin change with me. But to me, the absolute minimum a passenger can do for a driver is to say, "Keep the change." Patrick Kane, the star forward of the Chicago Black Hawks, nearly got jail time over 20 cents with a cabbie.

9. <u>Talking On Their Cell For The Whole Trip:</u> This, in and of itself, is pretty inconsiderate, but more importantly, I'm not a mind reader. If I need you to direct me, it helps if you pay attention.

8. <u>Smelling Bad:</u> I know if I smell bad, there is a good chance the passenger will call in to complain. Unfortunately, it doesn't go both ways.

7. <u>Asking Me To Surf Radio Stations:</u> This is a personal problem I have. We were told to do what ever the passenger wants. But I generally didn't have the radio on, except when I was alone in the cab. I didn't mind turning the radio on, but if a person doesn't know what station they want, it was just a way for them to exert control over me, and that bothered me.

6. <u>Wanting Me To Turn The Meter Off:</u> Cab drivers are paid for distance AND time. I had one occasion where a person tried to save $2 by calling me back after they ran their errand and I refused to come back for them. I heard they registered a complaint, but the company must have told them I wasn't obligated to come back for them.

5. <u>Asking For Discounts:</u> It's not that I'm not a nice guy and wouldn't have, at times, liked to cut certain people a break, but the problem was that ANY discount costs me money.

4. <u>Complaining About The Cost:</u> I quickly learned that this complaint was merely a ploy in hopes of talking me into offering a discount. My standard response became, "If you don't want to pay the fare then find another way to go."

3. <u>Not Tipping When I Carry Groceries:</u> It is pretty rude to have someone do work for you, and not pay him or her for the work.

2. <u>Not Having Enough Money:</u> I learned from experience

that, most of the time, this was done on purpose. There are real some weasels out there.

And the number one way passengers aggravated me was:

1. Rudeness: I have always felt lucky that only one out of maybe 500 passengers was rude to me for no real reason. I treated people with respect and it should be reciprocated.

Top Ten Places People Are Going When They Hire A Cab ━━━━━

I am of the opinion that the cab industry is recession proof, because the use of taxis is necessity-based. I'm guessing that in good times or bad, this list is consistent.

10. Wal-Mart: There are tons of people that don't have much that shop at Wal-Mart. A C-Book call in zone 363 is a call to the Wal-Mart at Pecos and Arizona 90% of the time.

9. Supermarket: There are plenty of older people that can't drive that need a way to get their stuff home.

8. MVD: If you drive without proper documentation here, you might as well have strangled a puppy. I had a lot of fares to and from the MVD so people could retrieve their driving privileges. Dozens of fares told me their licenses were suspended without their knowledge.

7. Emergencies: There are many situations that qualify, and not just health issues. Car won't start, missed a bus, car is in the shop, etc.

6. Mental Health Care Appointments: In an average week, I had at least five fares taking people to these agencies.

5. Physical Health Care Appointment: I took an average of 10 pregnant women to an OB-GYN every month. Also, there are chiropractors all over the Valley including Emergency Chiropractic, which pays for transportation. These are only a couple of examples.

4. Work: A large number of people have lost driving

privileges to DUI's, and they have to get to work somehow. Public transportation is not that great in the Valley.

    3. <u>Retrieving A Car:</u> The first half of every Saturday and Sunday was spent taking people to their cars after a night out drinking. Lots of people get their cars towed too, for some reason or another.

    2. <u>Going To Bars:</u> As one passenger told me, a good theory to live by is: if you don't drive your car to a bar, you can't drive it back.

    And the number one destination for which people will hire a cab:

    1. <u>Airport:</u> While I wasn't permitted to pick up from the airport, I could drive people to the airport. The absolute minimum metered fare I ever got was $8. Generally, the fare to the airport was at least $20.

Ten Fares I Knew, Or Knew Of, Before They Were Fares ━━━━━

    I knew that I would get to know some of my passengers as repeat customers. There have been, however, a handful of passengers that I knew, knew of, or recognized from their name from before they were a fare of mine.

    10. <u>Ramondo Stallings</u>: He was a defensive lineman in the NFL with the Bengals for five years, and in the CFL and XFL for one year each. He played with Marshall Faulk at San Diego State and he looked like he was ready to play.

    9. <u>Sean Mcnanie:</u> He played for three NFL teams after playing for Arizona State. He was here riding motorcycles in the desert that he rented from Eagle Rider in Scottsdale, which seems to be the premier motorcycle rental place in Phoenix.

    8. <u>Ashley:</u> She was an aide at the Smart for Life office I went to in Chandler, when I lost 74 pounds. She was in the last group of people I picked up on the New Year's Eve 2008.

7. <u>Fred Smerlas:</u> He was an All-Pro defensive lineman with the Buffalo Bills and New England Patriots in the 80's and 90's. He was riding with Sean Mcnanie. I knew that I knew him, but I might not have asked if I hadn't seen his name embroidered on his bag. He was huge and a very nice fellow.

6. <u>Herman Johnson:</u> A 2009 NFL draft pick, taken in the fifth round by the Cardinals. I gave him a ride from the Cards facility in Tempe to his hotel. He went to LSU, so he laughed when I told him I went to the Ohio State University. Unlike most Buckeye fans, I don't hate LSU or Florida. Herman was a very nice fellow, and he made the Cardinals roster.

5. <u>Tamara:</u> Worked at one of my hangouts. She was having trouble with her car, so I told her I would come back at closing time to give her a ride home. She bears a resemblance to both Jessica Simpson and Jaime Pressley.

4. <u>Mike:</u> A guy I've been friendly with since I moved here. He called me one night needing a ride home. He insisted on giving me way more than the meter said. It was a battle between my conscience and my wallet, and my wallet won in the end. His girlfriend later went out of her way to thank me.

3. <u>G-Mo:</u> A radio morning show host in the Valley. He was going to San Francisco for a vacation. He is from the east and G-Mo stands for Guillermo.

2. <u>Eric Owens:</u> Played eight years in the majors, mainly with the Cincinnati Reds. He is a roving instructor with the Angels, and he was traveling to the airport another Angels' roving instructor. I love talking baseball.

And the number one fare I knew or knew of:

1. <u>Kenny Britt:</u> He was a wide receiver from Rutgers and was the 30th pick in the 2009 NFL draft, taken by the Tennessee Titans. He was in Phoenix at a training facility preparing for the draft. I gave him a ride to his car, which had been towed. I told him I wished he hadn't left early, because RU really needed him. But, he seemed to make the correct choice, because he has played

extremely well so far, including catching a game—winning TD on the last play of the game to defeat the Cardinals.

My Top Ten Analogies, Anecdotes Or Theories ▬▬▬▬▬▬▬

These were the most common I would reference with passengers:

10. "Politician" Is A Euphemism For Crook: So many people are down on all politicians, so I thought this was funny. I know it's not true in EVERY SINGLE CASE. To hear Bill Maher tell it, it's only true of Republicans. To hear Bill O'Reilly tell it, it's only true of Democrats. My opinion is that it's non-partisan...and 97.4% true.

9. Nobody Knows Less Than The Person Who Thinks They Know Everything: I coined this one myself, or, at least, I've never heard anyone else say it. I don't feel shame in not knowing something. There are plenty who do, and they just can't admit it. Knowing what you know is important, but knowing what you DON'T know is more important.

8. Rainmaker – Acrimony Among Employees: This is one of my favorite movies. Matt Damon is a lawyer trying his first case, against a huge insurance company. His key witness, as played by Virginia Madsen, describes how separate departments within the company are kept at odds with each other purposefully. I believe this happens regularly in real life. The reason is to keep employees from unionizing, among other things. It's the old adage of "Divide and Conquer".

7. Homosexuality Is Not Genetic: I MUST REITERATE, THE FOLLOWING IS MY OPINION, BASED ON WHAT I'VE READ, EXPERIENCED, AND GUT INSTINCT. I HAVE DONE NO SCIENTIFIC EXPERIEMENTS IN THIS FIELD. I know this is not a popular belief. In fact, almost no passenger to whom I have ever said this agrees with me. Consequently, these discussions never

lasted very long. I based my opinion on a couple of things. Firstly, I think genetics is being "credited" with too many behaviors. I feel the genetics influence physical things and not much else. Secondly, I have been told the chances of having a homosexual child, genetically speaking, are one in ten. Based then on what I remember about probability in genetics, one out of 100 children should be gay. And yet, 10% of the population is gay. It just doesn't add up.

6. New Jersey Traffic: In the mid 80's, a study was conducted on the traffic issues that faced US Route 1 in New Jersey. The study said that at the current rate of growth, by the year 2000, it would take five hours to go from New Brunswick to Trenton (approximately 30 miles) during rush hour. The newspaper article reporting the study laid out the construction plan to build overpasses and remove traffic lights to prevent this from occurring. The construction started in 1986 and was completed around 2000. It was done so seamlessly and without interruption, it was incredible. I usually would tell passengers this story when I was stuck behind a backhoe.

5. Passive Smoke Causes Lung Cancer: As you might be able to guess, I don't buy this either. How could you even prove it? You want to tell me passive smoke is annoying, that's fine. I agree that passive smoke is annoying. Show me a study that PROVES it causes cancer.

4. Sometimes You Eat The Bear, Sometimes The Bear Eats You: All this means is that sometimes you win sometimes and sometimes you lose. I heard this from Salvo, one of the owners of Santino's in Marlton, NJ. Others have used similar lines, like "Sometimes you're the windshield, sometimes you're the bug".

3. Gay Marriage Is About Health Benefits: It could very well be that gay people love each other so much they feel the need to "make their love legal". I personally don't care whether anyone gets married, nor do I care whether someone is gay. I think marriage is only logical if you are going to have children. But, the

idea of gay people getting married was to get around the caveat of health benefits. Thieving insurance companies will do anything to not insure people, unless it's at a premium rate. Since these couples aren't married, they won't insure the "significant others".

2. <u>Charlie Weis:</u> This may only be meaningful to college football fans, but the former head coach at Notre Dame had one year of head coaching experience when he took the job at Notre Dame. He coached one season in the late 80's at my high school, Franklin Township in Somerset, NJ. He won a state championship, and then was hired by Bill Parcells to join the staff of the New York Giants.

And my number one analogy, anecdote or theory:

1. <u>My Grandfather Is Also My Uncle:</u> I love this! I've gotten a lot of mileage out of this story. My mother's mother divorced her husband shortly after my mom was born. She then remarried Dan Zissman, who was, among other things, my father's brother. This created a lot of confusion, because a number of my relatives are related to me in two different ways, INCLUDING MY PARENTS. My dad is also my great uncle and my mom is also my cousin. I promise you, there was no hillbilly shit going on here!

The next several lists will be about some of the pitfalls to driving a cab in the metropolitan Phoenix.

Top Ten Reasons Phoenix Leads The Planet In Per Capita Accidents:

When I first arrived here, I heard a radio report that of the top four cities for per capita accidents, three were Phoenix, Mesa and Tucson. Having driven here for almost three years, I believe it.

10. <u>Construction Is Endless:</u> I seem to be harping on this, but it's a huge problem. The detour signs are ambiguous, the construction vehicles think they always have the right of way,

there are port-a-johns in the middle of the road, and there aren't always people directing traffic.

9. <u>Stuff In The Road:</u> The DOT doesn't clean things off the road. I don't know how some of that stuff gets there, but it does.

8. <u>People Making Turns:</u> I can't tell you how many times I nearly hit someone because they practically came to a complete stop making a right-hand turn.

7. <u>SUVs:</u> Tell me you haven't seen some woman that can't even see over the dashboard driving one of these fucking tanks.

6. <u>Photo Enforcement Cameras:</u> These exist solely to tax the citizens of Phoenix, not to create a safer environment. How many times have you seen people slam on the brakes on the 51 because they see the warning sign for Photo Enforcement? Between that and the bright flashes, I'm sure that these Orwellian devices cause more accidents than they prevent.

5. <u>Dangerous Traffic Patterns:</u> The reverse lane on both Seventh Street and Seventh Avenue is the stupidest, most dangerous thing I've ever seen. A lane that changes what you can and cannot do for a three-hour period of time is totally insane. There is also the merge of the 60 and the 10 in Tempe. Seven lanes of traffic merging at high speed, it's incredible. Plus, the five-way stops and the light rail cause problems all over the downtown area.

4. <u>Snowbirds:</u> They drive 45 MPH in the left hand lane on I-10. What are you morons looking at?

3. <u>Look At This:</u> Once, I saw a woman in a convertible, trying to down shift while smoking a cigarette and talking on her cell phone. Plus, she was tailgating the person in front of her. I just laughed.

2. <u>Pedestrians:</u> People think it's their god-given right to walk in traffic, because "they have the right of way." WILL MY GETTING A TRAFFIC TICKET BE YOUR CONSOLATION WHEN YOU ARE LYING IN A FUCKING COMA? One time, I saw a woman running to the corner, hoping to beat me to the spot, so she would have the right of way. She even gave me the finger when I didn't let her go.

And the number one reason Phoenix leads the planet in per capita accidents:

1. <u>People Just Flat Out Don't Pay Attention:</u> Here is one perfect example. Valley Metro is the Phoenix bus line. Their stops are almost always immediately after traffic signals. The problem is only 10%-20% of the stops have pull-in areas, so the busses frequently block traffic. I saw a guy bounce his Volvo off of the back of a bus once. I saw it coming 20 seconds before it happened, because I knew he wasn't paying attention to the bus.

Top Ten Areas Under Construction

One thing I learned almost immediately out here is that when a city is constantly growing, there is always construction holding you up.

10. <u>Cave Creek Road By The 101 Loop:</u> It was never very obvious to me what they were doing here. This was a nightmare during rush hour, which is anywhere from 3-7 PM.

9. <u>Warner And Dobson:</u> This intersection was a huge problem for two years. They wanted to make it less accident-prone by widening it.

8. <u>Power Road, South Of Williams Field:</u> Luckily, I wasn't out that way in Mesa very often. A lot of the construction seemed to be accommodating the railroad.

7. <u>Scottsdale Road, North Of Cactus:</u> This went all the way up to the 101, approximately four miles. The signs were so ambiguous. I'm amazed I wasn't ever in an accident here.

6. <u>Rio Salado Between Rural And McClintock:</u> This really backed up the ASU campus area, and the streets around the Tempe Marketplace. I still don't know what they were trying to accomplish.

5. <u>Rural And Scottsdale By The Loop 202:</u> The widening of the 202 started around April 2009. It created a huge backup

because the traffic patterns had to change and the exit ramps from the 202 were narrowed. One day, it took four traffic light changes before I was able to make a left onto Scottsdale Road. Rural Road in Tempe becomes Scottsdale Road on the other side of the 202.

4. <u>The 101 Loop In Chandler, Mesa, Tempe And Scottsdale:</u> They are still adding an HOV lane. On the weekends, certain parts of the loop have been closed for construction. Sometimes traffic was so backed up I couldn't take it. The thing that really aggravated me was, WHY WASN'T THIS LANE BUILT WHEN THE LOOP WAS ORIGINALLY CONSTRUCTED?

3. <u>Route 60 in Tempe:</u> Another case of widening the road that could have been done when the road was being built in the first place. The westbound merge detours are particularly scary.

2. <u>Queen Creek Road In Chandler:</u> It seems that almost all of Queen Creek Road is under construction, but between Dobson and Gilbert Roads, it is especially annoying.

And the number one place under construction during my time as a cabbie:

1. <u>The Indians, Scottsdale:</u> Indian School and Indian Bend Roads. Rebuilding a bridge, in particular, has crippled Indian Bend. One time, I drove right over a newly paved area on a side street because I couldn't figure out the traffic pattern. Both have been impossible since early 2008.

Top Ten Bad Spots For The GPS Signal: ▬▬▬▬▬

There were plenty of nagging problems that made my life difficult when I was driving. The company would not spend money on strengthening the GPS signal. The following were the worst spots that the GPS signal would fail.

10. <u>Right Next To Buildings:</u> It was really a pain trying to run a credit card when parked too close to a tall building.

9. 32nd Street Exit Of The 51: The 51 was built around a mountain, and you lose the signal because of it.

8. Loop 202 Between Gilbert And Power Road: There is no logical explanation for this, except for it being a remote area.

7. Chandler Road And The Loop 101: Again, there is no obvious reason, but it's really bad here.

6. Between Mesa Drive And Stapley Road On Broadway In Mesa: During my final two months, when I frequently picked up Budd Light, the poor signal here often prevented me from getting follow-up fares.

5. Magellan, Alma School Road, Mesa: You would have to work hard to find decent reception after dropping someone off here. It was particularly difficult in the parking lot.

4. Chandler Road In The Foothills: South Mountain is in the way. The signal sucks, but it wasn't a huge problem because I didn't wait for a call there very often. I was usually going to pickups on the occasions I was there.

3. Wal-Mart At Pecos And Arizona Avenue: Another reason to hate zone 363.

2. The 101 Between Frank Lloyd Wright And Cactus: This is a tremendous area to get big fares. Unfortunately, the signal is so weak I hardly ever got any of them.

And the number one worst area for the GPS signal is:

1. Guadalupe: The town of Guadalupe is in the Yaqui Indian Reservation, and as I understand it, any kind of satellite signals are illegal there. There is no reception at all on I-10 between Baseline Road and Elliot Road. This was particularly a problem when I would get calls to Guadalupe. Seventy-five percent of the time, they would be cancelled and getting a no-show OK'd was next to impossible.

Top Ten Ways Dispatch Aggravated Me

I mentioned in the introduction that my purpose for writing this book was not to crush the cab industry. But the issues with the system that I experienced sometimes were so maddening that I have to mention them so I can keep a clear conscience about it.

10. <u>C-Booking Is Not Completely Fair:</u> I chased calls all the time, and my screen was at least 30 seconds behind. I know this because I have been rejected, booked back in, tried again, been rejected again, booked back in, and the fare still hadn't come off the screen.

9. <u>They Don't Approve No-Shows:</u> I had at least 30 occasions where a no-show was disapproved, only to discover it should have been approved. When I would call for an explanation they would never have a reason. Or I should say they didn't have a good reason.

8. <u>Accountability:</u> I could be wrong, but I never heard that any of these people have lost their jobs "because their mistakes screwed over a driver".

7. <u>They Have The Power To Suspend Me:</u> I was twice suspended because they presumed I blew off a fare. This wasn't necessarily their fault, but a fault in their system. For drivers, it's always "guilty until proven innocent".

6. <u>Stupid Messages They Send:</u> They send constant inane messages about safety, where to buy cheap gas, and to "Have a nice day". Fuck you! They always seem to come at an inopportune time. Plus, I don't care leave me alone.

5. <u>They Don't Admit Mistakes:</u> This was a problem that seemed to fade as time went along. But I would get so mad at one specific woman who would say anything to deflect blame when I wanted to discuss my issue. She once told me I must have hit C-Book by mistake. That was impossible. I stopped complaining, just because I knew I would NEVER get ANY satisfaction.

4. <u>They Don't Care That Mistakes Cost Drivers Money:</u> Every one in this company knows the only people that lose money because of mistakes are drivers. I never received an apology for

a typo on an address, a wrongfully disapproved no-show, a miss-zoned fare, or an incorrect amount on a voucher.

3. <u>I Can't Tell Them How I Feel:</u> There was no two-way communication, other than voice requests. Voice communication is frowned upon, in my opinion, for this very reason. A facilitator once told me he waited 45 minutes for a voice request. I doubted that, too. It's just a way to dissuade drivers from sending those messages.

2. <u>Calls Are Not 100% Random:</u> I was constantly being sent four to six miles for $6 vouchers. The company gets a payment on vouchers, so they are going to make sure those pick-ups are taken first. One day, I got six consecutive $6 vouchers.

And the number one reason dispatch aggravated me:

1. <u>They Ignore Requests For Help:</u> This is another thing I stopped doing because I got so frustrated. There are specific message to send, requesting dispatch's help finding passengers. Once, I sent the same message four times before they answered. They claimed they didn't get the first three messages and when they finally responded, their answer was way beyond useless to me.

Top Ten Places To Find A Panhandler ▬▬▬▬▬

I don't recall being asked very often for money by street people until I came here. More often than not, I believe it is a choice to be homeless. I don't give anyone money now. It is the only way to keep my conscience clean and not get mad.

10. <u>Arizona Mills Mall:</u> I'm not sure why they aren't rousted here. There are least 10,000 people a day in this mall. But every time I've picked up a fare here, I've seen at least one panhandler.

9. <u>Baseline Road Exit Of I-10:</u> They always *look* more like panhandlers at this location.

8. <u>Light Rail Stops:</u> The light rail just opened after Christmas 2008, and the stops have become a new spot for panhandlers.

7. <u>Circle K's:</u> Convenience stores are doomed to be fertile ground for beggars because customers always have spare change in their hands.

6. <u>Greyhound Bus Stations:</u> One of the more traditional spots.

5. <u>Behind The Kinko's At 48th And Ray:</u> There is one particular woman that hides in this corner and springs out of nowhere. She walks up and down the entire strip mall, and then across 48th Street to the Target strip mall. Her shopping cart is always full of assorted crap.

4. <u>Intersection Of I-17 And Peoria Avenue:</u> It seems there are laws for panhandlers. The only time I've ever seen a panhandler approached by police was here. This guy was on the island that divided the street, which presents a danger to him and drivers.

3. <u>Westbound I-10 At Ray Road:</u> There was always someone on this ramp. I remember one young woman that looked like a college student. That's when I stopped feeling bad for these people.

2. <u>The Corner Of 153 And University:</u> This is a pretty remote location, but beggars are always here. It is one of the main exits for the airport, so it makes sense for that reason.

And the number one place to find panhandlers:

1. <u>Any Quik Trip:</u> The thing I love about QT's is that every store is built the same way. Every item is in the exact same place in every store, INCLUDING THE PANHANDLERS. They are always next to a garbage can outside, out of the view of the cashiers.

My Top Ten Disappointments As A Cab Driver: ━━━━━

The up and downs of this industry are a given, a microcosm of life itself. It's never as good as it seems and it's never as bad as it seems. I did have a number of flat out disappointments. They didn't make me angry, they just left me feeling severely let down.

10. <u>Dating:</u> You would think with the volume of phone numbers I got, one of these situations would have led to something.

9. <u>Thieves:</u> I was stiffed at least once per month. There were always potential solutions, but I never followed through on these precautions. I just felt it would hurt with tipping. Still, it's hard to stomach that many people were looking to get one over on me.

8. <u>Missy:</u> I had her as a voucher fare once. She was a fantastic young woman who lived in Kearny, AZ. The disappointment was her trip was a $140 fare, but I only got it once. At least 10 other drivers knew about her, so it was tough to get.

7. <u>Kid's Dental:</u> The nurse asked for my phone number in September 2008, claiming she would call me with long fares a couple of times a week. In the end, she only called me six times in total. Plus, her number one concern was the huge discounts I should give them "because of all the business they were giving me."

6. <u>Cinemax After Dark:</u> I never saw one sex act in my cab.

5. <u>Crystal:</u> This woman was a passenger about six times. She had a degenerative eye disease, and I brought her to the clinic in North Phoenix. Her free transportation was being discontinued and she was going to have to pay for 20% of the fare via HHVs. She was going to give me a chance to bid for the fare. It was worth $70-$80 per day, but I never heard from her.

4. <u>Contempt:</u> There are many occupations in which bosses have historically treated independent contractors with contempt. Many other drivers have told me that they have been told: plenty of people want to drive for Discount and if they can find something better, go ahead. Nobody ever said that to me, but I was blown off several times when I questioned something.

3. <u>The $240 Letdown:</u> I was near the hospital on 10th and McDowell. I got a dispatch for a passenger going 165 miles. The fare was a voucher worth $240. It took me 20 minutes to contact

the fare. He was ready to go, but he hadn't been released and they told me the earliest he was going to be released was in six hours. I decided to no-show the call, because the round trip was at least seven hours, and I could make that much in 13 hours.

2. Socrates: I met him in October 2008. He was so impressed that I knew he was Greek. His name gave it away. He was losing his driver's license a while later and said he wanted to have me as a permanent driver. After talking his cell number and exchanging text messages for a few months, I only drove him two more times.

And, my number one disappointment as a cab driver:

1. Did They Know I Actually Drove For Them? I drove 360 shifts in a Discount Cab. Nobody has ever acknowledged that I don't work for the company anymore. That made me really sad.

Top Ten Things You Can Find Here On Almost Any Street Corner ▬

One of my favorite things about where I live is that I am never far from anything. A lot of the time, location isn't important.

10. Supermarkets: Fry's, Bashas', Safeway, Fresh and Easy, Albertson's, Food City. It doesn't matter which store you want, because you can always find one in a flash.

9. Construction: I know you're tired of it.

8. Banks: If you can't get cash, it's because you don't have any.

7. Gas Stations/Convenience Stores: QT is the best, but there is also AM/PM, Circle K, Sinclair, Valero, Shell and many others.

6. Car Washes: The dust is so bad out here that the vain people probably wash their vehicles every day. On weekends, there are at least a dozen places you can find cheerleading squads trying to raise money by washing cars.

5. Check Cashing: These places are everywhere. It is basically a way of giving credit to people that the banks won't deal with.

There was some legislation introduced to try and regulate this "industry", but I guess "Let the buyer beware" still holds true here.

4. <u>Pawnshops:</u> To me, another "phenomenon." You will be glad to know that they prohibit LOADED firearms. Electronics and jewelry seem to be the pawning items of choice.

3. <u>Panhandlers:</u> I said it before; every QT was built exactly the same way, including the panhandlers being in the exact same spot outside the store. One time, I saw one guy at QT 85 at 9:30 AM. When I went back there six hours later, he was still there; only he had gotten a Mohawk hair cut. Business must have been good for him that day.

2. <u>Mexican Food:</u> It is ubiquitous here; high-end, cheap, drive through, sit down, stand up, etc. I can't believe Taco Bell stays in business.

And the number one thing you can find on almost any street corner is:

1. <u>Bars:</u> Some of these places open at 6:00 AM. Some do their best business at 6:00 AM.

Top Ten Things I Wouldn't Have Guessed There Would Be So Many ━━━━━━━━━

It has taken me a while to get accustomed to a number of things here in the Valley. For starters, this is the first time I have ever really lived in a city. I have been back to New Jersey enough times to still not be fully used to all things Phoenix just yet.

10. <u>Trailer Parks:</u> I think 10% of people here live in trailer parks. Not that there's anything wrong with that.

9. <u>Cab Companies:</u> There are 85 listed in the on-line yellow pages. Some are dedicated strictly to the Spanish-speaking population.

8. <u>Fish And Chips Restaurants:</u> Pete's is the chain with the most outlets, but there are least 15 others. However, there is no Arthur Treachers.

7. <u>Drive-Through Liquor Stores:</u> I thought these only existed in Canada.

6. <u>Dollar Stores:</u> There are at least six different companies, including Dollar Tree, 99 cent store, and the Dollar Store.

5. <u>Guys Flipping Signs:</u> I remember once seeing a guy in New Jersey, dressed as the Statue of Liberty, advertising an income tax service by flipping a sign. Here in Phoenix, it seems that practically every business pays a guy to stand on a street corner, flipping a sign in the air, to get people to come in. Apartment complexes, restaurants and car dealers are among the businesses that often use this ploy.

4. <u>Auto Glass Salesman:</u> Gas stations permit these people to come up to you while you are pumping gas and try to get you to buy auto glass from them. They are relentless. I can't believe an established convenience store/gas station would allow this to happen. They must be in dire straits.

3. <u>Vanity License Plates:</u> I'm pretty sure one out of three people have these tags. People bragging; about their car, the way they look, their overall financial status, who they are, etc. Me, me, me, look at me, look at me.

2. <u>Parks:</u> One really smart thing this metropolis did when they decided to try to become a major city was to build dozens of parks for kids to play in. I've been told part of the reason was because they needed to temper the amount of concrete. It is 100 degrees at midnight during the summer out here. I think if these parks didn't exist, the temperature would never go below 100 degrees for a three-month period.

And the number one thing I would never have guessed there would be so many of:

1. <u>Farms:</u> I have been told that Gilbert, Chandler, Surprise, Avondale and Queen Creek, among others, were all farms 20 years ago. Well, there are still way more farms than I would've guessed. Just east of the 101 in Scottsdale, there are so many cotton fields, I felt like whistling Dixie the first time I saw them.

Top Ten Reasons I Like Phoenix ━━━━━━━━━

When I moved here, it was to try to start over, do some soul searching and reflect on my life. Having done that to a certain extent, I realized that I like living in Phoenix. Here are some of the more important reasons, excluding weather:

10. <u>The City Is Logical:</u> Even if you have never been here, you can find things easily, based on the address. It's not fool proof, but it is not difficult with a little thought.

9. <u>It Is Not Overly Expensive:</u> I have met a lot of people who think Phoenix is very expensive. As compared to New Jersey, though, it doesn't seem bad at all.

8. <u>Old Town Scottsdale:</u> There are tons of shops and restaurants to visit. It is a beautiful part of town to walk around and there is a lot of history. I have always done well there fare-wise and the people are pleasant. Generally, the people in this part of town don't think they are better than you because they have more money.

7. <u>Transportation:</u> Whether I'm going back to NJ or I want to travel, the airport is convenient. I have never had trouble with flights. Plus, the freeway system is very good. It connects to the entire city. Mass transit isn't very good, but I don't use it, so I don't care.

6. <u>Lots Of Stuff To Do:</u> There are sports teams, college and professional, a zoo, shopping, nightlife, motorcycle trips, race tracks, hiking trails and museums among the myriad of activities.

5. <u>Restaurants:</u> There are so many different ethnic foods; I defy anyone to not find one. The palate will always be satisfied. If you are a picky eater, standard fare is available everywhere.

4. <u>My Neighborhood:</u> I moved into my apartment after I found my first job. The complex, while not without problems, is quiet and convenient to everything, including the freeways.

3. <u>Different People:</u> So many people have transplanted

here from everywhere imaginable over the past 20-25 years, you constantly meet people with different ideas. Some people don't like change, but I love meeting people with new ideas and opinions. That's the only way to grow.

2. <u>Beautiful Women:</u> There are bushels of fabulously attractive woman in the Valley. What stands out to me is how many stunners there are in their 40's and older.

And the number one thing I like about Phoenix is:

1. <u>Year-Round Golf:</u> I have played more golf in Delaware than I have in Phoenix since I moved here. However, the IDEA that I can hit the links at any time of the year really appeals to me. I love golf, after all.

Top Ten Oddities Or Random Occurrences: ▬▬▬▬

I couldn't write a bunch of pages on every little thing that has happened to me. But a lot of odd things have accumulated quickly.

10. <u>Kelby Craig:</u> I was given this name by dispatch as a passenger's name on five occasions. Never once did I pick up a person with this name.

9. <u>How Many Berto's Can You Fit In A Volkswagen?</u> There are five million Mexican restaurants (give or take) here in the Valley. What I thought was strange was how many have names that end with "berto". Filiberto's, Poliberto's, Aliberto's, Roliberto's, Hilberto's and Eliberto's are among them.

8. <u>Have You Got A Lint Brush?</u> After I got a tip about the importance of having a cigarette lighter in the cab for passengers, I thought about what other courtesy items I could carry with me. I went out during a break one afternoon and bought a bunch of things, including a lint brush. Two passengers later, a guy said he had stuff all over him, so I offered him the lint brush. He gave me an extra five dollars. But, NO ONE ever

asked me for that lint brush again.

7. <u>Are You Sure You're The Voice Of The Badgers?</u> I have had at least 30 passengers from Wisconsin who claimed to be University of Wisconsin Badger fans. My friend Matt has done their radio broadcasts for nearly 20 years, yet none of these people knew his name. No offense intended, I just think that's strange. Maybe video did indeed kill the radio star.

6. <u>The Scarlet Knight In Shining Armor:</u> Wayne was a football player at Rutgers in 2006 and he was a passenger for me April 2009. He knew the aforementioned Kenny Britt. Incredibly, I found out he was dating a woman I know, shortly after I left the cab industry.

5. <u>You Only Need One Sock I Guess:</u> I had a woman with three children that were in town with a production of the "Lion King". I brought them from Scottsdale to the Chandler Fashion Square and back. It was a quite valuable trip. When we got back to their hotel, they got out and I noticed one of the infant's socks was lying on the floor of the back seat. The mother stopped and thanked me, because it was the only pair of socks she had for her baby. Two hours later, I noticed the other sock under the seat.

4. <u>Looking For Stars:</u> I had a passenger whose name was Peter Boyle. The weird thing was he LOOKED like Jerry O'Connell.

3. <u>I Know How To Win Friends And Influence People:</u> I had to stop by the cage in Mesa for a PM. They normally take an hour, so I went up to the front to ask for downtime and talk to Axel, one of the people who handled driver reconciliation's. As I was walking to the waiting room, a guy who was doing an orientation came up to me and asked what I thought of the job. Now, I remembered feeling angry when I asked the same question of another driver and he was an asshole to me. So I decided to be as honest as I could with this guy. I told him the facts as well as my opinions and he continued to ask more questions. After about 10 minutes that the entire class of orientation students surrounded me and picked my brains. I was holding court.

2. <u>I Bike EVERYWHERE:</u> I picked up a fare and brought him to the airport. It came up, as it frequently does, that I am originally from New Jersey. He asked where I am from, so I said a small town of which he had never heard. He insisted on me telling him the name of the town, so I told him Griggstown. He then told me he had ridden his bike on the bike path adjacent to the canal. You wouldn't know the bike path (actually, it was referred to as "the toe path") was there, unless you knew it was there. Small world.

And the number one random occurrence is:

1. <u>Deuce Coyote:</u> I stopped at this house to pick up a couple that was going to retrieve their car from the Sand Bar in Scottsdale. After they got in the cab and we had started out, a coyote ran into the middle of the road. Now, I had never seen one before. I was trying to find my camera, but I couldn't. I said, "Hey look, there's a coyote" and they looked. I was saying something else when the coyote stopped, squatted and took this enormous dump right on the center yellow line. I looked at them and I said, "Jeez, he's got good aim." After a couple of seconds, we all cracked up.

Top Ten Times I Was The Ass-clown:

As much as I'd like to think I'm a brilliant guy, I'm not. I do my share of stupid things every day and I did my share of stupid things as a cab driver.

10. <u>How About A Profile:</u> I brought back a camera from New Jersey after Thanksgiving 2008. I started taking pictures all over the place, hoping to have funny captions under them for this book. I was waiting at a gas station and I saw an attractive woman, so I took her picture. I had taken all kinds of pictures of woman for months. Unfortunately, a "security" person saw me do this. He told the woman, and then sent another security person out to question me about it. I just denied that I took her picture. I was convincing enough to where he walked away. I went home,

erased every picture of women I had on the camera, and never took another picture of a woman again.

9. <u>Swinging Doors:</u> I had just dropped off a couple at a leasing office in a gated apartment complex in Tempe. I was waiting for the gate to open. I looked down for a moment, and then heard a banging noise. I looked up to see the gate opening in, banging on the car. I thought about it for 20 minutes and decided to report it to the safety guy. He took pictures and told me I would probably be charged back for it. Luckily, I wasn't.

8. <u>Wrong Way Feldman:</u> On my last day, I was so paranoid that something bad would happen, something almost did. After I dropped off this couple, I saw a policeman at an intersection, and then turned right onto First Avenue. It was a one-way to the left, unfortunately. What was fortunate was either the cop didn't see it or he tossed me a bone.

7. <u>How Long Does It Take To Change A Flat?</u> I got a flat tire one day in cab 732 about four miles from the Glendale cage. It really sucked because I was having a great day to that point. I called for a tow, as instructed, and I was at the cage within 40 minutes. I didn't drive out of the Glendale cage, so I didn't want to ruffle feathers by continually asking when my car was going to be ready. I sat in the waiting area for two and-a-half hours before the safety guy asked about my car. He came back and said it was done 90 minutes ago. The person who was supposed to let me know about it just said, "Why didn't you ask me?" At least I got down time.

6. <u>Hey Dude, Where Is My Key?</u> On my first day, I compounded a no-show by locking my keys in the car with the engine running. I was only two miles from the cage, so I caught a break.

5. <u>I'm A Genius:</u> I realized there was a continuous voucher of $63 in South Chandler. I timed it perfectly to get the call. I was 20 minutes early, so I waited in front of the house. At 9:00 AM, I called the given number to have the passenger come out. At that very moment, she cancelled the fare. See how smart I am?

4. <u>She's Pregnant, Don't Mess With Her:</u> I got a $50 voucher, again in South Chandler, bringing this pregnant woman to Glendale. She made me wait 10 minutes for her to come out. She asked me how I was, so I told her how unfair these vouchers were, because the fare should be about $75. Then, we didn't talk the rest of the trip. As we got there, she said, "I hope the rest of your day is better." And I said, "Yeah, me too". When I got to the cage on Sunday, I found I was placed on "de-active" status. This woman complained about "how rude I was".

3. <u>You Are So Helpful:</u> I got a photo enforcement camera ticket in Tempe. I decided I was just going to pay it, because this was my job and I didn't want to get fucked with. I waited 20 minutes to pay, and after I did, the clerk in the window said, "Why didn't you wait for them to give you the summons? You don't have to pay unless they present it to you in person." Thanks for telling me now.

2. <u>I Know I Have Forgotten Something:</u> I went into a gas station to fill up right before I went to a pickup. I got a drink, a newspaper and $12 of gas. It wasn't until I dropped off my pas-senger and started towards my next fare that I realized I never pumped the gas.

And the number one time I was the ass-clown:

1. <u>"I'm Not As Think As You Drunk I Am":</u> I went back east for my annual Dewey Beach trip in September 2008, after two months as a cab driver. I had been on the cookie diet since March and I hadn't had an alcoholic drink during the entire time I was on the diet. I had four beers before my friend took me to the airport. After I checked in, I went to one of the bars in the airport and slugged five huge beers before my flight was called. After I got on the plane, I started to feel lousy and 10 minutes before the flight took off, I vomited. It went all over. The person next to me bolted from his seat and I just sat there, dazed. The next thing I knew, SIX security people were dragging me out of the seat and off the plane. I was pleading that I needed to be on the flight, but

they said no. They booked me on a flight the next day. They tried to get me to go to a hotel, but I insisted on staying in the airport. I smelled awful. When I later told the Dewey guys, they thought it was great.

My Top Ten Personality Quirks And Obsessions ━━━━━

I think I'm a pretty normal guy, but I'm sure there are people that think I'm strange. The following are some things about me that might seem "less than normal".

10. <u>Harry Potter:</u> I think reading is overrated. I never read fiction. For some reason, Harry Potter struck a chord with me. I have all seven books, all six movies and I'm in a Harry Potter meet-up group. I don't get it.

9. <u>I Must Text With Perfect Grammar:</u> I will not send a text message unless proper grammar is used, including capitalizing, punctuation and spelling. Every once in a blue moon I get lazy and don't use capital letters.

8. <u>Go To Sleep Four-Eyes:</u> I wear contact lenses. However, they are semi-hard gas permeable lenses so I can't sleep with them in. My sight without correction is so poor that I sleep with my glasses on, so I can see when I wake up. The Dewey guys have seen it so often they don't even goof on me anymore.

7. <u>Quarters:</u> I always have tons of coin change. I have to rummage through all of my change and spend the quarters that don't have states or Bi-Centennial markings on them first.

6. <u>Dry Napkins:</u> If I'm at a bar drinking beer, the napkin has to be dry. I will go through 50 napkins to make sure the one my beer is sitting on is dry.

5. <u>Milestones On My Odometer:</u> I have recorded where I was when the odometer of the vehicle I was driving reached a milestone, like 50,000 miles. During my time as a cab driver, I would take pictures of the odometer to record these milestones.

4. <u>People Liking Me:</u> I will let people take advantage of me, that's how abhorrent it is to me to have them dislike me. I know having everyone like me is impossible, but I can't help it. I think I know where it comes from, but it's not really worth explaining.

3. <u>Ziplock Bags:</u> These wonderful things are the only way I keep myself reasonably organized. To me, they were the greatest invention, EVER.

2. <u>Broadcasting:</u> I lost seven on-air spots over the course of time, through no fault of my own. Either the station was sold, or someone with power gave my spot to a friend. Every time I see that Pam Ward is calling a Big Ten football game, hear Baker Rink referred to as Baker Arena, or an interception return called a "Pick 6", I want to scream. I'm just as good as anyone doing play-by-play. You can call it whatever you want to call it and I know it's my problem. I just can't get over it.

And my number one personality quirk is:

1. <u>Pens:</u> I have so many pens; I wouldn't even hazard a guess as to how many I have. I bet 80% of them don't write. I need to have at least five pens in my car. I have them strategically placed throughout my apartment so I never have to reach more than six inches to have a writing instrument. It started with the NESF. We would make deliveries for pharmaceutical reps and they have the best pens. I started collecting them and the rest is history. Now, I take them from where ever I can.

Top Ten Team Fan Bases Here in Phoenix

One of the weird things about the Valley is that the local teams don't seem to have the majority of fans behind them. Most people that live here became fans of teams from their hometowns, so it is understandable. From my experience, these are the teams with the largest amount of fans:

10. <u>Chicago Cubs:</u> They haven't won the World Series in

more than 100 years. They haven't even been in the World Series in more than 60, yet attendance at Diamondback's games triples when they are in town.

9. <u>Denver Broncos:</u> I sat at a bar of 15 people for one game, and every single person aside from me had on a Broncos shirt.

8. <u>Michigan Football:</u> It follows, since half of Detroit has moved here in the past 20 years. TOO BAD, THOUGH, THEY BLOW.

7. <u>Los Angeles Lakers:</u> A lot of people from LA live here. It also appears some of the world has forgiven Kobe Bryant.

6. <u>Detroit Red Wings:</u> The Red Wings are the one Detroit team that has been consistently good for the past 15 or so years. Those fans also forgot how shitty they were for the 20+ years prior to that.

5. <u>Boston Red Sox:</u> I wasn't here before the Red Sox snapped their 86-year "curse", but I'm sure these fans were a lot more quiet before 2004.

4. <u>DA BEARS:</u> Rex Grossman leaving Chicago seemed to be more important than Jay Cutler coming to Chicago.

3. <u>New York Yankees:</u> I hoped that a miracle would happen in 2009 and they would figure out a way *not* to win. Once again, they completely disappointed me.

2. <u>Dallas Cowboys:</u> They will continue to be "America's team" as long as that pompous boob Jerry Jones is in charge.

And the number one team fan base here in Phoenix is:

1. <u>Nebraska Football:</u> One of the local all-sports radio stations carries their game broadcasts for god sakes! There are multiple sports bars in Phoenix dedicated to Cornhusker football, and I have met more than my fair share of Husker fans.

Top Ten People I Wish Would Go Away

As I may have stated earlier, one of the reasons for my move to Phoenix was the fact that I was going through a mid-life crisis.

Part of my mid-life crisis was that I was tired of certain famous people, generally Hollywood types, and their sense of entitlement. The following are people I'm tired of seeing.

10. <u>Jennifer Lopez:</u> Actually, it seems like she already has gone away. She is one of the many pretentious people in Hollywood who think they are ENTITLED to their fame and fortune. Jenny is a crock is more like it.

9. <u>The New York Yankees:</u> I thought the inevitable collapse was happening when they missed the playoffs last season. But, they signed the three most valuable free agents for zillions of dollars and they are back on top. It was bad enough in the mid-90s when they got good and all the fans in the metropolitan area crawled out from the rocks under which they were hiding. But I'm 2300 miles from NYC, and I still see Yankee hats and jerseys everywhere. You know the bandwagon jumpers are the ones wearing shirts with a player's name on it. No Yankee has EVER had their name on their uniform, EVER.

8. <u>Sean Penn:</u> I don't care if he's a great actor, he's still Jeff Spicoli whether he likes it or not. I am so-o-o-o grateful he's decided to be a US diplomat.

7. <u>Tyra Banks:</u> What a hypocrite. She made a lot of money to wear clothes and walk. Then she got pissed because she did the ONE thing she couldn't do if she wanted to keep her job. She got fat. Now, she thinks she's the second coming of Oprah Winfrey. Does ANYONE actually watch her show, other than the people who get free tickets?

6. <u>Tom Cruise:</u> Why do people in Hollywood think they speak for the masses? Scientology doesn't mean enlightenment. Just because you're a bankable Hollywood star doesn't mean anyone gives a shit what you think.

5. <u>Hillary Clinton:</u> I have no problem with a woman being president. I have a problem with THIS woman being president.

4. <u>Wanda Sykes:</u> SHE JUST ISN'T FUNNY.

3. <u>Rush Limbaugh:</u> How does this fucking guy continue to be allowed on the air? Did you honestly think the NFL was going to let this oral sewer become an owner? He is no worse than Sean Hannity, Bill O'Reilly, Glenn Beck or Ann Coulter, but he was the first of the most recent group of right wing shills.

2. <u>Mariah Carey:</u> Have you ever heard an interview with this nitwit? Saying they kissed her ass doesn't do the interviewers justice. Another person who thinks it's her entitlement to treat people like shit.

And the number one person I wish would go away:

1. <u>Miley Cyrus:</u> A couple of local radio guys bowed to this arrogant little twit. Like most pop "stars", she's nothing special as a singer. And, more importantly, what 16-year-old *deserves* to be a billionaire?

CHAPTER 12

Epilogue

I was told by an acquaintance that I needed to draw a conclusion about the cab driving industry. His argument to me was that, as a scientist, he can't see doing research on a subject and not drawing a conclusion. I'm sure that as far as science is concerned, you wouldn't do research unless you were trying to reach a conclusion. My involvement in the cab industry was hardly a scientific endeavor.

Even if I went into my career as a driver with the intention of "doing research", I would not be able to come to a conclusion that any other driver would necessarily be able to agree with. We all have different mindsets, goals, levels of motivation, levels of trust, etc. So, this is an Epilog, as opposed to a Conclusion.

There are factors that are true almost all the time, if not all the time. First, the cab company always gets the same amount, regardless of how much money the driver makes. Drivers pay a specific price for the lease to which they agree. The lease and the amount of money spent on gas are the expenses. Subtract those two figures from the total amount collected during the day and the net is the total amount that drivers make.

So, outside of the few advertising deals they make, the amount kept from vouchers and the pre-arranged cab stands they get paid for, the lion share of income for Discount Cab comes from the leases they have with their drivers.

Next, when a mistake is made, the driver is the one that loses, regardless of who makes the mistake. Wrong address, wrong phone, wrong time, it doesn't matter. Time is definitely money to a cab driver. If incorrect information costs a driver 40 minutes of their day, you don't know how much money will end up being lost.

Also, the cab industry is a necessity-based one; people that use cabs don't get enjoyment from it. A large portion of passengers are disabled (physically, mentally, or otherwise) to the point they can no longer drive, because of age, injury, lack of brains, birth defects, whatever. Some people can't drive because the state took away their driving privileges. Some try to avoid a DUI by taking cabs to and from bars. Hundreds of people every day use cabs to go to and from the airport. Add these factors with the fact that public transportation in Phoenix is mediocre at best and the taxi industry gets plenty of business.

Finally, driving a cab is an extremely dangerous job. Driving, in and of itself, is extremely dangerous, especially in Phoenix. There is constant construction, there are a large numbers of SUVs on the road and people don't pay attention to what they are doing. Also, you never know whom you are picking up. I've had the police involved in some way with my pick-ups seven different times. Plus, some people are always looking to get over on you. There is a lot of danger involved. And, if that wasn't enough, driving is among the most stressful things a person can do. I have been told that, statistically speaking, after a policeman, driving a cab is the second most dangerous job. According to the website www.taxi-library.org, nearly 3000 cab drivers have been murdered in the last 100 or so years, including 15 in Phoenix.

Having figured in the above finite factors, allow me now offer my assessment of the cab industry.

What are the positives of being a cab driver? First, you get to meet a lot of people. I enjoy talking. I am a talker by nature. I know a lot of inconsequential and trivial things, so it is easy for me to strike up a conversation with someone and find a topic of interest for them.

Plus, I will quote some great person by saying, "Everyone is my teacher, for I may learn from him". I not only can say that I gained a lot of book knowledge from my passengers, but I learned a lot about the lives of other people that live in Phoenix. There are so many people living "underground"; if you don't actually know them firsthand, you wouldn't ever know they exist at all. I learned so much about life from being a cab driver. I believe Al McGuire said, "Everyone should be either a cab driver or bartender at least once in their lives". I have done both and learned a lot from both.

The second positive thing is you can drive whenever you want to and as much as you want to. I chose to lease the cab on a weekly basis, because I knew I was going to drive as many hours as I could stand. After three or four days, generally every dime you bill is yours to keep.

After a while, I determined that driving four weeks on and one week off was a good plan for me. I did that for the last eight months I worked for Discount Cab. Looking back, it probably would have been better to do two on and one off, considering the hours I put in each week. That way, I could've driven 14-16 hours a day for two weeks, instead of four, and not burned out the way I did. The point is, you try stuff, some things work, some things don't and then you can set up the schedule that works best for you.

Another plus is that you can make some really decent money, if you are fortunate. I had several days that I made $200 plus. I cleared over $400 on New Year's Eve. Unfortunately, I had plenty of 12-14 hour days where I made less than $30 dollars.

If you are smart, you can really do well. For example, I got a $75 voucher that took me out to Buckeye. On the way, the guy told me his appointment was an hour long and that he would get a return voucher coming back. That zone was pretty remote, so I waited the hour and got his return trip. That doesn't make me a genius, but it was a long distance and a lot of miles worth of gas that I would have had to pay for had I not waited.

Also, it is really a pretty simple job. You take people from Point A to Point B. Sometimes there was a point C, D, E and F added. There was nothing hard about that. Sometimes you would have to carry groceries or other purchases for people. Since there are a lot of elderly people, you would sometimes have to help them get in or out of the cab, or unload a walker or a wheelchair. But how hard is that?

There were certain obstacles with the Crown Victoria's. It was more difficult negotiating those boats in certain situations. They also had a tendency to break down. From a mechanical perspective, learning the MDT was the hardest thing. But, this job was easy to learn and know how to do.

I also learned the city of Phoenix very quickly. There are plenty of things to do in the metropolitan area. The thing that stood out for me was finding some great places to eat. I also know where the many shopping malls are located. When it comes to the nightclubs in Scottsdale, Chandler, Mesa and Glendale, I know where they all are. Every trip for every fare is a place familiar to me now.

I would have to say in the end, the negatives outweighed the positives. First of all, the cab company always gets the same amount regardless of how much money the drivers make. Can you imagine working a whole week, for 40-60 hours, and not making a dime? That almost happened to me one week in the summer of 2009. I drove 65 hours one week and cleared $45. The cab company got its $846 dollars, and I made 70 cents an hour. While that was a rare occurrence, there were plenty of weeks that I made less than $3 an hour.

If I ever got the impression that dispatch cared that when they made a mistake, it cost the drivers, it probably wouldn't have bothered me so much. But, during my first six months, every time I questioned something, they just denied any responsibility. It was one of my first points on anger with the job. After a while, it became a huge problem for me.

In a way, the dangers associated with driving a cab are real. The stress involved with the job was *the issue* for me, far more than the danger. My blood pressure shot through the ceiling after a 12-14 hour shift. I was more concerned about my health than about my safety.

My overall health seemed to deteriorate in my tenure as a cab driver. I had been on the "Cookie Diet" and I went from 292 pounds to 218 in approximately six months. I went off the diet two months after I started working for Discount. Over the next six months, I gained back 48 pounds. I am not saying it was the fault of Discount Cab, but I can honestly attribute the weight gain to just sitting 12-14 hours per day. The sedentary nature of the job caused my metabolism to ground to a halt. Days of that length also do not inspire a person to then go to the gym. It can be done, but I know my weaknesses. I don't have that kind of discipline.

Another issue is that the cab companies do not provide drivers with health insurance. Drivers are independent contractors FOR THIS PRIMARY REASON. I have twice paid hefty amounts for health insurance since I moved here, although to hear others tell me, I was getting it cheaply. I cancelled the first plan after they bumped my rates 30% after the first year. The second time, I was cancelled because I didn't pay them, even though I never received an invoice to pay. That insurance company basically stole $600 from me. Bastards.

As I understand it, the cab industry used to be a unionized

business and drivers had health insurance. I learned this from a passenger (a gentleman that was in his 70's) that had driven a cab in San Diego for 20 years. I don't know if that was ever true here in Phoenix, but I haven't been able to find anyone that can confirm or deny it for me. However, I have decided that I need a job that pays me health benefits. I'm 47 years old, and while I have been very fortunate to this point (I've called out of work twice in 25 years), I can't rely on luck forever.

Another issue for me was the mentality of the cab company regarding money. They definitely take the maximum and give the minimum. When I went back to New Jersey in September 2008, I returned to Phoenix weeks later to find that the lease rates had gone up approximately 5%. Management taped a note on the cage explaining that this was the first rate jump in two years. Other drivers later told me that every time the rates go up, management says the same thing. I learned that this was the fourth rate hike in less than four years.

After six months, the IOI line was established to give credits to drivers when there was a system error, a duplicate order, or the address or phone number of the passenger was incorrect. We would get a $5 credit if it were determined that the mistake was the fault of one of the above. Now, generally you would lose anywhere from 15-45 minutes on a no-show. For me to make a reasonable amount of money, I needed to bill $20-$25 per hour. Five dollars for someone else's blunder was nothing more than a token. On top of that, management was very stingy with these credits. I had a conversation with the fellow that handles these credits. He told me he works hard to give as many credits as he can. The next time I went in for reconciliation, I saw I had called in eight mistakes that had been reviewed and I had one credit. Yeah, he was really working his ass off for me.

Another nickel and dime issue is downtime. Drivers get lease credit for preventative maintenance, flat tires, and other equipment breakdowns. We would get paid $8.50 an hour for downtime, less than half of what I would consider reasonable. That rate was based ON A 100-HOUR WORK WEEK. Does that sound reasonable to you?

Additionally, drivers were charged more than $100 per week extra to lease the Toyota Prius. We would get two to four times the gas mileage with the Prius as compared to any of the other cars, so the idea that the company would bank a part of that was to be expected. I went to management when gas was around $1.60 a gallon and said, "Look, we have to drive 1400 miles a week to break even with the cost of the Crown Vic rate. This is not an advantage to me." His response was that he just had this conversation with another manager and they were going to rectify the situation. I didn't believe that was ever a topic of conversation, but three weeks later, the rate dropped by $3.43 per day. I don't know if I had anything to do with that happening, but even if I did, I didn't take pride in it. THE LEASES FOR THESE CABS WERE STILL WAY TOO EXPENSIVE.

Another problem for me was quality of life. To make a reasonable amount of money, I had to work a bare minimum of 70 hours per week. Sometimes, that wasn't enough. I was spending anywhere from 35-55 hours a week paying off my lease and for gas. That's why no-shows and mistakes were so intolerable. When I started the stretch of time where I drove 19 weeks in a row with only one day off, I wondered how I was really going to able to do that after the first 10 days. I was so tired. Eighty to 100 hour workweeks are no way to live.

A lot of my co-workers could really "stretch the truth." I heard stories from other drivers about how well they do. One driver told me he made $40K the week the Super Bowl was in Phoenix in 2008 (this was before I started driving for Discount). I thought about that. For him to have made that much money, he would have driven 100 hours and cleared $400 per hour. He was totally full of shit. Then I thought, "Maybe he said $4K." That would mean he would have driven 100 hours, averaging $40 per hour cleared. I'm pretty sure that was a lie, too.

I completely understand why things are run the way they are. In an industry where cash is used as payment 40-80% percent of the time, it is very difficult to monitor whether drivers are being honest or not. I had dozens of passengers ask for a flat rate, hoping I wouldn't turn on the meter and give them, in essence, a discount. If I did that, I would be stealing from the cab company. It would be pretty easy for the cab company to get ripped off.

As independent contractors, the company is not obligated to pay drivers' health benefits. To me, that was totally reprehensible, but looking at it from the company's perspective, I understand why they do this. Approximately 90% of their "employees" are drivers, so it's a simple question of bottom-line economics. There have also been lawsuits argued from the perspective that the National Labor Relations Act does not protect cab drivers, since they are, technically, not employees. Again, I find this reprehensible, but I understand their perspective.

Most importantly, having been a driver for 15 months, I can also completely understand the reasons that drivers do some of the things they do, and why they are perceived as dickheads so often. I had at least 30 situations where a passenger tried to screw me over. I would bet that almost every time each one of those assholes called for the cab, they did so fully knowing that they were going to try to rip off the driver. After a short while, I easily noticed the signs of it.

Some drivers told me they would ask for a deposit, or ask the passenger to show them that they had money up front. I came to the conclusion that these rip offs were destined to happen occasionally. I figured if I went the deposit route, I would lose more money in tips for "offending" passengers than I would lose "protecting" myself from the rare thief. But I understand why the other drivers do what THEY do.

And I totally understand why passengers are paranoid about cab drivers. Dozens of passengers told me that some drivers would run up fares by taking the old "scenic route". One fellow told me a driver somehow turned a $7 fare into a $30 one. Then, when he refused to pay it, the driver called the police and he ended up spending the night in jail. Is that story really as simple as that? It could be, and that is an example of why I never got mad when people would give directions turn by turn, even though I knew where I was going.

Bottom line: The cab industry DOES have some negativity. There isn't a lot of trust regardless of whose perspective you take. It's dangerous and it takes crazy amounts of hours to make a livable amount of money. Everything considered, I would say for the most part that I enjoyed this profession and I was pretty good at it. For the long term, though, I decided to try something else. The main reason is because I was worried about the affects that 12-15 hours a day of being sedentary, everyday, would have on my long-term health. There are people, and I mean this in the most positive of ways, that are perfect for the job. I just don't feel that I'm one of them.

I have one final, humorous (to me) side note. About two months before my final day, I went to the cage on a Sunday to reconcile my receipts. The two regular clerks were there to check me out. Someone called in from the road on the speakerphone and referred to Adam as Aaron. For the remaining two months, I would call Adam any male name I could think that began with an A that wasn't Adam. I did the same thing throughout this book. *Did any of you notice?* Thank you so much for reading.

LaVergne, TN USA
09 May 2010

182020LV00003B/2/P